SOURCES OF GROWTH

D1522482

Since 1985 the International Center for Economic Growth, a nonprofit organization, has contributed to economic growth and human development in developing and post-socialist countries by strengthening the capacity of indigenous research institutes to provide leadership in policy debates. To accomplish this the Center sponsors a wide range of programs—including research, publications, conferences, seminars, and special projects advising governments—through a network of more than 230 correspondent institutes worldwide. The Center's research and publications program is organized around five series: Sector Studies; Country Studies; Studies in Human Development and Social Welfare; Occasional Papers; and Working Papers.

The Center is affiliated with the Institute for Contemporary Studies, and is headquartered in Panama with the administrative office in San Francisco, California.

For further information, please contact the International Center for Economic Growth, 243 Kearny Street, San Francisco, California, 94108, USA. Phone (415) 981-5353; Fax (415) 986-4878.

ICEG Board of Overseers

SOURCES OF GROWTH

A STUDY OF SEVEN LATIN AMERICAN ECONOMIES

Victor J. Elías

A Joint Research Project of
the Fundación del Tucumán and the
International Center for Economic Growth

 ICS PRESS
San Francisco, California

THE FUNDACIÓN DEL TUCUMÁN is a nonprofit organization created in 1984 with the purpose of spreading knowledge of socioeconomic issues. The members of the foundation are brought together by a firm belief in democracy, a love of freedom, and a deep faith in the creative spirit of the individual as a leader in social progress.

Inquiries, book orders, and catalog requests should be addressed to ICS Press, 243 Kearny Street, San Francisco, California 94108 USA. Telephone: (415) 981-5353; fax (415) 986-4878. For book orders in the contiguous United States: **(800) 326-0263**.

Distributed to the trade by National Book Network, Lanham, Maryland.

Cover designer: Lisa Tranter.

Indexer: Shirley Kessel.

Library of Congress Cataloging-in-Publication Data

Elías, Víctor Jorge.
    Sources of growth: a study of seven Latin American economies / Víctor J. Elías.
        p.   cm.
    "A joint research project of the Fundación del Tucumán and the International Center for Economic Growth."
    Includes bibliographical references and index.
    ISBN 1-55815-143-5 (paper)
    1. Latin America—Economic conditions—1945- 2. Latin America—Economic policy. 3. Industrial productivity—Latin America.
    4. Economic development. I. Title.
    HC125.E44 1992
    338.9—dc20   91-44983

To my wife, Ana,
my daughters, Georgina and Cecelia,
and my son, Julio

CONTENTS

List of Figures		ix
List of Tables		xi
Preface		xvii
Acknowledgments		xix
Chapter 1	Introduction and Overview	1
Chapter 2	Latin American Macroeconomic Performance	11
Chapter 3	Models and Methods for the Study of Economic Growth	19
Chapter 4	Sources of Economic Growth	33
Chapter 5	Output and Income Distribution	59
Chapter 6	Labor Input	71
Chapter 7	Capital Input	101
Chapter 8	Agriculture, Manufacturing, and the Public Sector	115
Chapter 9	Complementary Approaches to the Analysis of Latin American Economic Growth	131

Chapter 10   A Comparative Growth Analysis of
              Latin American and Other Countries   151

Chapter 11   Predictions and Policy Implications for
              Latin American Economic Growth   163

Appendix A   The Sources-of-Growth Methodology   169

Appendix B   Production Function Estimates   175

Appendix C   The Stock of Educational Capital   181

Appendix D   Occupation Classification II   183

Appendix E   Basic Data   187

Appendix F   Estimates of the Econometric Growth Model   231

              References   233
              About the Author   245
              Index   247

LIST OF FIGURES

Figure 1   Sources of Economic Growth for Seven Latin
             American Countries, 1940–1985   9
Figure 2   Average Annual Growth Rates of GDP,
             Population, and Per Capita GDP, 1900–1980   14
Figure 3   Average Annual Compound Rates of Inflation,
             1913–1980   15
Figure 4   Schematic Presentation of the Sources-of-Growth
             Methodology   32
Figure 5   Frequency Distribution of Output, Labor, and
             Capital Growth by Country-Decades, 1940–1985   42
Figure 6   Contribution of Labor, Capital, and Total Factor
             Productivity to Output Growth, 1940–1980   43
Figure 7   Contribution of Inputs to Output Growth by
             Decade, 1940–1980   44
Figure 8   Index of Total Factor Productivity, 1940–1985   46
Figure 9   Partial Productivity of Labor, 1940–1985   48
Figure 10   Partial Productivity of Capital, 1940–1985   49
Figure 11   Annual Rate of Change of GDP, 1948–1980   64
Figure 12   Average Annual Growth Rate of GDP and Public
             Output by Decade, 1940–1980   66
Figure 13   Schematic Presentation of the Labor Input   84
Figure 14   Average Annual Change in Labor Quality Based
             on Six Characteristics, 1940–1980   85
Figure 15   Schematic Presentation of the Capital Input   108

Figure 16   Average Annual Rate of Growth of Capital Stock
             by Decade, 1940–1985   109
Figure 17   Contribution of Land, Labor, and Capital to the
             Growth of Agricultural Output, 1950–1980   122
Figure 18   Labor Contribution Share in Manufacturing,
             1940–1980   123
Figure 19   Contribution of Labor, Capital, and Total Factor
             Productivity to Public Output Growth, 1940–1980   124
Figure 20   Growth of Output, Labor Contribution, and
             Capital Contribution by Sector, 1940–1980   125
Figure 21   Annual, Biannual, and Triannual Growth Rate of
             GDP in Argentina, Brazil, Chile, Colombia, and
             Mexico, 1900–1986   138
Figure 22   Annual Rate of Change of Total Factor
             Productivity in Latin American Countries, the
             United States, and Western Europe, 1948–1973   143
Figure 23   Profile Analysis: Argentina and Brazil, 1940–
             1980   146
Figure 24   Profile Analysis: Argentina and Colombia, 1940–
             1980   146
Figure 25   Profile Analysis: Brazil and Colombia, 1940–1980   147
Figure 26   Labor Productivity for Latin American Countries
             and Other Selected Countries, 1940–1984   157
Figure 27   Predicted Growth Rates of Labor, Capital, and
             GDP for the 1990s   168

LIST OF TABLES

Table 1   Expansion and Contraction Periods for Argentina,
           Mexico, and Venezuela, 1960–1984   17
Table 2   Average Annual Growth Rate of GDP and the
           Contribution of Inputs by Decade, 1940–1985   50
Table 3   Average Annual Growth Rate of GDP and Inputs
           by Decade, 1940–1985   53
Table 4   Average Annual Growth Rate of the Real Input
           Prices of Labor and Capital by Decade, 1940–
           1980   55
Table 5   Estimate of Average Annual Growth Rate of
           Productivity by Decade (Dual Approach), 1940–
           1980   56
Table 6   Average Annual Growth Rate of Capital Stock
           and the Contribution of Foreign Trade, 1940–
           1973   56
Table 7   Real GDP and Consumption and Investment
           Goods in Selected Years, 1940–1980   68
Table 8   Share of Investment Goods in Total GDP in
           Selected Years, 1941–1980   69
Table 9   Capital Income Share in GDP in Selected Years,
           1940–1985   69
Table 10   Labor Force Participation Rates for Selected
           Years, 1940–1980   87

Table 11   Employment, Population, and the Employment-
            Population Ratio for Selected Years, 1940–1985   87
Table 12   Average Number of Hours Worked per Worker per
            Week in Selected Years, 1960–1980   88
Table 13   Average Rate of Urban Unemployment, 1963–
            1985   89
Table 14   Labor Force Composition by Educational Level in
            Selected Years, 1940–1980   90
Table 15   Relative Wages by Educational Level in Selected
            Years, 1957–1969   92
Table 16   Average Annual Rate of Change of the Quality
            Component of Labor Based on Educational Level,
            1940–1980   93
Table 17   Share of Women in the Total Labor Force in
            Selected Years, 1940–1980   93
Table 18   Relative Wages by Gender in Selected Countries,
            1960 and 1970   93
Table 19   Average Annual Rate of Change of the Quality
            Component of Labor Based on Gender, 1940–
            1980   94
Table 20   Labor Force Composition by Age in Selected
            Years, 1940–1980   94
Table 21   Average Annual Rate of Change of the Quality
            Component of Labor Based on Age, 1940–1980   95
Table 22   Labor Force Composition by Occupation
            Classification I in Selected Years, 1940–1980   96
Table 23   Relative Wages by Occupation in Selected Years,
            1961–1968   97
Table 24   Average Annual Change of the Quality
            Component of Labor Based on Occupation, 1940–
            1970   97
Table 25   Labor Force Composition by Economic Sector in
            Selected Years, 1940–1980   97
Table 26   Relative Wages by Economic Sector in Selected
            Years, 1940–1970   98
Table 27   Average Annual Change of the Quality
            Component of Labor Based on Economic Sector,
            1940–1980   99
Table 28   Average Annual Change of the Quality
            Component of Labor Based on Regional
            Reallocation, 1940–1980   99

Table 29   Stock of Fixed Capital in Selected Years, 1940–
1985   111

Table 30   Composition of the Fixed Capital Stock according
to Various Criteria in Selected Years, 1940–1980   111

Table 31   Real Gross Rate of Return to Fixed Capital in Selected
Years, 1940–1985   113

Table 32   Gross Rate of Return to Total Fixed Capital and
Some of Its Components, 1960 and 1970   114

Table 33   Average Annual Growth Rate of the Quality of
Capital Based on Capital Composition, 1940–
1970   114

Table 34   Sources of Growth of Agriculture, 1950–1980   127

Table 35   Average Compound Rates of Change of the
Residual, Some Omitted Inputs, and Quality
Change Indicators, 1950–1980   128

Table 36   Average Compound Growth Rates of the Residual
and the Contributions of Modern Inputs, Public
Inputs, and the Net Residual, 1950–1980   128

Table 37   Sources of Growth of Manufacturing, 1940–1980   129

Table 38   Sources of Growth of Public Output, 1940–1980   130

Table 39   Signs Behavior of the Annual Rate of Growth of
the GDP, 1900–1986   148

Table 40   Simple Correlation Coefficients between the
Annual Rate of Change of TFP of Latin
American Countries and the United States and
Western European Countries, 1948–1973   148

Table 41   Average Annual Values for the Variables in the
Econometric Growth Model, 1940–1983   149

Table 42   Sources of Growth, Input Contribution Shares,
and Input Rate of Growth for Latin American
Countries, Japan, and the United States, 1940–1980   160

Table 43   Average Annual GDP Growth in Selected
Countries and Periods and Its Acceleration   161

Table B1   OLS Estimations of Cobb-Douglas Production
Function, with the Form $\ln(\text{GDP}/L)_t = a + bt +$
$c\ln(K/L)_t + d\ln L_t + u_t$ 179

Table B2   OLS Estimation of the Cobb-Douglas Production
Function, Pooling Time Series with Cross-
Country Data, with the Form $\ln(\text{GDP}/L)_t = a +$
$bt + c\ln(K/L)_t + d\ln L_t + \text{dummies} + u_t$ 180

Table C1   Stock of Educational Capital in Selected Years
and Its Average Annual Growth Rate by Decade,
1940–1970   182

Table D1   Labor Force Composition by Occupation
Classification II in Selected Years, 1960–1980   184
Table D2   Venezuela's Relative Wages by Occupation
Classification II, 1961   186

Table E1   Output, Consumption Goods, and Investment
Goods in Argentina, 1940–1980   188
Table E2   Output, Consumption Goods, and Investment
Goods in Brazil, 1940–1980   191
Table E3   Output, Consumption Goods, and Investment
Goods in Chile, 1940–1980   194
Table E4   Output, Consumption Goods, and Investment
Goods in Colombia, 1940–1980   197
Table E5   Output, Consumption Goods, and Investment
Goods in Mexico, 1940–1974   200
Table E6   Output, Consumption Goods, and Investment
Goods in Peru, 1940–1980   202
Table E7   Output, Consumption Goods, and Investment
Goods in Venezuela, 1940–1974   205
Table E8   Ratio of Investment Goods to Total GDP, 1940–
1980   207
Table E9   Share of Capital Income in GDP, 1940–1985   208
Table E10   Employment, Population, and Labor Force
Participation Rate in Argentina and Brazil, 1940–
1985   210
Table E11   Employment, Population, and Labor Force
Participation Rate in Chile and Colombia, 1940–
1985   213
Table E12   Employment, Population, and Labor Force
Participation Rate in Mexico and Peru, 1940–
1985   216
Table E13   Employment, Population, and Labor Force
Participation Rate in Venezuela, 1940–1985   219
Table E14   Stock of Fixed Capital, 1940–1985   221
Table E15   Partial Productivity of Labor, 1940–1985   224
Table E16   Partial Productivity of Capital, 1940–1985   226

Table E17   Index of Real Monthly Wages in Selected Years,
             1940–1980   228
Table E18   Real Gross Rate of Return to Fixed Capital,
             1940–1985   229

Table F1   OLS Estimates of the Reduced Form for the Rates
             of Growth of GDP (y) and Capital (k), Argentina,
             Colombia, and Mexico, 1956–1980   232

PREFACE

Economic growth is one of the primary goals of national economic policy, but for most of the Latin American countries this goal has been notoriously difficult to achieve in the past couple of decades. While scholars have conducted extensive studies on the sources of economic growth in the industrialized countries, few have applied the sources-of-growth method to Latin America. In this important book, Victor J. Elías examines the sources of growth, and the forces that underlie them, in Argentina, Brazil, Chile, Colombia, Mexico, Peru, and Venezuela. In so doing, he comes to some interesting conclusions about the roles of various factor inputs, such as capital, labor, and education, as well as economic sectors in contributing to growth.

Elías's findings shed light on why different growth behavior is observed in the developed and developing countries. The study presents useful guidelines for future investment by both the public and the private sector. Ultimately, his conclusions have important implications for policy in Latin America. Only by pursuing policies that promote growth will the countries of Latin America succeed in overcoming the economic stagnation and poverty that plague them.

In this volume, students of economic growth will find suggestions for future research; professors, a useful text for empirical economic growth courses; and policy designers, evaluations of different policy tools.

Through a joint research project with the Fundación del Tucumán of Argentina, the International Center for Economic Growth supported the study whose results are presented here.

Nicolás Ardito-Barletta
General Director
International Center for Economic Growth

Panama City, Panama
February 1992

ACKNOWLEDGMENTS

This work is the result of my research efforts during the years 1973–1989. It began during my stay at the Harvard Institute for International Development in 1973. I continued at my home institution, the National University of Tucumán, and at the many institutions I have visited over the years: the National Bureau of Economic Research at Stanford University (1975); the Instituto Torcuato Di Tella, Buenos Aires (1979); the Bellagio Study and Conference Center of the Rockefeller Foundation (1980); and the Food Research Institute at Stanford University (1988). My research included intensive agricultural sector investigations as part of a project developed for the International Food Policy Research Institute in Washington, D.C. (1978–1985).

Many people made important suggestions and encouraged me in my work. Some of them are Richard Mallon, Dale W. Jorgenson, Arnold C. Harberger, John W. Mellor, Larry Sjaastad, Jacob Mincer, and the late Oswald H. Brownlee and Carlos F. Díaz Alejandro. My colleagues and the administrative staff of the Institute of Economic Research at the National University of Tucumán provided constant support. Financial assistance came from many sources: the Research Council of the National University of Tucumán, the Social Science Research Council, the J. S. Guggenheim Memorial Foundation, the Ford Foundation, the Fulbright Commission, and the International Development Research Center of Canada. The final stages of this study were supported by the International Center for Economic Growth, through a subsidy granted to the Fundación del Tucumán. Rolf Lüders made important suggestions in the final drafting process during my very agreeable stay at the Institute of Economics of the Pontifical Catholic University of Chile. I appreciate the excellent editorial work of Jorge Cambias and Thomas Connelly.

My family has contributed greatly to my enthusiasm for concluding this task. They encouraged me at every stage, helping me to remain concentrated on the objectives of this study.

CHAPTER 1

Introduction and Overview

Economic growth, defined in terms of gross domestic product (GDP) per capita, has been one of the main objectives pursued by most countries throughout history. Economic growth can improve the well-being of a country's poor and bring an increase in social welfare for all members of a society.

But as an objective of economic policy, economic growth has not been easy to achieve. Many countries have experienced a significant level of economic growth only since the beginning of the nineteenth century. Economic history reveals how difficult it was for societies to achieve growth before the nineteenth century and how difficult it still is for many. Economic development theory provides many arguments to help explain these difficulties, but there are still important questions to be addressed by economic growth theorists.

Since 1950, many countries have registered strong and rapid economic growth, doubling their GDP per capita in a very short period. These experiences, which contrast with those in previous centuries, suggest that there is strong potential for the design of optimal economic growth policies and for increasing the number of countries that can benefit from economic growth in the last decade of this century and in the next.

The decade of the 1980s was difficult for most Latin American countries, in terms of both economic growth and stability (inflation and unemployment). Many of these countries not only suffered the worldwide growth slowdown that began around 1974, but also had several years of negative growth in the subsequent period of mild global recovery. Toward the end of the 1980s, some Latin American countries began slight recoveries, although the future of this recovery is still uncertain.

Many factors are at play in this situation, making it difficult to distinguish causes from effects. For example, in the economic debate, the elevated amount of foreign debt held by Latin American countries is blamed for poor growth performance. However, as some economists have pointed out, if all the loans had been used in investments providing normal rates of return, such as those observed in the past, those investments would have provided sufficient return not only to service the debt but also to pay the principal.

The aim of this book is to provide both a framework for understanding this situation and methodological tools for designing and evaluating economic policies.

My hope is that the findings and method presented here will help promote the design of better economic policies not only to lead to a recovery of the growth rates of the 1950s, 1960s, and early 1970s, but also to enhance the long-term growth potential of Latin American countries.

The Approach

Macroeconomics seeks to understand general movements in economic activity and to evaluate the role of economic policies, among many other factors, in those movements.

Economists have begun to analyze growth and stability problems jointly, rather than separately, as they did before. In business-cycle analysis, for example, macroeconomics examines the length of the cycles, the duration of their different phases (depression and expansion), and their intensity. In growth analysis, the main concern is to explain the diverse stages of growth and disparities within them, across countries and over time. Both of these approaches contribute insights to the more general macroeconomic effort to understand both business cycles and growth movements in a unified economic model. The evidence currently being processed by these two types of analysis is extensive and is being subjected to diverse types of methods and models.

This study investigates the growth experience of seven Latin American countries—Argentina, Brazil, Chile, Colombia, Mexico, Peru, and Venezuela—from 1940 to 1985 and identifies the main sources of that growth.[1] My analysis of growth performance is mainly empirical and builds on a frame of reference being developed in the specialized growth literature. I propose a methodological advance by quantifying the data for traditional sources of growth and provide some new empirical tools for measuring the role of other factors that seem significant in recent growth acceleration experiences.

I hope to participate in the development of comparative growth analysis by offering insights that will be useful for formulating policies to stimulate economic growth. Many such policies in the past have been designed without reference to the restrictions to growth that the sources-of-growth analysis reveals. Recent studies provide significant insights into the stages of growth, acceleration and slowdown phenomena, and sources of growth that may help close the gap in per capita income across countries, as well as into the many growth forces suggested by diverse growth models (such as economies of scale, division of labor, the role of market size, reallocation of resources, the role of foreign trade, and the productivity gap). As analyzed here, the actual experience of the Latin American countries contributes new factual material to the debate about economic policies needed for future growth.

The study of the sources of economic growth is a field of increasing relevance in the area of economic growth and development. Within this field, most studies have focused on developed economies; an analysis of the Latin American experience is, therefore, an important contribution that allows for comparison among countries.[2]

My analysis is done at an aggregate economic level (one-sector model) as is usually done for developed economies, and I codify the data for analysis in terms of diverse economic sectors (agriculture, manufacturing, public) without reference to the "traditional-modern" distinction, which has created problems for the analysis of Latin American growth behavior. I also offer a detailed study of the composition of labor and capital inputs, establishing links between growth and development analyses, which are so often considered mutually exclusive or antagonistic. In this way, I hope to contribute to the creation of a model and method that will permit accurate comparisons among Latin American economies and improved understanding of their diverse growth experiences.

Including the seven countries studied here, sources-of-growth analyses are currently available for around twenty-five countries in Europe, Asia,

North America, and Latin America. Studies are also in progress for Bolivia, Costa Rica, Paraguay, and Uruguay.[3]

Overview

The principal findings of this study stress the importance of accurately identifying the main factors in growth fluctuations among countries and over time. As a first approximation of the Latin American economic experience of the past forty years, Figure 1 (page 9) presents the overall average annual rate of change of each of the structural components considered by sources-of-growth method for the seven Latin American countries from 1940 to 1985.

These figures are not much lower than those reported for fast-growing economies, and they reveal the importance of both the quality and quantity of inputs and the relevance of each input for overall growth. Some of these elements (such as quality of labor, quantity of capital, and technological change, also called total factor productivity) respond more directly and more quickly to economic policies than others (such as gross labor, which is a function of population growth). A detailed analysis for each country and each decade from 1940 to 1985 is presented in Chapter 4.

In general, for all countries and decades, capital made the highest contribution to output growth (45.6 percent), while the contribution of labor was similar to that of total factor productivity (TFP). The schematic representation also shows that capital made a greater contribution to growth both because of the growth of its quantity and because of its share (or weight). The quality of labor played an important role in the growth of the labor input and, through it, in output growth.

The overall growth rate of output, or GDP, of around 5 percent per year implied a per capita growth rate of over 2.5 percent. Even though this is a reasonable growth rate for the long run, it seems low for a short period, especially in the light of the substantial gaps between Latin America and developed countries with respect to the per capita GDP. In the seven countries, the trends for labor and capital correspond closely with that for output. What diverges is the behavior of the TFP trend, which, in my analysis, includes technological change and some commonly omitted variables.

This study is organized in eleven chapters and six appendixes. In the chapters, I describe the main findings of my analysis, emphasizing their implications for the design of economic policies. Much of the analysis is contained in the tables and figures, which appear at the end of each chapter and are an important complement to the text. The appendixes contain complete tables for each of the variables considered and provide more technical explanations of my method. They will be helpful to those interested in using the data as research material or in furthering the analysis presented here. The notes contain some methodological discussions and suggestions for future research.

Chapter 2 provides a general picture of the performance of each of the seven Latin American countries in terms of output growth and stability (inflation and business-cycle performance). It offers a kind of quick economic geography of the seven countries, useful to help us find our way in their economies.

Chapter 3 presents the basic elements of the sources-of-growth methodology and a general discussion of the relevant economic growth literature. This review of the literature highlights the importance of diverse contributions to the sources-of-growth approach. As such, it is a very general description of the different models of and approaches to the study of economic growth.

Chapter 4, which is part of the set formed by Chapters 4 to 7, presents the main findings of my analysis of the sources of economic growth for the seven countries studied. In general terms, the analysis reveals that capital has had the highest share in contributing to output growth; TFP has been very important; and the quality of labor has an important role in labor's contribution to overall growth. However, important variations in these contributions occurred across countries and over time. Chapter 4 also presents a measurement of the TFP index and of the partial input productivities of labor and capital. These indexes are a useful complement to the study of the sources of growth because they tend to follow other indicators very closely, clearly defining a period of acceleration from 1940 to 1973, a slowdown until 1980, and a negative trend in TFP since then. The chapter ends with the results of the sources-of-growth analysis using the so-called dual approach, based on prices of output and inputs, which corroborates both the findings and the method.

Chapter 5 presents estimates of the output growth and functional income distribution that determine the weights given to the growth rates of each input in computing its contribution to overall output growth. It also describes the behavior of the annual growth rate of GDP, discussing the importance of the public sector in total GDP growth.

Chapter 6 presents a detailed analysis of the labor input. The measurement of labor quality is relevant for economic policy making because it reveals the main elements that explain labor income distribution. Chapter 6 looks at labor composition in terms of education, sex, age, occupation, economic sector, and regional distribution. Changes are computed by decade and weighted by the relative productivity of each category. The chapter thus provides an estimate of the rate of change of labor quality and determines the most important component in labor quality change. It also provides valuable information on the labor market in Latin American countries, which will be useful in the study of diverse labor economics problems and for the design of economic policies affecting the labor market.

In Chapter 7 I examine the capital input, estimating both the quantity and quality of capital. In all seven countries, capital stock (the gross component of the capital input) had a reasonable rate of growth over time, with countries like Brazil achieving capital accumulation similar to that of the high-growth countries of the Pacific Rim. The growth of capital stock produced an important increase in the capital-labor ratio, which was positively associated with the degree of importance of TFP in output growth. The quality component of capital, however, showed negative growth, diminishing capital accumulation. Chapter 7 also provides valuable information for the analysis of capital markets, which will be relevant for evaluating the role of economic policies connected with investment and saving decisions.

Chapter 8 applies the sources-of-growth method to the growth phenomena in the agricultural, manufacturing, and public sectors. This exercise complements the aggregate analysis in Chapter 4. First, it demonstrates the usefulness of the aggregate approach for the analysis of a particular economic sector. Second, it integrates, at least partially, demand- and supply-side approaches to the study of economic growth, by demonstrating the importance of observing changes in output composition in GDP growth. Finally, it provides a useful tool for evaluating the propositions arising from economic development literature, which, in many cases, argue for the importance of one particular sector or another for aggregate growth.

The sources-of-growth method used throughout this study is complemented by other econometric methods in Chapter 9. The chapter has two purposes. The first is to estimate the role of several factors that have been postulated as decisive by many growth theories, such as technological transmission across countries. The second is to present some methodologies that may be useful in the field of empirical economic growth studies, such as stochastic analysis of the behavior of the GDP over time, an econometric growth model that would allow us to integrate variables relevant for economic policy decisions with sources of economic growth, and profile analysis that allows us to discriminate between performance and policy variables across countries.

Chapter 10 presents a comparative analysis of the growth performance and sources of growth of the seven Latin American economies and those of many developed economies. The developed economies and the Latin American economies exhibit the same stages of growth acceleration and slowdown, with an important difference: the Latin American economies accelerated less but slowed down at rates similar to those of developed countries. The chapter also gives estimates of the productivity of labor for these economies for the period 1940–1980. Labor and capital, it appears, play different roles in Latin American and developed economies.

Finally, Chapter 11 presents some predictions for the future growth of Latin American economies. These broad predictions are based on particular predictions concerning the growth of labor and capital inputs, taken together with expected technological change. Although some Latin American economies currently seem to be leaving the slowdown period while others remain trapped within it, my predictions are based on long-term observations of the behavior of these economies. They should be taken with a grain of salt, for changes in these countries and in the world economy could produce a happier outcome than the one suggested here. The fact is that new economic policies will influence the growth processes of these countries. The analysis presented here provides a framework for evaluating current policies, which is a necessary step in the creation of adequate future economic growth policies.

Relevance for Economic Policy Design

An important aim of studies of this kind is to give an empirical and theoretical basis for tools used to design economic policies. To this end, I will show the relationship between the main results of this study and specific tools of economic policy design, in the hope that they will be useful to economic policy makers in Latin America and elsewhere.

For example, the quality component has been an important factor for labor input growth, and government expenditure policies can have an important role in improving labor quality through education. The quality component has not contributed to capital growth, however, indicating that little has been done to improve capital market efficiency and suggesting that future fiscal and regulatory economic policies will be key for the stimulation of that source of growth. Moreover, the fact that the public sector has reported lower capital rates of return and weaker growth in TFP than the private sector suggests that partial movements from the public to the private sector should also be the concern of economic policies. Other significant findings related to such economic growth factors as foreign trade, labor reallocation, and technological change are discussed in the relevant chapters.

Notes

1. I chose the period 1940–1985 for three reasons: it is recent; it is long enough to accommodate the sources-of-growth methodology; and reasonably accurate national accounts have existed only since 1940.

2. The design of economic policies requires not only the frameworks provided by economic models, but also an evaluation of those models in terms of their ability to predict growth behavior in diverse economies, in comparative terms and over time.

3. These studies are being conducted at the Universities of Tucumán and Montevideo.

FIGURE 1 Sources of Economic Growth for Seven Latin American Countries, 1940–1985
(average annual percentage)

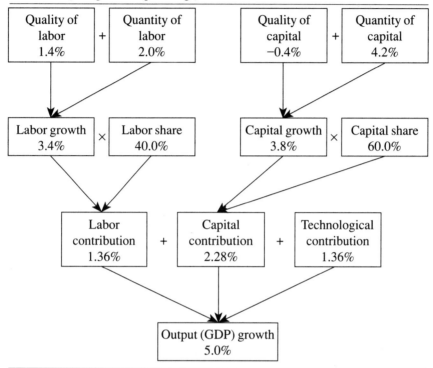

SOURCE: Table 2.

$$Labor + tech = .544 - 54.4\%$$
$$Capital = .456 - 45.6\%$$

CHAPTER 2

Latin American
Macroeconomic Performance

This chapter presents an overview of the economic performance of the seven countries studied here, analyzing them in terms of long-run growth and stability for the period 1900–1980. Long-run growth will be examined in terms of the average annual growth rate of GDP, population, and per capita GDP. (Chapter 9 gives a more detailed analysis of annual growth variation.) Stability will be analyzed in terms of inflation and business cycles, on the basis of the data concerning the average duration of the cycles and the average length of recovery and recession phases. (Another important indicator, the unemployment rate, is discussed in Chapter 9).[1]

The integration of growth and stability is a challenging task for economic analysis. This study contributes evidence helpful for understanding fluctuations in the long-run GDP growth rates. This kind of integral analysis is essential to a comprehensive understanding of the growth slowdown of the 1980s.[2]

Long-Run Economic Growth

Figure 2 (page 14) gives long-run trends in growth rates of GDP, population, and per capita GDP for the seven countries. This figure shows a

11

positive trend in the average annual growth rate of per capita GDP. The average rate for all the countries rose from 1.29 percent in the period 1900–1940 to 2.37 percent in the period 1940–1980.

Interestingly, population growth rates vary both between periods and among countries. All the countries except Argentina, however, show positive trends in the rate of population growth.

In the rate of overall GDP growth, Brazil, Chile, and Mexico show important increases, while Argentina and Colombia are relatively stable.

Stability

Expansion and contraction

Some recent studies on the business cycles of Latin American countries offer data that can be used to appraise economic stability. These studies include business-cycle quantifications for Argentina, Mexico, and Venezuela from 1960 to 1984 (see Table 1, page 17). In all three countries, expansionary periods lasted much longer than contractionary periods. The average duration, in months, for expansions and contractions was 41 and 15 respectively for Argentina, 45 and 20 for Mexico, and 43 and 29 for Venezuela. In this period, Argentina registered one more total cycle than Mexico.

Even though business-cycle phases in these economies are of similar duration, they are not synchronized. In a period of twenty-one years, for example, Argentina and Mexico were in different phases half the time. More advanced countries report a higher degree of synchronization not only in their business-cycle phases but also in their growth phases (Moore 1989).

Prices

The variability of the inflation rate is another important measure of economic stability. The Latin American countries have at times experienced high and variable rates of inflation.

Figure 3 (page 15) presents the average annual compound rate of inflation for selected periods. The 1940s show similar rates of annual inflation across countries, around 13 percent. In the 1950s, Argentina, Brazil, and Chile had accelerating inflation rates, while the other countries experienced low inflation, below 13 percent. In the 1960s, Brazil experienced an acceleration of its inflation rate, a phenomenon that spread to the rest of the continent in the 1970s.

Notes

1. The Latin American countries included in this study present a history of high and variable inflation rates and variable unemployment rates. These two indicators are a good index of stability, except in the case of a stable Phillips curve, where they are substitutes for each other.

2. The description of the performance of any specific national economy requires more detailed indicators than the ones presented in this chapter. Some, such as output and input composition, will be discussed in other chapters. Others, such as institutional and financial indicators, will not be discussed in this study. Income distribution analysis is incorporated in the sources-of-growth methodology, but its specific effects on growth through aggregate demand will not be considered.

FIGURE 2 Average Annual Growth Rates of GDP, Population, and Per Capita GDP, 1900–1980

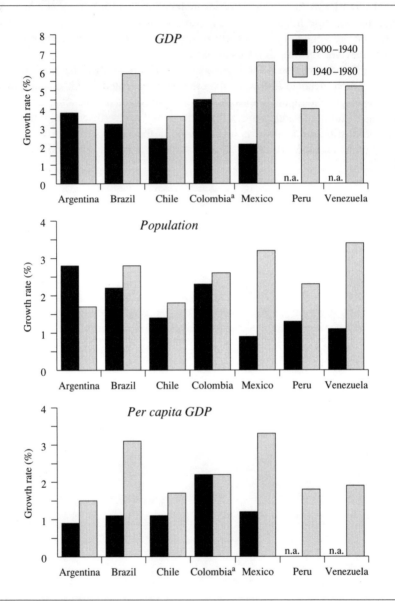

n.a. = not available.
a. Black bar covers the period 1925–1940.
SOURCES: Economic Commission for Latin America (1951); Ruddle and Barrows (1974); Banco Central de la República Argentina (1976).

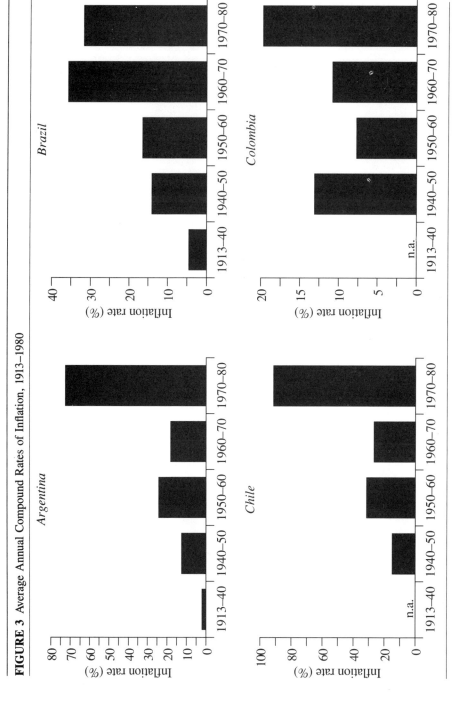

FIGURE 3 Average Annual Compound Rates of Inflation, 1913–1980

(continued on following page)

15

FIGURE 3 (continued)

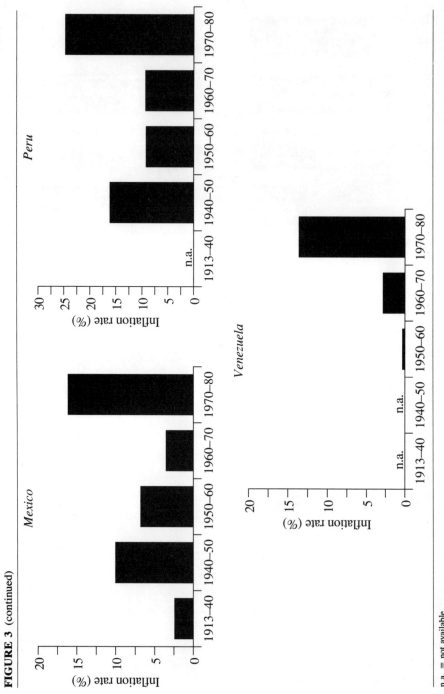

n.a. = not available.
SOURCES: Same as Figure 2.

TABLE 1 Expansion and Contraction Periods for Argentina, Mexico, and Venezuela, 1960–1984

Country	Expansions Period	Duration (months)	Contractions Period	Duration (months)
Argentina	July 1963 to May 1967	47	August 1961 to July 1963	23
	December 1967 to December 1974	84	May 1967 to December 1967	7
	November 1975 July 1977	20	December 1974 to November 1975	11
	March 1978 to February 1980	23	July 1977 to March 1978	8
	April 1982 to October 1984	30	February 1980 to April 1982	26
Mexico	April 1962 to February 1964	22	February 1964 to May 1967	39
	May 1967 to August 1970	39	August 1970 to April 1971	8
	April 1971 to July 1976	63	July 1976 to February 1977	7
	February 1977 to October 1981	56	October 1981 to December 1983	26
Venezuela	May 1973 to September 1978	64	June 1970 to May 1973	35
	August 1980 to June 1982	22	September 1978 to August 1980	23

SOURCES: Arranz and Elías (1984); de Alba and Trigueros (1986); Rosas Bravo (1983).

CHAPTER 3

Models and Methods for the Study of Economic Growth

This chapter presents the main ideas underlying several recent models that attempt to explain the growth behavior of developed and underdeveloped economies, highlighting the facets of these models that I have incorporated into my analysis. The discussion here is a summary and does not investigate all the implications of these theories.

I also discuss sources-of-growth methodology, which I employ in my study of the economic growth of seven selected Latin American countries. I discuss my method here in detail to enable the reader to critically appraise the main arguments that inform my analysis in the following chapters. This chapter also presents the main formula used in the sources-of-growth methodology. (See Appendix A for a detailed presentation of this formula.)

Long-Run Equilibrium Growth Models

There are many approaches to studying the economic growth processes of a given economy, depending on the analytical objectives and the kind of problem to be examined. In this section, I discuss the equilibrium theory of economic growth. This theory developed directly from static theory and is related to dynamic equilibrium problems.

Equilibrium theory attempts to explain the level and the determinants of the equilibrium growth of a given economy. This model shows whether or not an economy will grow in the long run in terms of total and per capita GDP. It also analyzes the stability of the equilibrium growth rate determined by the model and, in the case of displacement from equilibrium, suggests how equilibrium can be restored.

I distinguish between models that operate exclusively according to a given set of equations and those that are informed by a proposed optimization process from which the appropriate set of equations is derived. The former models derive the equilibrium solution directly from the equations proposed and the necessary equilibrium conditions. The latter propose an intertemporal welfare function that society wishes to maximize and, within the limits of given restraints, determine the optimum equilibrium growth rate. Both models are useful for exercises in balanced-growth simulations and for determining the main elements that will sustain the desired equilibrium growth.

The optimization method has an advantage in that it uses the underlying assumptions of the basic equations, explicitly justifying the incorporation of each equation and of the variables in those equations. In this way, it clearly restricts the basic parameters of the model.

In these two equilibrium models, total factor productivity (TFP) plays a significant role in determining the rate of growth of per capita GDP. The saving rate, in these models, does not affect the equilibrium rate of growth (even though it affects the level of per capita GDP and the adjustment path to equilibrium growth). The possibility of input substitution only increases the stability of the model's equilibrium. Recent studies of human capital and capital heterogeneity recover the role of saving in equilibrium growth analysis.

In general, equilibrium models use broad macroeconomic functions; very few begin their analysis from a microeconomic point of view. They also tend to use very simple macroeconomic functions with limited reference to information coming from empirical macroeconomics.[1]

Growth Theories

Growth theories are generally known as economic development theories in the specialized literature. Their main purpose is to explain the behavior of underdeveloped economies and reveal the main factors that would allow them to approach the behavior of developed economies. These theories have been closely associated with the design of economic policies for the purpose of accelerating the economic growth of a given country.

Different growth theories emphasize different aspects of the economy. I describe some of them here in a general way and make use of certain elements of them in my own analysis.

Some growth theories operate principally in terms of two economic sectors: modern and traditional. They argue that in order to grow an economy must develop its modern sector. The role of the traditional sector is to provide basic food, raw materials, and a flow of labor input for the modern sector. The modern sector must grow in order to provide employment for those migrating from the traditional sector.

Depending on the assumptions operating within the different models, the conditions necessary for the economy to start growing imply either a smooth pattern of advances or significant jumps in the behavior of the relevant variables.

These theories postulate that certain minimum conditions are essential for moving from economic stagnation to sustained growth. These conditions include high population growth, an accelerated rate of technological change, and increases in the marginal propensity to save and in the income share of labor.

In some theories, the traditional sector is identified with agriculture and the modern sector with industry—a distinction that has fallen into disuse in recent years. In some cases, an intermediate sector is introduced between the traditional and modern sectors, and the modern sector is sometimes divided into light and heavy industries.

Other growth theories seek the origin of underdevelopment at an aggregate level, attempting to show the causes of stagnation. Their principal concern is the high cost of the factors that have been responsible for growth in developed countries, particularly capital, which, if costly, inhibits adequate growth of fixed capital investment in stagnating economies.

Still other growth theories study economic growth patterns in an effort to identify those patterns that will be useful for the building of effective growth models. Most of these studies concentrate on demand. For this purpose, they analyze the importance over time of each economic sector in different economies. However, they also classify countries by their saving and investment rates, which some would consider part of a supply-side approach.

There are also growth theories that stress the importance of the foreign sector of the economy. Some of these attempt to discover the foreign-sector factors that should provide a targeted rate of economic growth. Others consider the actual behavior of the world market, showing how protectionism and terms of trade influence the growth potential of an underdeveloped economy. Generally, these theories seek to demonstrate that foreign-sector relationships between economies create dependencies that affect growth in these economies.[2]

These theories have paid great attention in recent years to the so-called limiting factors, such as nonrenewable resources. The incidence of these factors could notably diminish the high rate of growth characteristic of modern developed economies, thus compelling some countries to put restraints on their growth objectives.

Examples of the profuse growth theory literature appear in the References. I only wish to make critical mention here of the main aspects of these theories, relying on the existing survey articles to provide more detailed analysis. As I have mentioned, in this study I will use elements of these theories, especially those that seem to reveal growth sources.

The Sources-of-Growth Method

The sources-of-growth method is the method employed in this study. Its purpose is to identify the main determinants of the growth rate of the GDP or of any economic sector separately. Even though this method is mainly descriptive, it constitutes an important starting point for explaining the economic growth behavior of any economy. This is so because the method provides direct access to the determinants of growth (growth of inputs) and also to the underlying forces that explain growth (sources of input growth). Quantifying the contribution of each source of growth gives a clearer idea of the phenomenon I seek to explain.

The sources-of-growth method is mainly an accounting approach. As such, it has as its starting point the national accounts of the economies to be analyzed and the aggregate production function theory.[3]

The basic formula of the sources-of-growth method states that the rate of output growth (GDP) is equal to (1) the rate of growth of gross labor plus the rate of growth of its quality, times the labor income share plus (2) the rate of growth of gross capital input plus the rate of growth of capital quality, times the capital income share plus (3) total factor productivity change. This formula is presented schematically in Figure 4 (page 32).

Since this study will consider different kinds of labor and capital inputs, we need to define a gross and quality component for each of them. In the case of labor, the gross component is simply the arithmetic sum of employment across characteristics. For capital, it is the arithmetic sum of capital. The quality component of each input is established by a consideration of its diverse characteristics. The rate of change of the quality component is derived by applying the following calculation: The rate of change of the quality of labor is equal to the weighted sum of the changes in the share of each characteristic (such as education, sex, and age) considered for the composition of the labor force. The weights are the ratio of the unit wage of each kind of labor to the average wage rate for the whole labor force. This same formula is applied to capital, with the necessary adjustments.

The quality component, as defined here, captures changes in the composition of labor and capital. The difference between each input is reflected in its productivity, which is the basis for distinguishing between them. These distinctions, in turn, depend on many input characteristics. For example, in the case of labor, education level, age, sex, and occupation are important characteristics; in the case of capital, economic sector, "age" of capital, and different tax treatments of capital incomes for different sectors are important.

The differences in productivity are assumed to be reflected in the unit prices of each kind of input, which implies that we assume competitive equilibrium in the market for all inputs or that the same proportional distortions are present in the market for each kind of input.[4]

In this method, I also distinguish between two kinds of outputs: consumption and investment goods. Consequently, the total output rate of growth will be equal to the weighted sum of the growth rate of both outputs. This calculation captures the effects of changes in relative prices of consumption and investment goods.

Moreover, because the calculation of the quality of both labor and capital inputs may not capture all the changes stemming from the TFP, the main formula includes another element: the rate of change of the TFP.

The sources-of-growth method provides a structure for organizing the information in national accounts. The current state of these accounts was influenced by the development of macroeconomic models that emphasized the demand side of economic growth questions. This method attempts to complete the information, approaching the material from the supply side as well. In this way, the method gives the analysis of national accounts a more powerful role in the interpretation of the process of economic growth than was possible previously.

Even though this method is not a theory of economic growth, it provides a great deal of information that is useful for the design of economic policies, showing the role played by each component in the past and measuring the changes experienced by each variable, along with the effects to be expected from a change in each of them. This information is vital for the design of government expenditure and tax policies, many of which affect the quality of both labor and capital inputs.

A complete theory of growth will have to go beyond the input sources of growth and discover their determinants. Such a theory will have to account not only for the behavioral function underlying the determination of the level of each input, but also for the relevance of each of the elements as a determinant of growth.

Currently, the sources-of-growth methodology is still developing. At the end of this study, I will discuss some of the theoretical efforts being made at present and some initial analytical results obtained for Latin American countries (see Chapter 9).

This method can also be applied to each economic sector separately. Moreover, we can start at the level of economic sectors and then aggregate them. The method can therefore provide information about specific and aggregate economic sector composition that is very useful for certain policy-design purposes. For this analysis of seven Latin American countries, complete data for all economic sectors are not available. However, I will apply the sources-of-growth method to the available data in order to form a general picture of sector composition behavior.

Some Antecedents of the Sources-of-Growth Method

The roots of this methodology can be traced back at least as far as the work of Jan Tinbergen (1959), who in 1942 examined the national accounts of Germany, the United States, France, and Great Britain for the period 1870–1914. His studies, like many that followed, considered only part of the current main formula, working exclusively with the gross components of labor and capital inputs and with total GDP. One of the characteristics of these early studies was the important role of the growth of the TFP, calculated as the difference between the rate of growth of the GDP and the weighted average of the rate of growth of gross labor and capital inputs. This was the unexplained part of economic growth—literally, the residual—and has come to be equated with technological change, although other factors must be included. This residual is also known as total factor productivity.

Since the beginning of the century, the National Bureau of Economic

Research in the United States has compiled the statistical information necessary to apply the sources-of-growth method. In a pioneering work, D. Gale Johnson (1950) applied this method to the agricultural sector of the United States.

Robert Solow's (1957) analysis of the sources of economic growth for the United States is a milestone in this field. It drew the attention of many economists to the problems involved in analyzing the effects of technological change.[5] Solow's results challenged the profession. After him, many economists attempted to make more accurate estimates of the inputs, working toward more precise definitions of the element known as technology. As their estimates of inputs became more accurate, the amount of growth attributed to TFP fell.

Subsequent studies carried out for the United States have concentrated on productivity (the supply side) with approaches that have contributed to the current efficacy of the sources-of-growth method (Fabricant 1959; Abramovitz 1956; Kendrick 1961). Some researchers followed Solow's approach of estimating the aggregate production function, with emphasis on a more general functional form. These efforts produced great improvements in the area of production function, both in theory and econometrics, comparable to earlier developments in the econometrics of demand theory. Others followed a more direct sources-of-growth approach, mainly through recourse to national and sector accounts.

In a landmark work, Edward Denison (1962) contributed to the development of the sources-of-growth method by including in his measurements not only gross labor and capital, but also elements of input quality and other characteristics of the production function. In this way, Denison reduced a great deal of the TFP that remained in the work of Solow. For labor, he took into account education, the age and gender composition of the labor force, hours of work, and unemployment. For capital, he considered changes in the stock of capital composition by economic sector (see Kendrick 1961), alternative definitions of the capital input, and other components, such as the role of foreign trade and increasing return to scale. He included what today are considered the main determinants of GDP growth, and he devised effective ways of assigning a weight to each of them.

In 1967, Denison extended his work to cover many developed countries, allowing a comparative analysis of the sources of economic growth among countries. He covered Germany, Belgium, Denmark, the United States, France, Great Britain, the Netherlands, Italy, and Norway. In other works, he analyzed a more recent period in the United States and included other determinants, such as fluctuations in the agricultural sector (like weather) and ecological problems. In the case of Japan, which experienced a prolonged period of high growth, he analyzed the role of technological transfer.

An important contribution to the methodology was made by Dale W. Jorgenson and Zvi Griliches (1967), who developed the approach used in this study. They were able to explain nearly all the TFP in their analysis of the United States. They also presented a consistent method for the study of outputs and inputs, mainly by calculating net output and capital stock, which permits the explicit consideration of capital depreciation and replacement. The differences between the approach of Jorgenson and Griliches and that of Denison may explain the differences in their results. Jorgenson and Griliches' residual was reduced to less than 10 percent of GDP growth, while Denison's was slightly higher (see Abramovitz 1988).

A number of researchers wrote comparative works on sources of economic growth in several countries, mainly the United States and European countries (Domar et al. 1964; Barger 1969; Kuznets 1971; Bergson 1974). The comparative analysis made by Christensen, Cummings, and Jorgenson (1980) is very important. They covered Germany, Canada, the United States, France, Great Britain, the Netherlands, Italy, Japan, and South Korea, extending, for comparative purposes, the previous study of the United States made by Jorgenson and Griliches. In their work on the United States, these economists developed a complete set of accounts appropriate for the sources-of-growth method that provides the necessary information in four categories: production, expenditure, distribution, and accumulation. Furthermore, they extended the range of defined components of physical capital to cover different kinds of assets, such as production and household assets, although they limited their distinctions to the private sector only. They also integrated the production function approach into their investigations, using the logarithmic approximation of the production function, creating a flexible method and providing a specific framework for the verification of the underlying assumptions with respect to the substitution of inputs and the return to scale.

Kendrick (1976) made an important effort to establish a concept of total capital, including human and nonhuman elements, basing his definition on the work of Frank Knight (1944), I. Fisher (discussed in Knight), and Theodore W. Schultz (1953). Kendrick's results support the idea of a constant capital-output ratio, for those cases in which all the elements that could be considered capital are included. A recent development in this approach with important macroeconomic implications is that of Jorgenson and Fraumeni (1988).

Irving Kravis and his associates (1975) also made an important methodological contribution by attempting to estimate the national income of a great number of countries, which could, subsequently, be compared. They developed purchasing-power parities for the products for many countries, which are necessary for eventual comparative analyses.

Currently, there is concern among economists about the decrease in the importance of the TFP as a source of growth, a phenomenon that appeared in the 1970s, along with the global slowdown of GDP growth. This contrasts with the relatively great importance of the TFP in the 1950s.

Many studies have also been made of Latin America. Work by Henry J. Bruton (1967) covered Argentina, Brazil, Chile, Colombia, and Mexico. In 1970, Héctor Correa included the same countries and added Peru, Venezuela, Ecuador, and Honduras. Bruton covered the 1940–1964 period and Correa, 1950–1962. Both studies focused exclusively on long-run changes, without considering annual behavior. Other studies have been made for particular countries or sectors.[6] I began my work in 1973 and have, since then, published parts of it.

Recent Contributions to the Sources-of-Growth Method

In recent years, the sources-of-growth methodology has been refined in order to consider different problems. And its usefulness has been questioned (Abramovitz 1988).

In his last work on the United States, Denison (1985) incorporated new elements, such as treatment of fluctuations in the agricultural sector and the role of management as partial determinants of the behavior of the TFP in an effort to obtain an improved account of the GDP.

The treatment of fluctuations in agriculture is an important factor for this study, because the agricultural sector plays an important role in the growth processes of Latin American countries. Because there are many fluctuations in the agricultural sector, mainly due to weather, TFP values could be considered to be unaffected by technological changes. For the United States at least, Denison found that these weather-caused fluctuations are not important in accounting for the TFP.

Denison also considered ecological problems, which were mentioned in another context by W. Nordhaus and J. Tobin (1973). They attempted to calculate a welfare indicator instead of the GDP, taking into account the fact that there were many elements commonly being calculated for the GDP that generally should not, strictly speaking, be considered consumption output (for example, air and water preservation, which are important indirect economic factors, require a great deal of investment). Denison also tried to include this element in a separate account. The sources-of-growth method used here studies almost all the determinants of production, even though some output of this production is not so much for consumption but rather for the consumption of other elements.

In the case of these and other adjustments, such as the inclusion of sectors that are not captured by the national accounts (such as the informal sector), the calculations must be made on both sides of the formula for the sake of accuracy.

The work of Christensen, Cummings, and Jorgenson aimed at providing a complete set of national accounts and at using the production function theory to record all quality relationships. As mentioned above, they integrated the production, expenditure, distribution, and accumulation accounts, providing a complete picture of the most important aspects of the economy.

Their approach can easily take into account the financial aspects of the economy and the investment process of some elements that are relevant for the quality indicator. In this study, I measure both quantities and prices in order to have effective control over the estimates. Calculations of the accounts in terms of prices have been used in very few previous studies (see Peterson 1967 on the poultry industry in the United States and Griliches 1971 on hedonic prices).

Jorgenson endeavored to make appropriate measurements of factor prices in terms of their units of services. This is clearly seen in his work on physical capital, for which he applied the findings of investment theory, relating the prices of investment goods, the price of capital, and the prices for their services, including the rate of return, the depreciation rate, and capital gain or loss.

Jorgenson also investigated the corresponding relationship between the replacement and depreciation aspects of the output and accumulation accounts. He emphasized the assumptions necessary to make their treatment symmetrical in both accounts.

He was also interested in developing an econometric model of economic growth from this set of accounts, giving a more analytical role to the sources-of-growth method. This model will be an important aspect of future research, though not an easy one to apply, as advances will have to be kept within a reasonably simple structure.

This book attempts to broaden the growth-accounting approach in order to evaluate the role of the foreign sector in the economic growth of the study countries. This has been an interesting effort because the foreign trade sector plays such an important role in the economies of Latin America. My analysis was presented, in preliminary form, in two papers published in 1972 and 1978 (Elías 1972, 1978a).

The measurement of the foreign sector contribution to growth as such is not measured by traditional international trade theories in terms of productivity, so it has been necessary to develop new approaches that allow us to identify the importance of this source of growth. I have attempted to develop this integration through two approaches. The first relies on the elements of the cost of foreign trade protection and the terms of trade effect. The second approach measures the contribution of foreign trade to the growth of the capital stock of the economy. This measurement is made in terms of economies that export consumption goods and import investment goods. In this case, foreign trade introduces a greater amount of investment goods into the economy than would be the case for a closed economy. This approach makes it possible to estimate this additional investment and its contribution to the growth of the capital stock and therefore to evaluate the foreign trade contribution to economic growth. In this study, only the second approach was followed.

I mention here in passing an alternative approach that builds separate capital stocks for domestic and foreign-origin investment goods. This approach would allow for an estimate of their separate effects through the production function approach (see Sturm 1977). This alternative is helpful for identifying the effects arising from the public sector, including the government's role as a public enterprise and its administrative role, which should, however, be treated separately. Government expenditures would be considered a process of investing a kind of public capital, which will influence private sector production.

I also want to mention the analysis of economic interrelationships among countries. Countries affect each other through international trade, producing effects that can partially explain the behavior of the TFP. This mechanism of transmission and interaction could be an important element in explaining the TFP as a component source of growth. In some cases, the correct accounting for the payment of the so-called royalties paid by countries for the use of a particular technology could account for these effects. In other cases, we have to explore other channels that are not so clearly identifiable.

Chapter 9 explores the relevance of some of these recent advances for the case of Latin America.

Country Comparative Analysis

In order to make a cross-country comparative study of the results obtained for the countries included in this study, the data must be homogenized, through the application of one of several methods. One interesting approach is to use the purchasing power parity alternative for output and inputs. Another is to evaluate output and inputs at common international prices across countries. (This will require very detailed information for output and inputs.) A simpler approach will be to use the U.S. dollar exchange rate of each country, even though this could have an important bias when it differs much from the one that will correspond according to the purchasing power parity. However, when comparative analysis is done in terms of the rate of growth of output and inputs, fewer accounting problems can be expected.

Moreover, country accounts can be analyzed separately, over time, or a number of countries and periods can be considered together, as a single sample. In the first case, I do the comparative analysis by contrasting the results obtained for each country. In the second, I analyze all the country observations at the same time, trying to derive their implications. In this study, I combine both approaches, first, by accumulating a sample of cases defined by certain characteristics, and second, by applying statistical tools in order to summarize the assembled data and draw conclusions.

The Latin American experience can be analyzed by itself or in comparison with analyses of other countries, especially those of developed economies. This broad sources-of-growth analysis would make creative methodological use of the findings already available in the literature.[7]

Notes

1. Given the presence of monetary assets, many efforts have been made to integrate the real and monetary sectors of the economy in order to study the effects of the growth rate of the money supply on the growth rate of GDP within the different models discussed in this section.

2. In the past decade, the economic behavior of developed and under-

developed economies has become increasingly similar, suggesting that analysis of certain "typical" and exceptional growth national economies, within the global context, would demonstrate whether the growth of a given country is a direct result of growth in other countries or not.

3. Under certain conditions of invertibility of cost and production functions, both approaches are equivalent. This problem is addressed by the "dual approach."

4. Thus, quality is defined on the basis of the weighted sum of changes in the proportion of each kind of input in the total gross input. For example, for analytical purposes, the quality term will be zero if there is no change in the composition of each kind of input. It will also be zero if there is no difference in unit prices between the different categories of inputs (that is, if inputs are homogeneous). Quality change will be positive if there is an increase in the proportion of labor inputs with high unit prices.

5. Solow used a Cobb-Douglas aggregate production function on the gross concepts of labor and capital. Then he used a constant income share for computing the weighted average of the rate of growth of labor and capital inputs. He also, however, ended up with important values for the TFP.

6. See, for example, M. Selowsky (1967) for Chile and Mexico; C. Langoni (1970) for Brazil; R. Hertford (1969) for Mexican agriculture; V. Elías (1969) for Argentinean industry; Orozco (1977) for Colombian agriculture; and Valdés (1971) for Chilean agriculture.

7. Some new techniques have been developed to study the comparative data in a more rigorous way. For example, Jorgenson used some particular forms of production function for two or more countries, deriving from them a measurement of approximation together with the sources of this approximation. However, since this approach requires great homogeneity in the cross-country information, I am not able to use it here.

FIGURE 4 Schematic Presentation of the Sources-of-Growth Methodology

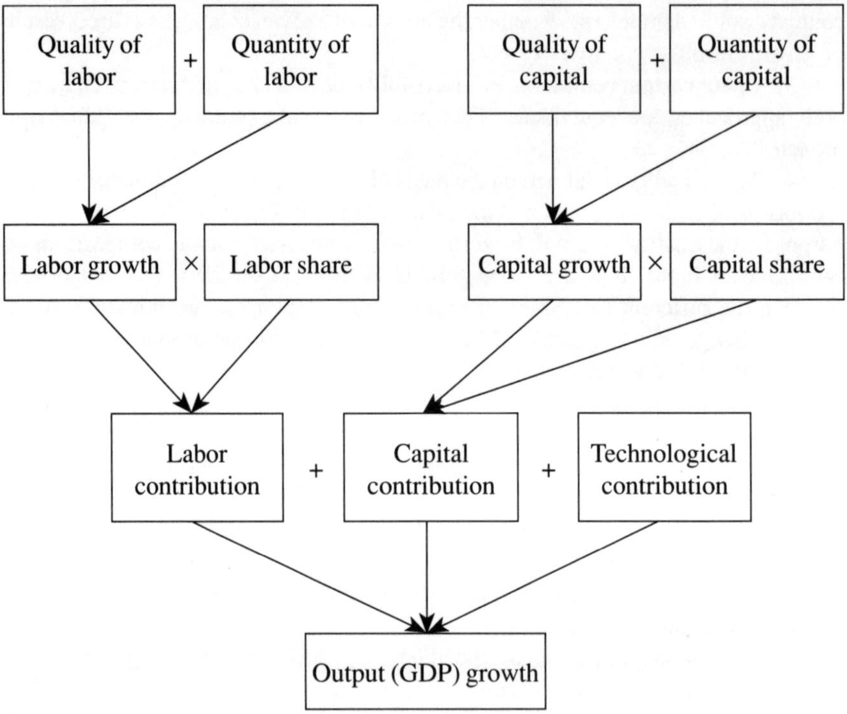

SOURCE: Author.

CHAPTER 4

Sources of Economic Growth

This chapter discusses the main results of my research into the sources of the economic growth of the seven Latin American countries selected for this study. These results are organized according to the formula presented in Chapter 3: Output growth equals labor contribution plus capital contribution plus technological contribution, which is equal to labor income share by gross and quality growth of labor plus capital income share by gross and quality growth of capital plus technological contribution. These same relationships are shown graphically in Figure 4 (page 32).

I will present, first, an overview of the data for the seven countries together and then for each country separately. The productivity indexes, on a yearly basis for each country, will be added to further the analysis of that particular source of growth. I will discuss also alternative approaches to my analysis, based on prices of output and inputs, in order to corroborate my findings. Finally, I will discuss, by way of explanation of TFP change (that is, the change of output per unit of total input), some of the sources of growth that are usually discussed as important factors in growth accelera-tion, such as the external sector.

A useful way of presenting an overall picture of performance of Latin American growth is to consider the country-decade as the unit of observation and draw a histogram for the frequency distribution of output, labor, and capital growth, arranged on the basis of all the available data (thirty-four observations for output and capital and thirty-five observations for labor). Figure 5 (page 42) presents the results of this exercise.

There is considerable dispersion in the growth rates of output and capital inputs and less dispersion in the growth rates of labor inputs. Capital input growth also appears more dispersed than output growth. This figure suggests that variations in output growth should be explained by variations in capital inputs.

The results in Table 2 (page 50) and Figure 5 give us an idea of how the growth rates experienced by these countries differ, both among each other and over time, and serve as a starting point for critical appraisal of economic policies.

Sources of Growth of the Seven Countries

Figure 6 (page 43) summarizes the contribution of each source to the total output growth of the seven countries for the period 1940–1980. The simple average contribution share for labor input (including both gross and quality components) for all countries was 27.7 percent, while the average capital input contribution share was 48.0 percent. The contribution of total factor productivity to growth was also important, at 24.3 percent.

Figure 7 (page 44) shows the contribution share of each input by decade. Here we can observe greater variability in the contribution share of each input across countries and over time. The variability of the labor contribution share, across countries and periods, was a little higher than the variability of the capital contribution share.[1]

In most of the countries and decades, the capital contribution share has been larger than the labor contribution share. Over time, a trend toward a larger capital contribution share can be observed in Argentina, Brazil, Chile, and Mexico. However, in Mexico, Peru, and Venezuela, the labor contribution share has grown during the decades under consideration. These diverse trends are mainly due to the growth rate of the overall contribution of the corresponding inputs in the different countries.

The contribution share of the TFP shows a negative trend over time, reflecting the rise of the labor and capital contribution shares. This rise is due in part to improved identification of input growth over time and, probably, to a declining trend in the technological contribution itself.[2]

However, it is interesting to observe that the contribution share of the TFP is positively related to the rate of growth of GDP.

Following the schematic presentation of the sources-of-growth methodology, I will analyze the elements underlying the contribution share of each input, presenting, first, the absolute contribution of each input and then the rate of growth of each input and its income share. I will also analyze each element of the sources of growth separately, which will better demonstrate the method and will present the data in a way that renders them useful for other applications.[3]

Table 2 presents the contribution of each input to GDP growth. Here it is possible to observe that, even after taking into account changes in the quality of the labor and capital inputs, the TFP is nevertheless important. Of the nineteen countries and decades for which there are estimates of the labor quality contribution, the TFP contribution was higher than the total labor and capital input contribution to output growth in four cases.

Total capital input made a greater contribution than labor in twelve cases, and a lower contribution in seven cases. So, in general, both inputs have been important contributors to output growth.

As expected, the size of the contribution of total inputs to growth has a clear positive association with the size of the output growth. This positive association also prevails in the contribution of each of the inputs.

Meanwhile, the quality of the labor contribution seems to have been an important factor in the growth of labor (the growth of each input is equal to the sum of the growth of its gross and quality components), while the quality component of capital was not very significant for capital growth. In eight of nineteen observations, the quality of labor could be considered as important as the gross labor contribution to output growth. The quality of capital, however, in most cases made a negative contribution to output growth; in other words, capital did not move easily to sectors with higher social rates of return.

Table 3 (page 53) presents the average annual rate of growth of both output and inputs (gross and quality components). In general, the combined growth of gross labor and capital accompany the growth of output. In other words, the increase in the growth of output required an increase in the growth of both inputs.

As for most of the particular observations, the capital input grew at a higher rate than that of labor, as the capital-labor ratio increases in the period 1940–1980. As an average for all countries and for the whole period 1940–1980, the capital-labor ratio grew at a rate of 1.6 percent per year.

This means that the growth of the capital-labor ratio was an important determinant of the growth of the per capita GDP.[4]

Of the input quality components, only labor quality had an important effect on growth performance. The quality of capital changed at a very low rate. Indeed, greater change in labor quality was associated with less change in capital quality, perhaps because of government policies (on education, labor and taxes, and credit and foreign investment) favoring the development of the quality of labor but not the development of efficient capital markets.

An important determinant of total input growth and of the contributions of each input to total output growth is the weight of each input. Table 3 shows estimates of the capital income share of GDP. The capital income share varies more among countries than through time. Argentina, Brazil, Chile, and Venezuela have a capital income share around 50 percent, while Colombia, Mexico, and Peru have a value around 65 percent.

Of the seven countries, Mexico has the highest capital income share in its GDP, which is why the labor input makes a small contribution to output growth, in spite of its high rate of growth. Brazil has the lowest capital income share, which explains, in part, the lower values observed for the contribution share of capital to GDP growth. (Remember that each input contribution is equal to the product of its rate of growth by its income share.)

Changes in capital income shares in GDP are not as high between decades as between years (as shown in the data in the appendixes). Therefore, most of the input income share movements happened within a given decade. And even though the capital income share does not change much from decade to decade, it is, nevertheless, an important element in determining total input growth.

Total Factor Productivity Index

The total factor productivity index is the ratio of the GDP to the total inputs.[5] The total inputs, as defined in this section, include gross labor and gross capital inputs only and do not include the quality components of those inputs. As such, this index shows the behavior of the TFP, revealing, for a given period, the amount of total inputs needed for a given level of output.

This index demonstrates more clearly the role of productivity in output growth. Figure 8 (page 46) presents the data in terms of five-year periods, which is useful from a historical perspective.

The index shows a positive trend in the period 1940–1973 except in Peru. After 1973, the trend was negative except in Colombia and Peru, and after 1980 the negative trend became general. Before 1973, Brazil and Mexico showed the steepest rise. From 1950 to 1985, more or less similar behavior for this index can be observed in all the countries, suggesting that their productivity was being affected in a similar way by common forces, including changes in labor quality and the growth patterns of developed countries (see Christensen, Cummings, and Jorgenson 1980; Maddison 1987).

Partial Productivity

The partial productivity of labor and capital are defined as the ratio of GDP to labor and capital, respectively. The concept "partial labor productivity" has been used more frequently in comparative productivity studies than total factor productivity because it does not require the calculation of capital inputs for which there are seldom sufficient data, especially for studies covering a long period of time. In this case, I was able to achieve estimates of both inputs for a reasonably long period of time, although there are many countries in the world for which this is not yet possible.

Unlike TFP, whose movement is explained exclusively by technological change, variation in partial productivity is also explained by movement in the capital-labor ratio, a fact to keep in mind in interpreting this variable.

This analysis will help us understand better the behavior of the TFP over time and will allow for the comparison of the study countries with many of the other countries for which this index is usually computed.

Figure 9 (page 48) presents the estimate of the partial productivity of labor, expressed, for comparative purposes, in 1960 U.S. dollars per worker per year.

The partial productivity of labor had a positive trend for the whole period in all countries. In some countries, it doubled, and in others, tripled. The value of this productivity varies from a low of US$500 (Brazil in 1955) to almost US$4,000 (Venezuela in 1974), while the average annual rate of change for the whole period varied from 0.88 percent for Venezuela to 3.22 percent for Brazil.

Much of the increase of the partial productivity of labor was due to the increase in the capital-labor ratio. This ratio explains not only the positive trend in all countries but also the differences among countries. The capital-labor ratio, in terms of 1960 U.S. dollars per worker, varies from US$600 (Peru in 1945) to US$8,000 (Venezuela in 1974). The highest increases in this ratio, in the period 1940–1985, occurred in Venezuela, Argentina, and Brazil (for Brazil, especially since 1960). The lowest increases were observed in the cases of Chile, Peru, and Mexico.

Figure 10 (page 49) presents the partial productivity of capital, also known as the output-capital ratio, for each decade from 1940 to 1985 in terms of percentages per year. The partial productivity of capital has also increased in most of our study countries throughout the whole period, although, as is to be expected, not as much as the partial productivity of labor.

Its value varies across countries and periods from about 40 percent to about 60 percent. Note that since the value of rural land is not included in the estimation of capital input, this ratio overestimates its true value.

The annual average growth rate of partial capital productivity varied from −1.54 percent for Peru to 0.85 percent for Chile during the entire period studied. However, it is also important to realize that this output-capital ratio exhibits highly variable behavior and cannot be considered a fixed parameter, even in the long run, as many growth models for Latin America have done. These models, which use fixed output-capital ratios to predict future growth or to evaluate the impact of an important increase in the rate of investment, clearly give incorrect predictions or esti-mates, misguiding economic policy design. In view of this, alternative growth models should be considered for analyzing the Latin American experience that incorporate the possibility for output-capital ratio flex-ibility, as neoclassical growth models do. Such models would have im-proved predictive power and would be more appropriate for the evaluation of the effects of economic growth policies. In fact, the sources-of-growth approach allows for less restricted assumptions about the output-capital ratio.

Dual Estimate of TFP

The sources-of-growth methodology provides an alternative approach for estimating the TFP index, based on the comparison of changes in the prices of inputs and outputs. This approach not only is useful for corroborating TFP estimates, but also provides new information that is useful for the study of the effects of growth on income distribution.

According to this approach, the rate of change of the TFP index can be computed by the following equation: the rate of change of total factor productivity index is equal to the weighted average of the rate of change of the unit prices of labor and capital minus the rate of change of the price of output. This is equal to the weighted sum of the rate of change of the real prices of labor and capital.

Table 4 (page 55) presents the average annual rate of growth of the real price of labor and capital for the period 1940–1980. There is not a definite pattern in the behavior of real prices. The growth rates of the real prices of both inputs were high and widely dispersed both among countries and over time. This evidence suggests that large changes in income distribution took place, probably in part because of the inflation observed in most Latin American countries.[6]

Table 5 (page 56) combines the information about the rate of change of both input prices provided in Table 4, according to the equation above. This table provides an estimate of the average annual rate of growth of the TFP for each of the seven countries, by decade.

The results presented in Table 5 should be compared with those of Figure 8. The estimates of the TFP index in Figure 8 are similar for most countries in most decades. The index indicates considerable expansion in the period 1940–1973 and a slowdown in the period 1973–1980. This pattern is also present in the data presented in Table 5.

Foreign Trade as a Source of Growth

In the economic literature foreign trade is considered not only a way of increasing economic welfare, but also an important source of economic growth. The international trade literature offers many models in which the foreign sector plays a crucial role in determining the growth rate of GDP. Development economists have also stressed the importance of exports for economic growth.

Foreign trade generally has a positive effect on economic growth through several channels: (1) production expansion, which provides benefits from economies of scale; (2) direct trade in technology, which allows for increases in TFP; (3) trade in capital goods, which allows for investments that will embody new technologies or are superior to capital goods produced domestically; (4) factor mobility in any one of the inputs; and (5) some short-run multiplier effects for countries with unemployed capital or labor.

This section will focus on trade in capital goods, using the traditional two-goods country model, according to which the two goods, at a given international price, are consumption and investment goods. In our case, the seven Latin American countries will be considered exporters of consumption goods and importers of investment goods.[7]

In the countries included in this study, exportation of capital goods has not been very significant with respect to the total production of investment goods. In many cases, their capital goods exports were taken into account in the estimate of the total net investment acquired through foreign trade.

Table 6 (page 56) presents the average annual rate of growth of the capital stock and the foreign trade contribution to that growth. The rate of growth of the total capital stock is a weighted average of the rates of growth of the capital coming from investment allowed by a closed economy case and the capital coming from the additional investment goods allowed by an open economy. The weights are subject to the same measurement problems mentioned in note 7 because I do not initiate my observations from true closed-economy positions.

This table shows that the foreign trade contribution to the growth of capital stock was very important (that is, more than 20 percent) for all countries except Peru. This contribution to capital growth was stable through time in Chile, Mexico, and Venezuela; and unstable in Argentina, Brazil, and Colombia. In general, the period 1950–1955 reported the highest contribution by foreign trade.

Among the factors that could explain the variability of the foreign trade contribution to capital accumulation is the behavior of the terms of trade between consumption and investment goods. In the period 1950–1975, the movement in the terms of trade was consistent with the degree of variability of the foreign trade contribution to capital accumulation in the cases of Brazil, Chile, Colombia, Mexico, and Venezuela.

In general, the contribution share of foreign trade in the growth of overall capital stock is higher than 20 percent. The fact that the capital input contribution share in output growth was higher than 40 percent, as seen earlier in this chapter, implies that the foreign trade contribution share in output growth has been only a little higher than 8 percent.

Notes

1. The range-to-arithmetic mean ratios for labor and capital were 1.3 and 1.2, respectively.

2. This trend is probably due to greater accuracy in national accounts and censuses.

3. The production function approach to studying the determinants of

output growth will become important for confirming the input weights implied by national accounts used in the above calculations of the sources of growth, because it gives direct estimates of both labor and capital shares.

4. The growth of per capita GDP mainly depends on the growth of technology and of capital per worker.

5. In order to compute the TFP index, we need to define total input, itself an index of labor and capital inputs. In this case, I used an arithmetic index, with fixed weights. Other types of indexes could be defined according to the underlying production function considered relevant, such as geometric or Divisia. The divergence between various types of indexes depends on differences in the behavior of labor and capital inputs over time in the data being considered.

6. Fluctuations in the functional income share for cases other than Cobb-Douglas production function depend, usually, on changes in the relative values of both inputs.

7. In the case of a closed economy, the country to be studied will have a bundle of consumption and investment goods, determined by the production transformation curve and the social indifference curve. The comparative advantage of this country, given its economic structure, is in consumption goods.

Foreign trade would allow this country to acquire more investment goods than if it were to remain closed. Thus foreign trade will produce greater capital accumulation. The additional capital accumulation will be considered a source of growth of capital input and, in the production process, of output.

Applying this approach, however, presents some empirical problems. First, we do not know the closed economy's initial position. Second, every country exports some capital goods. Both factors, which depend on the shape of the transformation curve and the social indifference curve, will cause some bias in the estimation of the additional part of the investment acquired through foreign trade. We can expect the rate of growth of the capital stock, built with the correct additional investment figures, to behave in a way similar to the one built with all the investment components coming from abroad. This similarity will depend on many factors, including capital-labor ratio differentials in the production of consumption and investment goods; movements in the total capital-labor ratio; and the behavior of the terms of trade between consumption and investment goods.

Some additional bias comes from situations of unbalanced foreign trade, where capital movements allow additional investment. This kind of bias can be expected to work in either direction and to cancel out over a reasonable period of time, such as five years.

FIGURE 5 Frequency Distribution of Output, Labor, and Capital Growth, by Country-Decades, 1940–1985

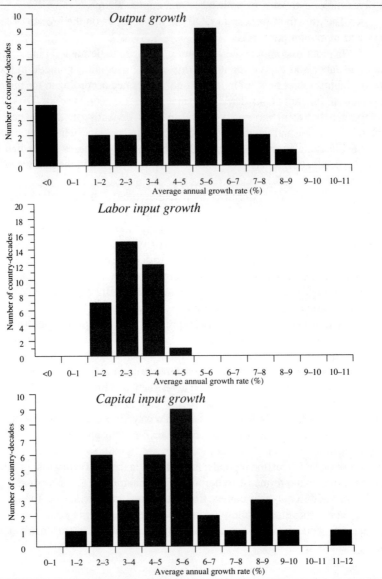

SOURCE: Table 2.

FIGURE 6 Contribution of Labor, Capital, and Total Factor Productivity to Output Growth, 1940–1980 (percentage)

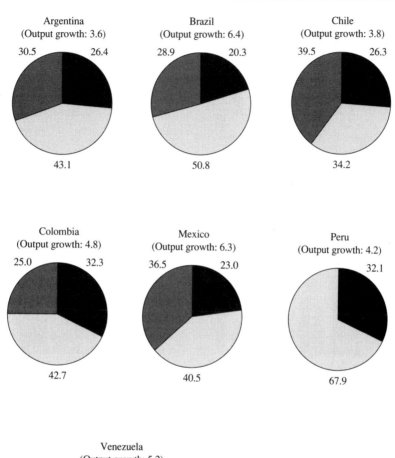

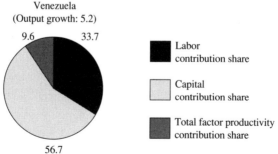

SOURCE: Table 2.

FIGURE 7 Contribution of Inputs to Output Growth by Decade, 1940–1980 (percentage)

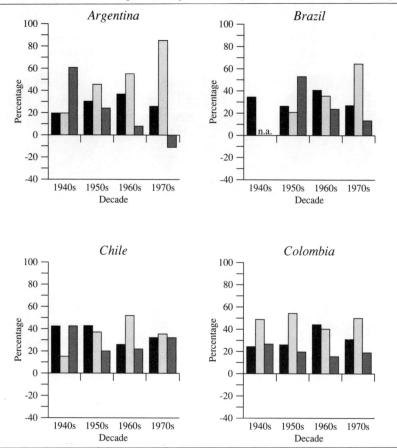

(*continued on next page*)

FIGURE 7 (continued)

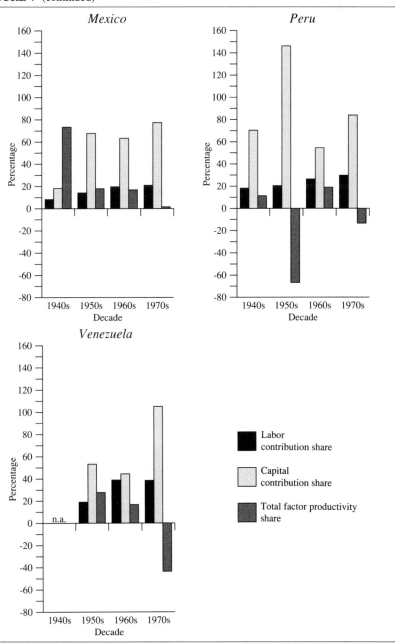

n.a. = not available.
SOURCE: Table 2.

FIGURE 8 Index of Total Factor Productivity, 1940–1985 (five-year average, 1960 = 100)

(continued on next page)

46

FIGURE 8 (continued)

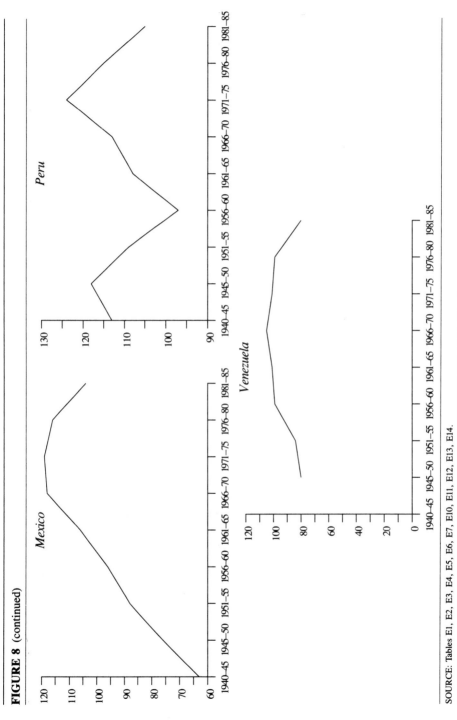

SOURCE: Tables E1, E2, E3, E4, E5, E6, E7, E10, E11, E12, E13, E14.

47

FIGURE 9 Partial Productivity of Labor, 1940–1985 (average value for each decade in 1960 U.S. dollars per worker per year)

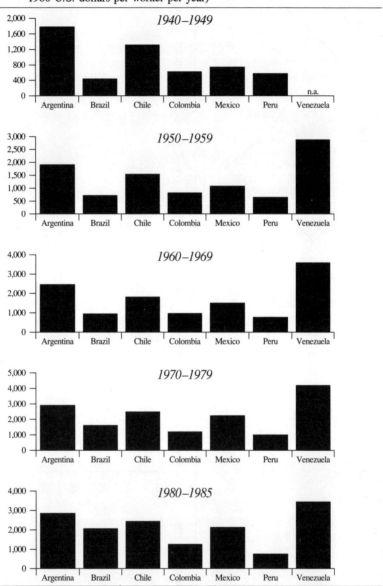

n.a. = not available.
SOURCE: Table E15.

FIGURE 10 Partial Productivity of Capital, 1940–1985 (percentage)

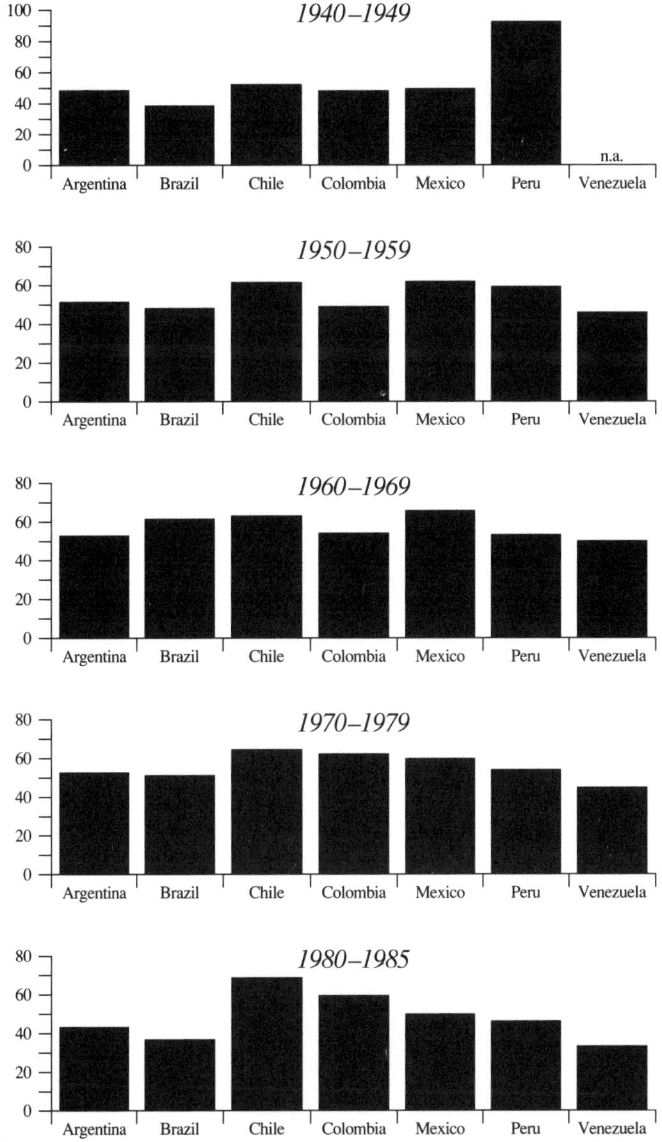

n.a. = not available.
SOURCE: Table E16.

TABLE 2 Average Annual Growth Rate of GDP and the Contribution of Inputs by Decade, 1940–1985 (percentage)

Period and component	Argentina	Brazil	Chile	Colombia	Mexico	Peru	Venezuela
1940–1950							
GDP (output)	5.1	5.5	3.3	4.1	6.0	4.4	n.a.
Total inputs	2.0	n.a.	1.4	3.0	1.6	3.9	n.a.
Labor input	1.0	1.9	0.8	1.0	0.5	0.8	1.4
Employment (L)	0.9	1.1	0.9	0.8	0.6	0.8	1.4
Quality (Q_L)	0.1	0.8	-0.1	0.2	-0.1	n.a.	n.a.
Capital input	1.0	n.a.	0.5	2.0	1.1	3.1	n.a.
Gross (K)	1.0	n.a.	0.5	2.3	1.1	3.1	n.a.
Quality (Q_K)	n.a	n.a.	n.a.	-0.3	n.a.	n.a.	n.a.
Total factor productivity	3.1	n.a.	1.9	1.1	4.4	0.5	n.a.
1950–1960							
GDP (output)	3.3	6.8	3.5	4.6	5.6	3.9	7.9
Total inputs	2.5	3.2	2.8	3.7	4.6	6.5	5.7
Labor input	1.0	1.8	1.5	1.2	0.8	0.8	1.5
Employment (L)	0.5	1.5	1.3	1.0	0.7	0.8	1.7
Quality (Q_L)	0.5	0.3	0.2	0.2	0.1	n.a.	-0.2
Capital input	1.5	1.4	1.3	2.5	3.8	5.7	4.2
Gross (K)	1.5	1.5	1.3	2.8	3.8	5.7	4.1
Quality (Q_K)	n.a	-0.1	n.a.	-0.3	n.a.	n.a.	0.1
Total factor productivity	0.8	3.6	0.7	0.9	1.0	-2.6	2.2

(continued on following page)

TABLE 2 (continued)

Period and component	Argentina	Brazil	Chile	Colombia	Mexico	Peru	Venezuela
1960–1970							
GDP (output)	3.8	5.9	5.0	5.2	7.1	5.3	5.4
Total inputs	3.6	4.5	3.7	4.4	5.9	4.3	4.0
Labor input	1.4	2.4	1.3	2.3	1.4	1.4	2.1
Employment (L)	0.8	1.6	0.9	1.2	1.0	0.9	1.2
Quality (Q_L)	0.6	0.8	0.4	1.1	0.4	0.5	0.9
Capital input	2.2	2.1	2.4	2.1	4.5	2.9	2.4
Gross (K)	2.1	2.2	2.6	2.2	4.5	2.9	1.9
Quality (Q_K)	0.1	−0.1	−0.2	−0.1	0.0	0.0	0.5
Total factor productivity	0.2	1.4	1.3	0.8	1.2	1.0	1.4
1970–1980							
GDP (output)	2.7	8.2	3.1	5.8	6.2	3.7	3.9
Total inputs	3.0	7.1	2.1	5.2	6.1	4.2	5.6
Labor input	n.a.	n.a.	n.a.	2.3	n.a.	n.a.	n.a.
Employment (L)	0.7	1.8	1.0	1.8	1.3	1.1	1.5
Quality (Q_L)	n.a.	n.a.	n.a.	0.5	n.a.	n.a.	n.a.
Capital input	n.a.	n.a.	n.a.	2.9	n.a.	3.1	4.1
Gross (K)	2.3	5.3	1.1	2.9	4.8	3.1	4.1
Quality (Q_K)	n.a.	n.a.	n.a.	n.a.	n.a.	n.a.	n.a.
Total factor productivity	−0.3	1.1	1.0	0.6	0.1	−0.5	−1.7

(continued on following page)

51

TABLE 2 (continued)

Period and component	Argentina	Brazil	Chile	Colombia	Mexico	Peru	Venezuela
1980–1985							
GDP (output)	-2.2	1.7	-1.0	2.3	1.9	-0.4	-1.3
Total inputs	0.7	2.7	1.7	4.0	4.3	2.2	1.9
Labor input	n.a.	n.a.	n.a.	n.a.	n.a.	n.a.	n.a.
Employment (L)	0.6	1.3	1.2	1.2	1.3	1.1	1.1
Quality (Q_L)	n.a.	n.a.	n.a.	n.a.	n.a.	n.a.	n.a.
Capital input	n.a.	n.a.	n.a.	n.a.	n.a.	n.a.	n.a.
Gross (K)	0.1	1.4	0.5	2.8	3.0	1.1	0.8
Quality (Q_K)	n.a.	n.a.	n.a.	n.a.	n.a.	n.a.	n.a.
Total factor productivity	-2.9	-1.0	-2.7	-1.7	-2.4	-2.6	-3.2

n.a. = not available.
SOURCE: Table 3.

52

TABLE 3 Average Annual Growth Rate of GDP and Inputs by Decade, 1940–1985 (percentage)

Period and variable	Argentina	Brazil	Chile	Colombia	Mexico	Peru	Venezuela
1940–1950							
GDP (output)	5.1	5.5	3.3	4.1	6.0	4.4	n.a.
Employment (gross labor)	1.9	2.1	2.0	2.2	2.3	2.2	3.0
Quality of labor	0.2	1.5	-0.2	0.6	-0.2	n.a.	n.a.
Gross capital	1.8	n.a.	1.0	3.6	1.5	4.9	n.a.
Quality of capital	n.a.	n.a.	n.a.	-0.4	n.a.	n.a.	n.a.
Capital share	54.0	48.2	53.0	64.0	74.0	64.0	52.0
1950–1960							
GDP (output)	3.3	6.8	3.5	4.6	5.6	3.9	7.9
Employment (gross labor)	1.1	2.8	2.5	2.8	2.6	2.7	3.7
Quality of labor	1.1	0.6	0.3	0.5	0.3	n.a.	-0.4
Gross capital	2.7	3.2	2.6	4.3	5.3	8.2	7.4
Quality of capital	n.a.	-0.2	n.a.	-0.4	0.0	0.0	0.1
Capital share	54.0	46.0	50.0	64.0	72.0	69.0	55.0
1960–1970							
GDP (output)	3.8	5.9	5.0	5.2	7.1	5.3	5.4
Employment (gross labor)	1.8	2.7	1.9	3.1	3.1	2.7	3.4
Quality of labor	1.4	1.3	0.9	2.9	1.2	1.6	2.1
Gross capital	3.7	5.3	4.7	3.6	6.7	4.4	3.5
Quality of capital	0.2	-0.3	-0.3	-0.2	0.0	0.0	0.9
Capital share	57.0	42.0	55.0	61.0	67.0	66.0	55.0

(continued on following page)

53

TABLE 3 (continued)

Period and variable	Argentina	Brazil	Chile	Colombia	Mexico	Peru	Venezuela
1970–1980							
GDP (output)	2.7	8.2	3.1	5.8	6.2	3.7	3.9
Employment (gross labor)	1.5	3.1	1.9	4.6	3.6	3.1	3.6
Quality of labor	n.a.	n.a.	n.a.	1.2	n.a.	n.a.	n.a.
Gross capital	4.3	12.3	2.2	4.9	7.3	4.7	7.1
Quality of capital	n.a.	n.a.	n.a.	n.a.	n.a.	n.a.	n.a.
Capital share	54.0	43.0	50.0	60.0	65.0	65.0	58.0
1980–1985							
GDP (output)	-2.2	1.7	-1.0	2.3	1.9	-0.4	-1.3
Employment (gross labor)	1.2	2.4	2.4	3.0	3.6	3.1	2.5
Quality of labor	n.a.	n.a.	n.a.	n.a.	n.a.	n.a.	n.a.
Gross capital	0.2	3.2	1.0	4.6	4.6	1.7	1.3
Quality of capital	n.a.	n.a.	n.a.	n.a.	n.a.	n.a.	n.a.
Capital share	n.a.	45.2	n.a.	n.a.	n.a.	n.a.	n.a.

n.a. = not available.
SOURCES: Tables E1, E2, E3, E4, E5, E6, E7, E10, E11, E12, E13, E14; Chapters 6, 7, and 8.

TABLE 4 Average Annual Growth Rate of the Real Input Prices of Labor and Capital by Decade, 1940–1980 (percentage)

Period and input price	Argentina	Brazil	Chile	Colombia	Mexico	Peru	Venezuela
1940–1950							
Labor	2.93	0.42	n.a.	-1.02	-1.82	n.a.	n.a.
Capital	5.83	n.a.	2.85	n.a.	n.a.	n.a.	n.a.
1950–1960							
Labor	-1.05	8.22	n.a.	3.86	4.03	n.a.	n.a.
Capital	-0.57	4.38	0.90	2.96	1.32	-2.93	-0.28
1960–1970							
Labor	4.06	-6.38	3.36	0.61	5.32	3.34	-2.46
Capital	-1.45	2.63	-1.65	1.95	-0.02	-2.84	1.90
1970–1980							
Labor	0.50	-1.35	-3.36	2.06	0.03	-2.75	-4.00
Capital	-0.14	-4.28	2.81	-0.34	-2.28	1.73	-4.40

n.a. = not available.
SOURCES: Tables E17 and E18.

TABLE 5 Estimate of Average Annual Growth Rate of Productivity by Decade (Dual Approach), 1940–1980

Period	Argentina	Brazil	Chile	Colombia	Mexico	Peru	Venezuela
1940–1950	4.38	n.a.	n.a.	n.a.	n.a.	n.a.	n.a.
1950–1960	−0.81	6.30	n.a.	3.41	2.68	n.a.	n.a.
1960–1970	1.31	−1.88	0.86	1.28	2.65	0.25	−0.28
1970–1980	0.18	−2.82	−0.28	0.86	−1.13	−0.51	−4.20

n.a. = not available.
SOURCE: Table 4.

TABLE 6 Average Annual Growth Rate of Capital Stock and the Contribution of Foreign Trade, 1940–1973

Period and variable	Argentina	Brazil	Chile	Colombia	Mexico	Peru	Venezuela
1940–1945							
Growth of capital stock	−0.5	n.a.	−0.8	n.a.	−0.5	n.a.	n.a.
Foreign trade contribution	−1.5	n.a.	−0.2	n.a.	−0.3	n.a.	n.a.
1945–1950							
Growth of capital stock	4.0	n.a.	2.3	n.a.	3.4	n.a.	n.a.
Foreign trade contribution	0.6	n.a.	1.0	n.a.	0.9	n.a.	n.a.
1950–1955							
Growth of capital stock	2.4	2.8	2.4	5.4	5.1	10.1	8.4
Foreign trade contribution	1.4	0.7	1.2	1.5	1.0	0.3	1.7

(continued on following page)

TABLE 6 (continued)

Period and variable	Argentina	Brazil	Chile	Colombia	Mexico	Peru	Venezuela
1955–1960							
Growth of capital stock	2.9	3.4	2.8	3.1	5.3	5.2	6.0
Foreign trade contribution	0.8	0.1	0.8	0.3	1.0	0.2	2.0
1960–1965							
Growth of capital stock	3.3	3.7	4.9	3.1	5.8	5.0	2.2
Foreign trade contribution	0.9	0.2	0.8	0.6	0.6	0.1	0.0
1965–1970							
Growth of capital stock	4.1	6.7	4.3	3.9	7.3	3.7	4.8
Foreign trade contribution	0.7	0.0	1.1	0.7	0.7	0.0	1.9
1970–1973							
Growth of capital stock	n.a.	14.0	n.a.	4.9	n.a.	3.1	7.1
Foreign trade contribution	n.a.	2.6	n.a.	n.a.	n.a.	0.0	2.0

n.a. = not available.

NOTE: The weights of the growth rate of capital coming from the additional investment allowed by foreign trade were 0.15 for Argentina, 0.20 for Brazil, 0.30 for Chile, 0.25 for Colombia, 0.20 for Mexico, 0.02 for Peru, and 0.20 for Venezuela.

SOURCES: *Argentina:* Banco Central de la República Argentina (1975); *Brazil:* Langoni (1970); Fundação Instituto Brasileiro de Geografia e Estatística (1974); *Chile:* Oficina de Planificación Nacional (1973); Muñoz (1971); Davis (1966); *Colombia:* Banco de la República (1973); Economic Commission for Latin America (1967); *Mexico:* Banco de México (1969); Nacional Financiera (1969); Reynolds (1970); *Peru:* Banco Central de la Reserva (1961, 1968); Vandendreis (1967); *Venezuela:* Inter-American Development Bank (1968); Ministerio de Fomento (1974); Banco Central de Venezuela (1974, 1975).

CHAPTER 5

Output and Income Distribution

The aggregate output of a country's economy—the gross domestic product—defines that country's economic size. The aim of this study is to explain how it grows. This chapter will present GDP estimates, at the aggregate level and for some components, for the periods and countries selected for this study.

Since this study is concerned with the production side of the economy, GDP will be defined at factor costs, excluding some indirect taxes (for example, sales tax).[1] The basic information used to estimate the GDP comes from the national accounts, which in Latin America exclude the value of the services provided by some durable goods, such as cars and some home appliances.[2] A more complete set of data for the GDP would include these kinds of services.

For the case of Latin America, I analyze GDP by aggregating the private and public sectors for two reasons: first, there is not enough information to separate these two sectors clearly and, second, the public sector in most of the study countries has a high share in the GDP, mainly because of the size of public enterprises. This aggregation creates some problems for the comparison of my findings with those of studies of other countries because the latter tend to include only the private sector in their sources-of-growth analyses.[3]

According to the method presented in Chapter 3, I will present estimates of the aggregate GDP and of its two components, consumption and investment goods (see Jorgenson and Griliches 1967). This form of calculation allows for applying growth models that link output policy decisions with capital accumulation. It also allows for taking into account changes in the relative prices of investment and consumption goods when estimating the growth rate of the GDP.

This chapter will also present the functional income distribution of the GDP corresponding to labor and capital inputs, which complements the production side of the national accounts discussed above and makes it possible to estimate the contribution of labor and capital to growth. This also allows us to estimate unit prices for the services provided by labor and capital inputs.[4]

Estimate of Output (GDP) and Its Components

Table 7 (page 68) presents estimates of real aggregate output and its components—investment and consumption goods.[5] Aggregate GDP is estimated from its rate of growth computed as a weighted average of the rate of growth of investment and consumption goods.[6]

Since the national accounts generally do not provide a ready description of GDP in terms of consumption and investment goods from the viewpoint of production, I found it necessary to derive this estimate indirectly. Where necessary, I used information for capital goods imports and exports to establish an estimate of the production of investment goods and, from that, the corresponding estimate of consumption goods production (GDP minus investment goods production).

I will begin my analysis of Table 7 by examining the behavior of consumption and investment goods. Table 8 (page 69) provides an overview of the share of investment goods in the total GDP. (More complete information appears in the appendixes.)

Across countries and over time, the share of investment goods in GDP was, in general, below 20 percent. The overall average for this share was around 15 percent. The lowest average value appeared in Chile. Brazil and Mexico showed a positive trend, whereas Venezuela showed a negative trend. The remaining countries do not exhibit a definite pattern.

The annual series data provided in Appendix Table E8 show considerable instability in the investment goods share for most of the countries and for some periods. This instability is greater than that in developed economies (see Christensen, Cummings, and Jorgenson 1980). This phenomenon could be due in part to the fact that the share of investment goods in total GDP was much lower in Latin American countries than in developed countries and, therefore, has been quite volatile. It could also be due to the much greater fluctuation in the terms of trade between investment and consumption goods, owing to changing protectionist policies in Latin America that have caused the domestic investment-consumption price ratios to differ substantially from the corresponding world ratio.[7]

Figure 11 (page 64) shows the annual rate of change of the aggregate GDP for the period 1948–1980.[8] There are many differences across countries and over time in the behavior of the annual rate of growth of the GDP. For example, Argentina reports both the highest number of years with negative rates of GDP growth and also the greatest rate of variability. Chile's GDP also exhibits high variability and many years of negative growth rates. The highest sustained rate of growth occurs in Brazil, and high rates of growth occur in Colombia, Mexico, and Venezuela as well.

A growth slowdown took place in most Latin American countries after 1978 and, as I will show later, in all of them after 1980. This behavior is similar to that observed at global levels, including developed economies.

However, the high variability of GDP growth rates in Latin American countries is not observed for the United States and many European countries.[9] Moreover, some variability, although much less than in Latin America, can also be observed in the high-growth countries of the Pacific Rim (South Korea, Taiwan, Hong Kong, and Singapore). This sort of shared variability might indicate that fluctuations are a necessary condition for increasing rates of growth and that there are some common cross-country economic forces.[10]

The data also allow us to explore the relevance of including both private and public sectors in our definition of the GDP.[11] Figure 12 (page 66) presents the average annual rates of change of the total GDP and public output. The fluctuations in the rates of growth of both aggregate GDP and public output have been similar, though more pronounced in the public sector. From this data, I conclude that a GDP measurement that includes only the private sector should report slightly less fluctuation than the measurement used here. This figure does not reveal an increase in the public sector from the point of view of output.[12]

Functional Income Distribution

The sources-of-growth method given here calculates the functional income distribution between labor and capital in order to weight the rate of growth of both inputs (see Chapter 3). Therefore, this section considers capital income share in the GDP for the period 1940–1980. (Since the percentage shares of the two inputs add up to 100, the labor income share will be 100 minus the capital income share.)

Table 9 (page 69) gives estimates of the capital income share in GDP. The capital income shares in GDP are very high in comparison with those commonly observed in many developed economies. This difference could be due partly to the exclusion, in the calculation of the labor income, of the income of many independent and executive workers, for which there are few data in Latin America.[13]

The capital income share was very unstable in Argentina, had a reasonably smooth negative trend in Mexico, and had a positive trend in Venezuela. In Brazil this share was stable until 1969, when a considerable increase occurred.[14]

Notes

1. Other studies (such as Christensen, Cummings, and Jorgenson 1980) add some direct taxes, especially taxes on capital input, to the factor-cost evaluation of the GDP, achieving a GDP definition based on estimates that are intermediate between factor costs and market prices.

2. For this calculation, one should construct capital stock series for the different capital goods and estimate from them the services provided.

3. There are two main arguments for including only the private sector in sources-of-growth analyses. First, it is difficult to give values to public output (such as public administration) because of the absence of a market for such a product. Second, public output derives from decisions made according to criteria that are different from those of the private sector. In other words, in the private sector, firms operate to maximize profits, whereas in the public sector, the criteria that orient decisions are less clear.

4. For comparative studies, the GDP of each country must be expressed in homogeneous units, such as those provided by calculations of output purchasing-power parity, which make the evaluation of the output of one country in the currency of another country possible. However, such a comparative study is not possible for Latin America because very few calculations of that kind have been done for the countries of this continent, although significant efforts have been made along these lines (see ECIEL studies from the 1970s and Kravis, Kennessey, Heston, and Summers 1975). I analyzed some of the results of these studies in order to weigh their implications for my research. This analysis revealed that because I am more interested in rate-of-growth analysis, my results will not be

greatly affected by the heterogeneity of the data; since the *degree* of heterogeneity does not change over time, the comparison of rates of growth is possible.

5. The appendixes give both the nominal and real values of these variables and their corresponding implicit prices (price indexes derived from the ratio of nominal to real value of the GDP).

6. In this computation, I follow the Divisia index approach (see Chapter 3).

7. It is also interesting to note that these fluctuations coincide with those expected from the theory of the demand for durable goods and the Austrian capital theory (for the first, see Harberger 1960).

8. This rate of growth was computed as a weighted average of the rate of growth of consumption and investment goods, using variable weights through time, as the Divisia index indicates.

9. These growth rate fluctuations could be due in part to variations in the use of the available inputs. One possible way to eliminate this source of fluctuation is to consider average rates of growth for periods longer than one year. On doing this, I found that only part of this problem was eliminated. The results are explained in greater detail in Chapter 9, where I analyze GDP growth rates as a time series, using a statistical method of analysis. The relevance of this phenomenon can be seen directly in the ever-increasing information about capacity use at the firm level for the industrial sector, but it was not necessary to take this into account in this part of my analysis.

10. See Moore (1989) for the identification of common business cycles in developed economies.

11. Chapter 7 treats public sector output in greater detail. Here, I offer a summary of the behavior of public output in order to clarify the results obtained for the total GDP (private plus public).

12. In fact, most of the estimates that establish an increase in the output share of the public sector in recent decades come from research into the expenditure side of national accounting, using the distinction between private and public consumption, on the one hand, and private and public investment expenditure, on the other.

13. Overestimation of the capital income share would create serious distortions in the estimation of each input contribution to output growth, overstating the role of capital input in the overall growth process. This must be kept in mind in the analysis of the results.

14. The production function approach allows for an alternative estimate of the labor and capital income share to be used for sources-of-growth analysis which corroborates the estimate presented in Table 9. For a more precise analysis of the diverse sources of economic growth, more detailed functional income distribution measurements are required than the ones used here, which use only two aggregate inputs. Such measurements should take into account different components of labor and capital, such as those presented in Chapters 6 and 7 (see Stone 1986 and Jorgenson, Gollop, and Fraumeni 1987).

FIGURE 11 Annual Rate of Change of GDP, 1948–1980 (percentage)

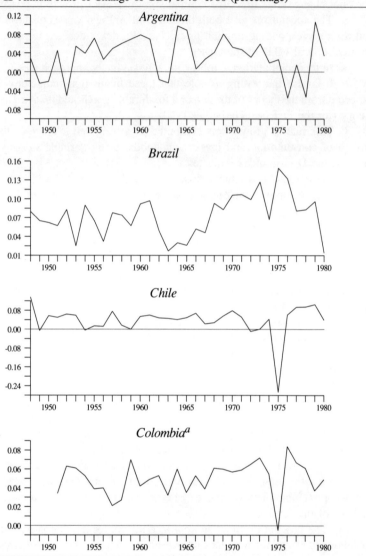

(*continued on following page*)

FIGURE 11 (continued)

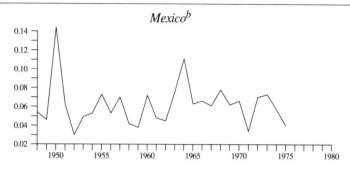

Mexico[b]

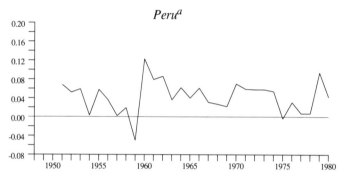

Peru[a]

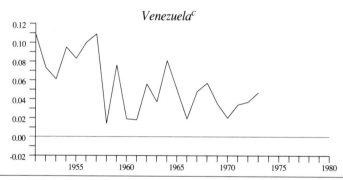

Venezuela[c]

a. Data for 1948–1950 are not available.
b. Data for 1974 and 1976–1980 are not available.
c. Data for 1948–1950 and 1974–1980 are not available.
SOURCE: Tables E1, E2, E3, E4, E5, E6, E7.

FIGURE 12 Average Annual Growth Rate of GDP and Public Output by Decade, 1940–1980

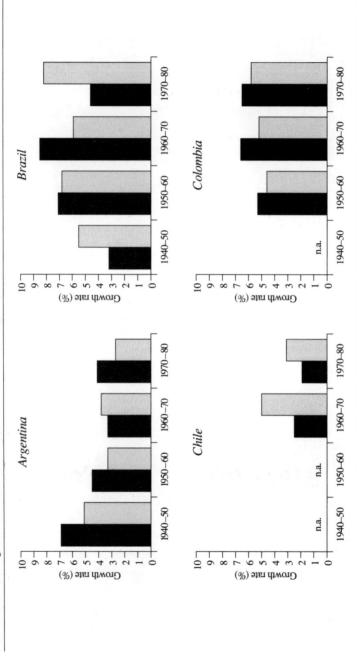

(continued on following page)

FIGURE 12 (continued)

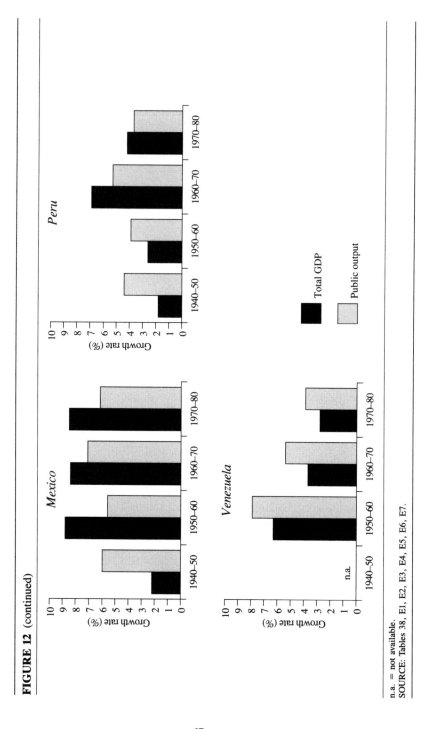

n.a. = not available.
SOURCE: Tables 38, E1, E2, E3, E4, E5, E6, E7.

67

TABLE 7 Real GDP and Consumption and Investment Goods in Selected
Years, 1940–1980 (millions of 1960 U.S. dollars)

Country and variable	1940	1950	1960	1970	1980
Argentina					
GDP	5,839	9,082	12,227	18,670	23,416
Consumption goods	n.a.	7,907	10,199	15,046	17,495
Investment goods	n.a.	1,175	2,028	3,624	5,675
Brazil					
GDP	6,108	10,471	20,227	36,237	95,190
Consumption goods	n.a.	9,128	17,725	28,422	71,532
Investment goods	n.a.	1,343	2,502	7,814	20,650
Chile					
GDP	2,043	2,817	3,966	6,529	8,098
Consumption goods	n.a.	2,620	3,574	5,907	7,211
Investment goods	n.a.	198	392	623	913
Colombia					
GDP	1,763	2,641	4,158	6,922	11,872
Consumption goods	n.a.	2,254	3,601	6,453	10,498
Investment goods	n.a.	387	557	468	1,333
Mexico					
GDP	3,309	6,959	12,041	23,723	40,975
Consumption goods	2,979	6,275	10,561	19,883	n.a.
Investment goods	330	684	1,480	3,840	n.a.
Peru					
GDP	n.a.	1,437	2,106	3,529	5,385
Consumption goods	n.a.	1,264	1,904	3,099	4,674
Investment goods	n.a.	173	202	430	643
Venezuela					
GDP	n.a.	3,710	7,767	11,850	17,520
Consumption goods	n.a.	2,902	6,682	10,185	n.a.
Investment goods	n.a.	809	1,085	1,665	n.a.

n.a. = not available.
SOURCES: Tables E1, E2, E3, E4, E5, E6, and E7.

TABLE 8 Share of Investment Goods in Total GDP in Selected Years, 1941–1980 (percentage)

Country	1941	1950	1960	1970	1980
Argentina	11.4	17.5	16.6	18.2	24.0
Brazil	n.a.	12.2	14.8	22.5	22.1
Chile	8.5	7.6	10.1	9.3	10.9
Colombia	n.a.	11.0	13.3	7.5	12.2
Mexico	7.5	8.1	12.3	16.2	n.a.
Peru	n.a.	11.5	9.6	9.2	11.0
Venezuela	n.a.	23.0	14.9	14.7	n.a.

n.a. = not available.
SOURCE: Table E8.

TABLE 9 Capital Income Share in GDP in Selected Years, 1940–1985 (percentage)

Country	1940	1950	1960	1970	1980	1985
Argentina	58.0	50.3	62.0	54.2	62.9	n.a.
Brazil	n.a.	49.1	42.6	59.2	62.1	n.a.
Chile	52.9	53.5	56.7	50.1	56.6	n.a.
Colombia	n.a.	64.0	63.3	58.9	53.8	54.7
Mexico	n.a.	73.8	67.5	65.5	61.0	68.4
Peru	n.a.	63.8	67.9	62.1	67.2	71.8
Venezuela	n.a.	52.0	50.0	57.4	57.3	58.2

n.a. = not available.
SOURCE: Table E9.

CHAPTER 6

Labor Input

Labor is a major source of economic growth in Latin America. This chapter will discuss in detail the measurement of labor, in terms of both quantity and quality, providing insights into the dynamics of this input. In this way, some implications for growth-policy design will emerge.

The labor input is defined as the total number of homogeneous hours worked in a given period. This will be equal to the total number of workers multiplied by the annual average number of hours worked per worker, and multiplied by a quality factor that takes into account differences in productivity among workers.[1] The schematic presentation of the labor input in Figure 13 (page 84) helps show how this is actually estimated.

The quality component of labor, according to the growth accounting methodology, reflects labor composition based on those characteristics that explain productivity differences among workers. Many studies in the field of labor economics suggest that the most important of these characteristics are education, age, sex, occupation, economic sector, and geographic region.

The Gross Component of Labor Input

I will begin by providing a detailed estimate of the first two components of labor input: the number of workers and the annual average of hours worked per worker. These two components make up the gross component of labor.

The number of workers is, by definition, equal to the total population times the labor force participation rate. To give a clearer understanding of this component, I will analyze the two elements of this definition separately. This separation provides an interesting link with population theory as a part of the explanation of the growth of labor, a factor seldom integrated into economic growth models for Latin America.

The annual weighted average of hours of work, per worker, requires information about the hours of work of each kind of worker and about the overall composition of labor. In general, information is available only about certain kinds of workers—mainly blue collar workers—and serves as the basis for estimating the average number of hours worked.[2]

Number of workers, population, and labor force participation rate

Since most of the information for estimating the number of workers in Latin America is based on the concept of the labor force (employed plus unemployed labor), I will discuss first the estimate of the labor force participation rate (equal to the labor force divided by population).

In general, the labor force participation rate does not change substantially over time for the aggregate of the population, even though it can be very different across countries and among different components of the population (mainly groups that differ in sex and age). In the short run, this rate is not extremely accurate because of fluctuations in the rate of unemployment. However, for long-run aggregate analyses within each country, like those in this study, this rate is very reliable for deriving an estimate of the number of workers from the total population. I will complement this information with data on unemployment rates to better demonstrate my results.

According to Table 10 (page 87), the labor force participation rate in the study countries varied from about 42 percent to about 57 percent for selected years from 1940 to 1980. These are high values compared with those found in developed and other underdeveloped countries. All seven countries show declining values over time, and Chile and Mexico experience important decreases. Changes in this rate can be explained, in part, by changes in the labor force participation rate among women and young people.[3] Chile and Mexico presented not only the largest decline in the labor force participation rate but also the lowest absolute values among the seven countries in 1980.

Table 11 (page 87) shows estimates of total population, number of workers, and the employment-population ratio for selected years. (The complete series appears in the appendixes.) The average annual rates of growth of employment and population in Argentina were 1.8 and 1.6, respectively; in Brazil, 2.9 and 2.7; in Chile, 1.9 and 1.8; in Colombia, 3.5 and 2.8; in Mexico, 2.7 and 2.9; in Peru, 2.7 and 2.3; and in Venezuela, 3.4 and 3.6. In five of the seven countries, employment grew at a much higher rate than population, implying a positive rate of growth for the employment-population ratio. Only Mexico and Venezuela experienced negative growth in the employment-population ratio. Moreover, the annual rates of growth of employment and population for all Latin American countries were both high in comparison with developed countries. Higher rates of growth of the gross component of labor can be observed in only a few countries, such as Japan and Korea (see Christensen, Cummings, and Jorgenson 1980; Maddison 1987).[4]

Average hours of work and rate of unemployment

According to the sources-of-growth literature, the average number of hours worked per worker per week has been an important determinant of the growth of the gross labor input. Some information gathered for Latin American countries gives a general picture of its importance.

Table 12 (page 88) shows a slightly declining trend in the average number of hours worked and important differences in its level across countries. This trend corresponds to the negative contribution of the hours worked to the growth of the gross labor input usually observed.

As noted in the previous section, the labor force participation rate is not accurate for short-run analysis of employment because of yearly changes in the rate of unemployment. Therefore, I believe it is useful to present annual statistics as a complement to the analysis of short-run fluctuations in employment.

In Latin America, the available information covers only unemployment in the urban sector (see Table 13, page 89). The rate of unemployment varies more across countries than over time, except in Chile and Venezuela, indicating that care should be taken even for long-run analysis of employment trends in these countries.

The Quality Component of the Labor Input

According to the growth-accounting methodology, the rate of change of the quality component should capture the effects of changes in the composition of the labor force. According to this method, the rate of change of the quality component is equal to the weighted average of changes in the share of each kind of labor in the total labor force. The weights are the wages for each kind of labor with respect to the average wage for the whole labor force. For example, if there is no change in the composition of the labor force, the rate of change of quality will be zero. If there are changes in favor of groups with higher relative wages, the quality will increase.

For the purposes of this calculation, each component of labor corresponds to a well-defined category. The category is defined by a set of characteristics such as education, age, sex, occupation, economic sector, and economic region. These have proven to be the most important elements in the explanation of labor income.

The education component

The education component of labor could be defined in a way that covers both formal education (schooling) and informal education (job training). The estimates presented in this section, however, will be based on the formal component only, because only those data are available for Latin America.

Table 14 (page 90) reveals considerable disparity in labor composition by education at the beginning of the period. Even though the share of those without schooling was large initially, it decreased considerably between 1940 and 1980. Among the seven countries, Argentina and Chile have the lowest percentage of people with no formal education.

In addition, there was a uniform increase in university-educated workers in all countries, which will have an important effect on the calculation of the growth of the labor quality component. Computing that component requires data on relative wages by education. Although increased attention has been given to this subject in the past decade, this information is still scarce for Latin American countries. The available data are presented in Table 15 (page 92). Relative wages by education are similar across countries. These countries, however, have a higher relative wage for those with secondary and university level education than do the United States and some European countries (Denison 1967; Christensen, Cummings, and Jorgenson 1980).

The range of variation in relative wages shown in Table 15 indicates that changes in the educational composition of labor will imply high values for the rate of change of the quality component. Even a small increase in the share of the upper part of the labor distribution will produce important positive changes in the quality of labor.

In recent decades, developed countries reported a decrease in the range of variation of relative wages according to educational level. This phenomenon was reflected in a decrease in the rate of return to investment in higher education and was due in part to an increase of the skilled-unskilled ratio in the labor force. Since Latin American countries can be expected to experience this same phenomenon, changes in the educational composition of the labor force will in the future have a smaller impact on the quality of the labor force.

The estimates presented in Tables 14 and 15 allow us to compute the rate of change of the quality component of labor. The results, given in Table 16 (page 93), show that the rate of growth of the quality component (education only) has been an important part of the rate of growth of the whole labor input, often growing at a rate higher than 1 percent. Some negative values in the rate of growth of the quality component occur, but they are very small.

An interesting element contributing to the high values in the increase of labor quality is the considerable influence of the decrease of illiteracy in the value obtained for the rate of growth labor quality.

Because of changes in the composition of the labor force and the wide range of relative wages, the contribution of labor quality to the growth of the labor input was not uniform across decades, as was the case in many developed countries.[5]

The gender component

A general phenomenon observed in many developed and developing countries is the increase in the share of women in the total labor force. Detailed studies reveal that this increase has been due mainly to increases in the women's labor force participation rate, while the men's rate has remained rather constant (see J. Mincer 1962, 1968). In this section, I will not study the reasons for this trend but instead examine its implications for the quality component of the labor force.

Another important phenomenon is the persistence of the wage differential in favor of men. Some of the determinants of this differential suggested in the labor economics literature are differences with respect to hours of work, education, productivity, and sex discrimination. In other studies, after correcting for hours worked and education, an important difference persists, explained by the productivity differential and sex discrimination. For my purposes, the available data have not allowed me to separate the effects of these four elements in the wage differential. However, as I use the ratio of the wages of each sex with respect to the average wage (which includes both men's and women's wages), I expect that some of these determinants will cancel out and will highlight productivity as the major cause of the wage differential.

Following our method, in this section the quality component of the labor input will be estimated in terms of the sex composition of the labor force. For this purpose, the wage differential between men and women will be assumed to be explained mainly by the productivity differential.

Table 17 (page 93) presents the composition of the labor force by sex. In 1970, in almost all countries, women represented approximately 20 percent of the total labor force. The greatest positive trend in this share was observed in Brazil and Mexico. Argentina presents some fluctuations, Colombia a small positive trend, and Venezuela an important positive trend since 1950.

Women's share in the labor force is larger in developed countries (Christensen, Cummings, and Jorgenson 1980; Denison 1967), which could indicate that, in the coming decades, a higher positive trend in this share will develop in Latin America.

Relative wages by sex are presented in Table 18 (page 93). In the cases of Brazil and Colombia, there is a substantial difference between men's and women's wages, with men earning almost double women's wages. In Venezuela, the difference is very small.

Applying the same formula used for the education component, the rate of change of the quality of labor can be computed for this component. The results are presented in Table 19 (page 94).

For most countries, and for most periods, the annual rate of change of the gender quality component of labor was very small or negative, with values of less than 0.1 percent per year. This does not mean, however, that the increase in the number of women in the total labor force had a negative total impact on the growth of labor, because the increase in women workers raised the total number of workers (the gross component of the labor force). Because of the wage differential in favor of men, this increase has had a negative effect on the overall quality of the total labor force. Nonetheless, both effects taken together are positive.

As mentioned before, the interaction effects among the quality components under consideration here are ignored. However, if I were to take into account interaction effects with other characteristics, I could expect the sex component to become more important in the overall indicator of the quality of the labor force than Table 19 seems to indicate (see Chinloy 1980).

The age component

Age constitutes the third main determinant of the labor-earning function, which explains wage differentials among workers (see Mincer 1974). Age seems to be as important as education in the determination of this function, at least in developed countries. In general, the 1974 Mincer study shows that earnings with respect to age increase up to forty-five years of age, other factors being equal.[6]

Since changes over time in labor force composition by age are very slow, substantial changes in the quality of labor due to age in the short run are unlikely, even though there are large differences in wages across ages.

Table 20 (page 94) indicates similar age distribution in the labor force, both across countries and over time. The age composition of the labor force is highly dependent on the rate of growth of the population, especially on the fertility rate. Other important forces are the share of young people who want to go to school (as in the case of Brazil) and the labor force participation rate of women.

Reliable data for relative wages were obtained only for Brazil for the years 1960–1970 (see Langoni 1970). These data reveal an increasing relative wage until the age bracket of forty to forty-nine.[7] The largest differences occur between the ten- to nineteen-year-old age group and the twenty- to twenty-nine-year-old age group. As in developed countries, a decline in the relative wages of people over sixty can be observed.

Using the data available for Brazil, Table 21 (page 95) presents the estimate of the annual growth rate of the quality component according to age. The contribution of the age quality component was very small, mainly because changes in age-labor composition were small. Only Brazil shows an important positive contribution by the age quality component. In Argentina and Venezuela, the contribution was negative.

As in the case of the gender component, the age characteristic effect could gain importance in interactional measurements. The literature on age, education, and earnings could lead one to believe that the interactional effect between education and age was very important (see, for example, Mincer 1974). Surely, however, considering education alone would overestimate the value of that quality component in the total quality of labor.

The occupation component

Both *The Wealth of Nations* by Adam Smith and *Principles of Economics* by Alfred Marshall mention occupation as an important factor in the explanation of wage differentials. These studies define occupation in terms of health risk, hours of work, and stability, most of which were not associated with a productivity differential, such as I am using here. Current statistics on occupation classification, however, are generally organized according to other criteria (usually related to education, age, and economic sector aspects of the labor input), rendering them more useful for productivity differential analysis.

Two principal methods of classifying occupations can be found in statistical sources. The first one divides labor into employers, employees, professionals, independent (or self-employed) workers, and unpaid family workers. The second, which is more appropriate for productivity differential analysis, uses the following categories: (1) professional, technical, and related workers; (2) administrative, executive, and managerial workers; (3) clerical workers; (4) sales workers; (5) farmers, fishermen, and hunters; (6) miners and quarrymen; (7) transport and communications workers; (8) craftsmen and production processes workers; and (9) service, sport, and recreation workers.[8]

Table 22 (page 96) presents the occupational distribution of labor according to the first kind of classification. This classification reveals some variablity through time and considerable disparities across countries, some of which could be due to different classification criteria across countries.[9] The employers' share is highest in Argentina and Colombia, with a declining share in Argentina. Brazil reports the highest share for independent workers, with a value around 34 percent, while, in other countries, it is around 20 percent. In the case of unpaid family workers, Brazil and Peru report the highest percentages.

In Table 23 (page 97), relative wages by labor occupation classification are given. Relative wages show important differences across categories, especially in the case of Peru. Relative wages of employers present high differences across countries. Unpaid family workers have very low relative wages (less than 0.5), which could imply that most of them belong to the rural sector.

The estimates for the average annual rate of change of the quality component for occupation are presented in Table 24 (page 97). Except for the cases of Brazil and Peru in the 1960s, in most of the countries and most periods, the occupation quality contribution was negative.

Appendix D shows the results of using method 2 to classify occupations. The estimates of quality changes according to this method will be much less than those obtained with method 1, mainly because it finds lower disparity of wages among different occupations. Changes in labor composition over time were not as large as differences observed across countries, which are results very similar to those obtained using method 1.

The economic sector component

In this section, I will divide the labor force into primary, secondary, and tertiary economic sectors to analyze the data (see Table 25, page 97). These criteria make possible the integration of patterns of development (based more on demand factors) with the sources of growth (based more on supply factors), thus complementing the growth-accounting approach.[10]

There are some differences in the economic sector composition of the labor force across countries, with important changes over time that tended to make the composition of the labor force more similar across countries.

Overall, the primary sector makes up 40 percent of the total labor force, except in Argentina and Chile. The largest component of this sector is agriculture in some countries and mining in others. The tertiary sector has increased its share significantly in all countries, mainly because of growth in the service and government components.[11]

Relative wages by sector are similar across countries and, in most cases, relatively stable through time (see Table 26, page 98). In most countries and periods, the tertiary sector has the highest relative wage, while the primary sector has the lowest relative wage. One explanation for this phenomenon may be that these sectors are composed differently in terms of education, age, and sex. Primary sector wages may also be underestimated because payments-in-kind are not calculated, and the higher proportion of unpaid family workers is not taken into account.[12]

The average annual rate of change of the quality component of labor, based on economic sector, is shown in Table 27 (page 99).[13] For most countries and periods, the average annual rate of change of the quality component of labor by economic sector was very high and positive, except in the cases of Colombia and Venezuela in the 1960s. The size of these changes is similar to that obtained for the education quality component (see Table 16).

Brazil, Chile, and Mexico show the greatest values in the growth of this quality component, while Argentina shows very low values (a result somewhat inconsistent with the results obtained for the education characteristic).

The reallocation component

Labor reallocation by region is an element of the internal migration phenomenon. This has its effect on the quality component of labor input as labor moves from lower to higher wage regions, or vice versa.

Economic sector classification takes into account reallocation among sectors, but not among regions, although it often has a high correlation with regional classifications.[14] This section emphasizes reallocation by region as a distinct category of the quality component of the labor input.

The study of migration takes into account not only productivity, which is the specific interest of the sources-of-growth methodology, but also consumption, investment, and the rate of growth of the population, which are important elements for the study of the dynamic effects of migration. This section considers only domestic migration, defined as migration that occurs within the boundary of a country.[15]

The statistical sources for migration provide classifications that are useful for this study: rural-urban migration, migration among states, and migration among economic regions. The rural-urban classification is adequately covered by the economic sector classification discussed above, so only the other two are considered here as separate categories.[16]

Following the method used in the analysis of other characteristics, I focus on changes in the composition of the labor force by region, which are due, in part, to labor reallocation, as well as to different rates of change in the amount of labor coming from the same region. Since migration information is scanty, this approach is very useful.

Table 28 (page 99) presents estimates of the rate of change of the labor quality component due to labor reallocation across different regions. Data are available for only a few countries but give a general idea of the importance of this quality component. The reallocation factor has been especially important in the case of Mexico.

Summary of the quality component of the labor input

An overall picture of the importance of the quality component in the growth of the labor input can be presented by observing the contribution of each characteristic during the whole period from 1940 to 1980. Figure 14 (page 85) presents the average annual rate of growth of labor quality due to different characteristics.

Overall, the average annual rate of change for total labor quality was around 1.5 percent, a high value compared with the other source of labor input growth (that is, employment, which grew at an overall rate of 2.7 percent).

Education was by far the main source of labor quality change. The gender characteristic made a negative contribution in all seven countries, while the age characteristic had diverse effects across countries (positive for Brazil, Chile, Peru, and Venezuela, and negative for the others). The economic sector characteristic made an important positive contribution in most countries.

A comparison of the growth of labor quality with employment growth across countries for the whole period reveals no definite relationship between these two components, suggesting that a high rate of growth of labor quality is not necessarily associated with high or low employment growth.[17]

Notes

1. This is the formula for calculating labor input (*L*):

$$L = N \times h \times Q(L)$$

where N is the number of workers, h is the annual weighted average of hours worked per worker, and $Q(L)$ is the quality factor.

2. I obtained estimates of weekly hours of work for only a few countries and part of my study period. These estimates cover low-wage worker categories. It is expected that these estimates will not differ much from the one suggested by sources-of-growth method. For comparative analysis with other countries, the limitations of these estimates should be kept in mind.

3. There are other difficulties in the measurement of this element, such as the one created by rural-urban migration. Many people, especially women, appear in the rural labor force, but not in the urban force, after they migrate.

4. A more detailed description of employment is presented in Table E10 (page 210). Argentina shows the greatest variability in the rate of growth of

employment, as it does in the growth rate of GDP. After the mid-1960s, Chile also presents highly variable employment growth.

5. The quality of labor can be estimated using a different methodology, based on the concept of the stock of educational capital (see Appendix C). This methodology yields a higher value for the rate of change of the quality of labor due to education. Some of the reasons for this difference are discussed in Appendix C.

6. In many studies, the age effect was not easily separated from that of experience, so both are generally incorporated into the age effect.

7. For example, in 1970, the relative wages were 0.327 for the age bracket 10–19; 0.846 for the bracket 20–29; 1.209 for the bracket 30–39; 1.355 for the bracket 40–49; 1.259 for the bracket 50–59; and 0.936 for the bracket 60 and over.

8. Some special surveys use a more detailed system of occupation classification. Since my main sources are economic and population censuses, I will use the two kinds of classification discussed in the text.

Studies of occupational mobility have relied on more detailed occupation classifications, providing a good source of information and a basis for comparison with the results presented here (for instance, Berry 1973).

9. Data with respect to independent and unpaid family workers are scanty and unreliable. Unpaid family workers are more common in the agricultural sector than in other sectors. The national accounts also underestimate the contribution these kinds of workers make to the GDP.

10. Classification of labor input by economic sector can indicate differences in productivity among labor in different economic sectors in those cases in which labor mobility is not perfect or when labor composition within each sector is not the same. In the first case, classification by sector provides some estimates of the quality component of labor input that are not captured in the analyses of other characteristics. Kendrick (1961) uses economic sector as a main factor in labor quality in his studies of productivity for the U.S. economy. Like occupation classifications, economic sector classifications can be performed according to different criteria. For example, in census classifications, one can study the sector at the two- or at the four-digit level, which allows better measurement of the interaction effects. Dale W. Jorgenson and M. Kuroda (forthcoming) pursued this approach in their analysis of the U.S. and Japanese economies. Many studies of developing economies try to determine the appropriate share of each economic sector for each stage of development. Pattern-of-development studies show that, for example, the tertiary sector increased its share in GDP according to increases of the GDP per capita. These studies suggest that some developing countries had a tertiary sector much larger than expected for their stage of development, with labor in this sector working at a much lower rate of productivity than in the other two sectors. There have also been numerous studies to verify the hypothesis that there are substantial differences in labor productivity between sectors (see Fuchs 1964). It is not clear from these studies whether increases in the share of the tertiary sector were demand or supply determined. Some recent theoretical developments

explain the share of independent workers (most of them in the tertiary sector in Latin America) in the total labor force, based on behavioral decisions (see Blau 1987).

11. The pattern of labor composition in economic sectors observed for Latin American countries is not very different from that observed in many other countries, although it is somewhat different from the composition predicted by patterns-of-growth studies. It is possible to separate the tertiary sector from the public sector, as I have done in the discussion of the product account and capital input in Chapter 8. Labor employed in the administrative part of the public sector (excluding public enterprises) can represent more than one-third of the tertiary sector. For this reason, it is important to treat it separately. In this section, the public sector is not considered separately. However, in Chapter 8, when sources of growth for certain economic sectors are estimated, it will receive separate treatment.

12. Earning function estimates made for some Latin American countries confirm, in part, the arguments made above (see the journal *Ensayos ECIEL*, many issues).

13. Changes in the composition of the economic sector can also have consequences for functional income distribution, thus affecting the weights given to the growth of each input. Part of this problem is taken into account by using variable weights in a discrete approximation to Divisia indexes of price and quantity change.

14. Reallocation understood in terms of economic sector can capture part of the phenomenon of regional reallocation, if one interprets the primary sector as mainly rural and the tertiary sector as mainly urban.

15. International migration should be considered in the analysis of the sources of growth of population so that its effects can be incorporated into studies of some of the different components considered here.

16. A direct way of measuring the change of the GDP due to migration (labor reallocation) is given in the following equation:

$$\Delta GDP = \sum_i \sum_j (w_i - w_j) \, L_{ij}$$

where L_{ij} is the amount of labor from region *j* which moved to region *i*, in a given time period.

This approach requires information on the amount of labor from region *j*, in all categories, that moved to region *i* in a given time period. In order to measure interaction effects, the data would have to be organized according to diverse characteristics.

17. In order to determine whether the quality of labor, especially in terms of the education component, is related to employment growth in other countries, one should take into account some differences in the labor quality components in the different countries.

FIGURE 13 Schematic Presentation of the Labor Input

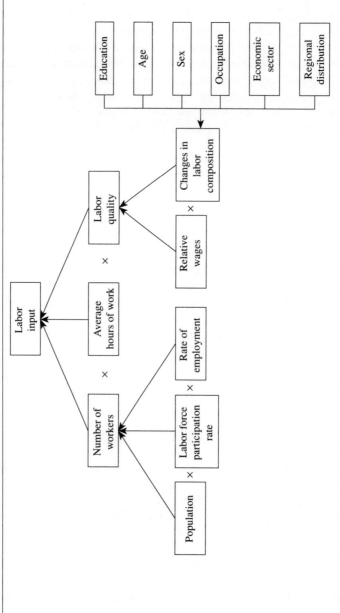

SOURCE: Author.

FIGURE 14 Average Annual Change in Labor Quality Based on Six Characteristics, 1940–1980 (percentage)

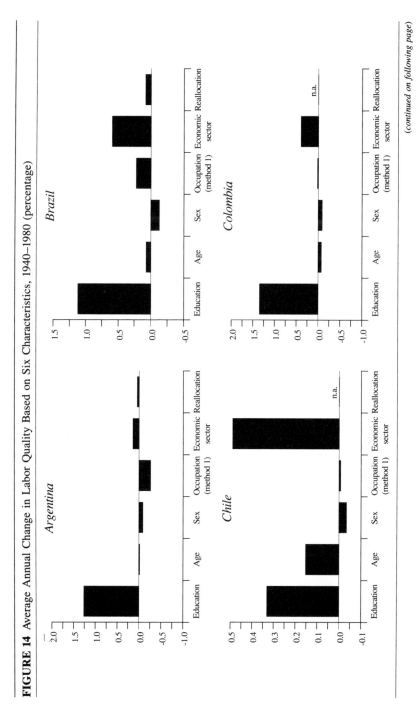

(continued on following page)

85

FIGURE 14 (continued)

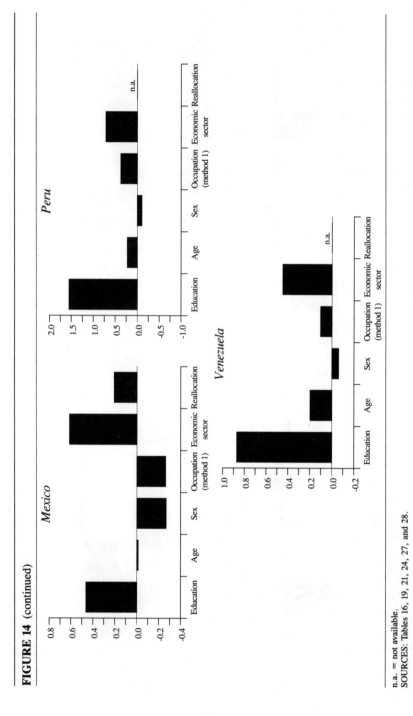

n.a. = not available.

SOURCES: Tables 16, 19, 21, 24, 27, and 28.

TABLE 10 Labor Force Participation Rates for Selected Years, 1940–1980 (percentage)

Year	Argentina	Brazil	Chile	Colombia	Mexico	Peru	Venezuela
1940	n.a.	49.70[a]	50.10[a]	n.a.	50.70[a]	47.60[a]	50.80
1950	51.36	48.41	49.19	48.81	47.09	56.82	49.10
1960	50.18	46.96	45.73	45.93	45.55	51.54	47.35
1970	48.36	45.53	41.66	44.89	43.29	47.21	43.39
1980	48.16	45.56	42.97	46.01	43.97	46.72	44.65

n.a. = not available.
a. My estimate is based on the related series method of interpolation.
SOURCE: Programa Regional del Empleo para América Latina y el Caribe (1982).

TABLE 11 Employment, Population, and the Employment-Population Ratio for Selected Years, 1940–1985

Country/variable	1940	1950	1960	1970	1980	1985
Argentina						
Population						
(thousands of people)	14,169	17,093	20,666	23,364	27,900	30,115
Employment						
(thousands of people)	n.a.	5,066	5,633	6,752	7,806	8,288
Ratio (%)	n.a.	29.6	27.3	28.9	28.0	27.5
Brazil						
Population						
(thousands of people)	41,114	51,973	69,797	92,764	119,056	134,268
Employment						
(thousands of people)	13,969	17,117	22,651	29,545	45,459	n.a.
Ratio (%)	34.0	32.9	33.4	31.8	38.2	n.a.
Chile						
Population						
(thousands of people)	5,089	6,120	7,375	8,853	10,522	11,448
Employment						
(thousands of people)	1,605	1,957	2,494	3,011	3,636	4,061
Ratio (%)	31.5	32.0	33.8	34.0	34.6	35.5

(*continued on following page*)

TABLE 11 (continued)

Country/variable	1940	1950	1960	1970	1980	1985
Colombia						
Population						
(thousands of people)	9,094	11,244	15,416	20,636	25,892	28,826
Employment						
(thousands of people)	n.a.	3,513	4,616	6,239	9,905	11,481
Ratio (%)	n.a.	31.2	29.9	30.2	38.3	40.0
Mexico						
Population						
(thousands of people)	19,654	25,791	34,923	50,600	67,396	76,025
Employment						
(thousands of people)	5,858	7,373	9,559	12,955	18,484	21,601
Ratio (%)	29.8	28.6	27.4	25.6	27.4	28.4
Peru						
Population						
(thousands of people)	7,033	8,674	10,204	13,586	17,743	20,172
Employment						
(thousands of people)	n.a.	2,431	3,162	4,189	5,718	6,676
Ratio (%)	n.a.	28.0	31.0	30.8	32.2	33.1
Venezuela						
Population						
(thousands of people)	3,710	4,974	7,364	10,275	n.a.	17,324
Employment						
(thousands of people)	n.a.	1,600	2,300	3,213	4,601	5,201
Ratio (%)	n.a.	32.2	30.1	30.0	n.a.	30.0

n.a. = not available.
NOTE: The employment-population ratio is less than the labor force participation rate given in Table 10 because here people under age fourteen are excluded.
SOURCES: Tables E10, E11, E12, and E13.

TABLE 12 Average Number of Hours Worked per Worker per Week in Selected Years, 1960–1980

Year	Argentina	Brazil	Chile	Colombia	Mexico	Peru	Venezuela
1960	n.a.	n.a.	50.5	50.0	n.a.	n.a.	n.a.
1964	42.1	n.a.	n.a.	48.9	45.6	47.3	n.a.
1970	n.a.	44.3	45.3	49.6	45.1	47.1	n.a.
1980	43.5	n.a.	n.a.	n.a.	46.6	45.6	44.2

n.a. = not available.
SOURCES: Same as Tables 14, 17, and 20.

TABLE 13 Average Rate of Urban Unemployment, 1963–1985 (percentage)

Year	Argentina	Brazil	Chile	Colombia	Mexico	Peru	Venezuela
1963	8.8	n.a.	4.9	n.a.	n.a.	n.a.	n.a.
1964	5.7	n.a.	5.3	n.a.	n.a.	n.a.	n.a.
1965	5.0	n.a.	5.4	n.a.	n.a.	n.a.	n.a.
1966	5.7	n.a.	5.3	n.a.	n.a.	n.a.	n.a.
1967	6.2	n.a.	6.1	n.a.	n.a.	n.a.	9.5
1968	5.0	3.2	6.0	n.a.	n.a.	n.a.	7.4
1969	4.0	3.0	6.1	n.a.	n.a.	n.a.	8.4
1970	4.9	3.7	7.1	n.a.	n.a.	6.9	7.8
1971	6.0	n.a.	5.7	n.a.	n.a.	7.5	7.1
1972	6.6	2.8	3.7	n.a.	n.a.	7.6	n.a.
1973	5.3	3.6	4.8	n.a.	7.2	5.0	n.a.
1974	3.4	n.a.	9.7	12.7	7.0	4.1	7.6
1975	2.6	n.a.	16.2	11.0	7.0	7.5	8.3
1976	4.5	2.3	16.7	10.6	6.7	6.9	6.8
1977	2.8	3.0	13.2	9.0	8.1	8.7	5.5
1978	2.8	6.8	14.0	9.0	7.0	8.0	5.1
1979	2.0	6.4	13.6	8.9	5.7	6.5	5.8
1980	3.5	6.3	11.8	9.7	4.5	7.1	6.6
1981	4.5	7.9	9.0	8.2	4.2	6.8	6.8
1982	4.7	6.3	20.0	9.3	4.1	7.0	7.8
1983	4.2	6.7	18.9	11.8	6.7	8.8	10.5
1984	3.8	7.1	18.5	13.5	6.0	n.a.	14.3
1985	5.3	5.3	17.2	14.1	4.8	n.a.	14.3

n.a. = not available.

SOURCES: Programa Regional del Empleo para América Latina y el Caribe (1982); Economic Commission for Latin America (1986).

TABLE 14 Labor Force Composition by Educational Level in Selected Years, 1940–1980 (percentage of the labor force)

Highest educational level attained	Argentina	Brazil	Chile	Colombia	Mexico	Peru	Venezuela
1940							
Illiterate	n.a.	53.3	n.a.	42.1	n.a.	n.a.	n.a.
Primary	n.a.	42.6	75.1[a]	n.a.	93.3[a]	n.a.	n.a.
1–3 years	n.a.	36.9	56.3[a]	n.a.	70.4[a]	n.a.	n.a.
4–6 years	n.a.	5.7	18.8	n.a.	22.9	n.a.	n.a.
Secondary	n.a.	3.2	22.2	n.a.	4.4	n.a.	n.a.
7–9 years	n.a.	n.a.	11.0	n.a.	2.9	n.a.	n.a.
10–12 years	n.a.	n.a.	11.2	n.a.	1.5	n.a.	n.a.
University	n.a.	0.9	2.7	n.a.	2.3	n.a.	n.a.
13–16 years	n.a.	0.1	1.7	n.a.	1.2	n.a.	n.a.
17 years and more	n.a.	0.1	1.0	n.a.	1.1	n.a.	n.a.
Unspecified	n.a.	0.7	0.0	57.9	0.0	n.a.	n.a.
1950[b]							
Illiterate	14.4	48.3	n.a.	37.7	n.a.	n.a.	n.a.
Primary	76.9	44.0	77.4[a]	54.8	93.5[a]	n.a.	89.7[a]
1–3 years	n.a.	27.7	51.8[a]	36.4	72.0[a]	n.a.	n.a.
4–6 years	n.a.	16.3	25.6	18.4	21.5	n.a.	n.a.
Secondary	7.5	6.6	20.2	5.4	4.4	n.a.	8.1
7–9 years	n.a.	4.8	10.4	n.a.	3.2	n.a.	n.a.
10–12 years	n.a.	1.8	9.8	n.a.	1.2	n.a.	n.a.
University	1.2	1.1	2.3	1.1	2.1	n.a.	2.2
13–16 years	n.a.	0.3	1.3	n.a.	1.1	n.a.	n.a.
17 and more	n.a.	0.8	1.0	n.a.	1.0	n.a.	n.a.
Unspecified	0.0	0.0	0.1	1.0	0.0	n.a.	0.0
1960[c]							
Illiterate	10.5	41.5	n.a.	27.1	n.a.	33.0	47.8
Primary	71.6	50.5	75.1[a]	63.7	92.0[a]	52.6	43.9
1–3 years	n.a.	30.8	39.5[a]	41.8	68.8[a]	n.a.	18.8
4–6 years	n.a.	19.7	35.6	21.9	23.2	n.a.	25.1
Secondary	14.7	6.8	22.3	6.1	5.7	11.2	6.5
7–9 years	n.a.	4.5	12.0	n.a.	4.4	n.a.	n.a.
10–12 years	n.a.	2.3	10.3	n.a.	1.3	n.a.	n.a.
University	3.2	1.2	2.6	0.8	2.3	2.3	1.8
13–16 years	n.a.	0.1	1.3	n.a.	1.2	n.a.	n.a.
17 and more	n.a.	1.1	1.3	n.a.	1.1	n.a.	n.a.
Unspecified	0.0	0.0	0.0	2.3	0.0	0.9	0.0

(*continued on following page*)

TABLE 14 (continued)

Highest educational level attained	Argentina	Brazil	Chile	Colombia	Mexico	Peru	Venezuela
1970[d]							
Illiterate	5.0	28.3	8.3	4.5	n.a.	24.2	20.2
Primary	69.1	58.1	52.2	56.3	83.4[a]	52.7	55.6
1–3 years	n.a.	37.4	15.5	n.a.	n.a.	n.a.	16.9
4–6 years	n.a.	20.7	36.7	n.a.	n.a.	n.a.	38.7
Secondary	20.3	11.7	31.5	30.6	13.9	17.8	17.0
7–9 years	n.a.	7.4	13.6	n.a.	n.a.	n.a.	n.a.
10–12 years	n.a.	4.3	17.9	n.a.	n.a.	n.a.	n.a.
University	5.6	1.9	3.3	8.6	2.7	5.3	3.5
13–16 years	n.a.	0.4	n.a.	n.a.	n.a.	n.a.	n.a.
17 and more	n.a.	1.5	n.a.	n.a.	n.a.	n.a.	n.a.
Unspecified	0.0	0.0	4.7	0.0	0.0	0.0	3.7

n.a. = not available.

a. Includes illiterate.

b. 1947 for Argentina and 1951 for Columbia.

c. 1964 for Colombia and 1961 for Peru and Venezuela.

d. 1969 for Brazil and 1967 for Colombia.

NOTE: Illiterate here refers to people who cannot read and write. The data for Colombia for 1980 are as follows: illiterate, 5.1 percent; primary, 48.6 percent; secondary, 33.7 percent; university, 12.6 percent; and unspecified, 0.0 percent.

SOURCES: Argentina: Instituto Nacional de Estadisticas y Censos (1947, 1960, 1970, 1980); Brazil: Langoni (1970); Chile: Selowsky (1967); Colombia: Departamento Administrativo Nacional de Estadisticas (many publications); Economic Commission for Latin America, *Statistical Yearbook for Latin America and the Caribbean* (many issues); International Labor Organization (1971); Mexico: Selowsky (1967); Peru: Economic Commission for Latin America, *Statistical Yearbook for Latin America and the Caribbean* (many issues); Venezuela: United Nations, *Demographic Yearbook* (many issues).

TABLE 15 Relative Wages by Educational Level in Selected Years, 1957–1969 (ratio to average wage of entire work force)

Highest educational level attained	Brazil		Chile		Colombia		Mexico	Venezuela
	1960	1969	1960	1965	1965	1967	1963	1957
Illiterate	0.553	0.538	n.a.	n.a.	n.a.	0.230	n.a.	n.a.
Primary	1.088	0.814	0.598	0.708[a]	0.916	0.560	0.835[a]	0.736[a]
1–3 years	0.841	0.710	n.a.	0.662[a]	n.a.	n.a.	0.680[a]	n.a.
4–6 years	1.335	0.917	n.a.	0.755	n.a.	n.a.	0.989	n.a.
Secondary	2.020	1.340	1.862	1.376	1.394	1.120	2.023	2.287
7–9 years	1.652	1.030	n.a.	1.011	n.a.	n.a.	1.743	n.a.
10–12 years	2.388	1.650	n.a.	1.741	n.a.	n.a.	2.303	n.a.
University	3.960	3.545	4.717	5.233	1.455	n.a.	5.126	9.868
13–16 years	3.111	2.304	n.a.	4.153	n.a.	2.840	3.435	n.a.
17 years or more	4.808	4.786	n.a.	6.313	n.a.	4.570	6.816	n.a.

n.a. = not available.
a. Includes illiterate.
SOURCES: Harberger and Selowsky (1966); Selowsky (1967); Langoni (1970); Schultz (1968); International Labor Organization (1971); Carnoy (1964).

TABLE 16 Average Annual Rate of Change of the Quality Component of Labor Based on Educational Level, 1940–1980 (percentage)

Period	Argentina	Brazil	Chile	Colombia	Mexico	Peru	Venezuela
1940–1950	n.a.	1.46	−0.24	0.64	−0.17	n.a.	n.a.
1950–1960	1.10	0.56	0.32	0.48	0.32	n.a.	−0.35
1960–1970	1.42	1.33	0.91	2.85	1.24	1.55	2.09
1970–1980	n.a.	n.a.	n.a.	1.41	n.a.	n.a.	n.a.

n.a. = not available.
SOURCE: Computed from Tables 14 and 15.

TABLE 17 Share of Women in the Total Labor Force in Selected Years, 1940–1980 (percentage)

Year	Argentina	Brazil	Chile	Colombia	Mexico	Peru	Venezuela
1940	n.a.	14.62	24.43	n.a.	n.a.	35.18	22.48
1947	20.21	n.a.	n.a.	n.a.	n.a.	n.a.	n.a.
1950	n.a.	14.70	24.24	18.35	13.64	n.a.	17.80
1955	23.25	n.a.	n.a.	n.a.	n.a.	n.a.	n.a.
1960	21.70	17.77	24.89	19.23	18.02	20.87	18.61
1970	25.40	20.48	21.36	19.97	19.03	22.00	22.23
1980	26.90	27.22	27.30	21.91	27.00	24.20	27.50

n.a. = not available.
SOURCE: Same as Table 14.

TABLE 18 Relative Wages by Gender in Selected Countries, 1960 and 1970 (ratio to average wage of all labor)

Year	Brazil	Colombia	Venezuela
1960			
Male	1.063	n.a.	1.007[a]
Female	0.687	n.a.	0.963[a]
1970			
Male	1.085	1.250[b]	n.a.
Female	0.660	0.500	n.a.

a. 1961.
b. 1967.
SOURCE: Same as Table 15.

TABLE 19 Average Annual Rate of Change of the Quality Component of Labor Based on Gender, 1940–1980 (percentage)

Period	Argentina	Brazil	Chile	Colombia	Mexico	Peru	Venezuela
1940–1950	n.a.	−0.003	0.007	n.a.	n.a.	n.a.	0.176
1950–1960	−0.056a	−0.115	−0.024	−0.066	−0.165	n.a.	−0.004
1960–1970	−0.139	−0.102	0.133	−0.056	−0.038	−0.043	−0.016
1970–1980	−0.064	−0.286	−0.252	−0.146	−0.598	−0.165	−0.395

n.a. = not available.
a. 1947–1960.
SOURCES: Tables 17 and 18.

TABLE 20 Labor Force Composition by Age in Selected Years, 1940–1980 (percentage)

Year/age group	Argentina	Brazil	Chile	Colombia	Mexico	Peru	Venezuela
1940							
10–19	n.a.	26.97	16.40	n.a.	n.a.	n.a.	n.a.
20–29	n.a.	27.15	29.44	n.a.	n.a.	n.a.	n.a.
30–39	n.a.	18.99	22.87	n.a.	n.a.	n.a.	n.a.
40–49	n.a.	13.67	16.35	n.a.	n.a.	n.a.	n.a.
50–59	n.a.	7.95	9.88	n.a.	n.a.	n.a.	n.a.
60 and over	n.a.	5.27	5.06	n.a.	n.a.	n.a.	n.a.
1950a							
10–19	n.a.	23.75	15.45	16.81	n.a.	n.a.	n.a.
20–29	n.a.	29.08	30.19	30.10	n.a.	n.a.	n.a.
30–39	n.a.	20.00	21.82	21.55	n.a.	n.a.	n.a.
40–49	n.a.	13.99	16.91	15.22	n.a.	n.a.	n.a.
50–59	n.a.	8.12	10.48	9.29	n.a.	n.a.	n.a.
60 and over	n.a.	5.06	5.15	7.03	n.a.	n.a.	n.a.
1960b							
10–19	13.16	20.48	15.73	16.99	18.54	15.39	15.66
20–29	26.02	28.48	29.00	29.28	28.54	30.17	29.76
30–39	42.66c	21.30	23.04	22.38	20.13	36.83c	23.42
40–49		15.07	16.66	15.85	14.06		15.83
50–59	11.93	8.91	10.66	9.78	10.14	9.56	9.68
60 and over	6.23	5.75	4.91	5.72	8.59	8.05	5.65

(*continued on following page*)

TABLE 20   (continued)

Year/age group	Argentina	Brazil	Chile	Colombia	Mexico	Peru	Venezuela
1970[d]							
10–19	12.81	14.25	10.42	17.32	17.96	12.43	16.69
20–29	26.45	29.52	30.88	29.60	29.86	32.32	30.52
30–39	22.24	23.02	23.52	21.86	20.84	23.79	21.92
40–49	19.80	17.18	17.65	15.35	14.94	15.89	15.63
50–59	12.68	10.05	10.87	9.31	9.30	10.71	9.45
60 and over	6.02	5.79	6.66	6.56	7.10	4.86	5.79
1980							
10–19	10.78	19.80	6.88	17.35	17.90	10.95	10.59
20–29	27.02	31.46	34.69	34.48	30.30	31.40	32.83
30–39	25.11	21.14	27.28	21.72	20.80	24.75	27.36
40–49	19.46	14.76	17.44	13.30	14.30	16.43	16.34
50–59	13.39	8.67	9.91	7.77	9.00	11.21	9.12
60 and over	4.24	4.17	3.80	5.38	7.70	5.26	3.76

a. 1947 for Argentina and 1951 for Colombia.
b. 1965 for Colombia and 1961 for Peru.
c. Includes 40–49 age group.
d. 1971 for Venezuela.
SOURCES: Same as Table 14.

TABLE 21 Average Annual Rate of Change of the Quality Component of Labor Based on Age, 1940–1980 (percentage)

Period	Argentina	Brazil	Chile	Colombia	Mexico	Peru	Venezuela
1940–1950	n.a.	0.170	0.051	n.a.	n.a.	n.a.	n.a.
1950–1960	n.a.	0.246	0.025	0.036[a]	n.a.	n.a.	n.a.
1960–1970	−0.237[b]	0.387	0.287	−0.049[c]	0.014	0.288	−0.124[d]
1970–1980	0.206	−0.535	0.244	−0.206	−0.038	0.163	0.518

n.a. = not available.
a. 1951–1965.
b. 1964–1970.
c. 1965–1970.
d. 1960–1971.
SOURCES: Table 20, and data specified in the text.

TABLE 22 Labor Force Composition by Occupation Classification I in Selected Years, 1940–1980 (percentage)

Year/occupation	Argentina	Brazil	Chile	Colombia	Mexico	Peru	Venezuela
1940							
Employers	n.a.	2.60	n.a.	n.a.	n.a.	n.a.	n.a.
Employees	n.a.	43.04	73.50	n.a.	n.a.	n.a.	n.a.
Own-account	n.a.	33.64	26.50[a]	n.a.	n.a.	n.a.	n.a.
Unpaid family	n.a.	19.90	n.a.	n.a.	n.a.	n.a.	n.a.
Others	n.a.	0.82	n.a.	n.a.	n.a.	n.a.	n.a.
1950[b]							
Employers	17.10	3.79	n.a.	10.14	n.a.	n.a.	3.80
Employees	72.30	49.11	75.30	52.90	n.a.	37.00	54.00
Own-account	7.50	29.37	24.70[a]	24.00	n.a.	63.00[a]	27.30
Unpaid family	3.10	17.51	n.a.	8.15	n.a.	n.a.	8.20
Others	0.00	0.22	0.00	4.81	n.a.	0.00	6.70
1960[c]							
Employers	13.20	3.60	1.40	n.a.	2.20	n.a.	2.70
Employees	71.30	50.00	73.90	n.a.	62.50	50.08	60.10
Own-account	12.40	28.10	18.80	n.a.	32.80	49.92[a]	31.00
Unpaid family	3.10	16.80	n.a.	n.a.	n.a.	n.a.	4.50
Others	0.00	1.50	5.90[d]	n.a.	2.50[d]	0.00	1.70
1970[e]							
Employers	5.71	1.57	3.11	8.18	6.15	n.a.	4.40
Employees	70.80	54.80	70.09	57.27	62.18	53.41	65.70
Own-account	16.23	34.14	19.25	24.99	25.14	46.59[a]	23.80
Unpaid family	3.17	9.32	1.65	8.20	6.53	n.a.	6.10
Others	4.09	0.17	5.90	1.36	0.00	0.00	0.00
1980							
Employers	n.a.	n.a.	n.a.	n.a.	n.a.	n.a.	n.a.
Employees[f]	71.60	64.20	76.90	n.a.	59.50	50.30	76.60
Own-account	25.20	30.50	19.20	n.a.	36.30	44.20	22.20
Unpaid family	3.20	5.30	3.90	n.a.	4.20	5.50	1.20
Others	0.00	0.00	0.00	n.a.	0.00	0.00	0.00

n.a. = not available.
a. Includes employers and unpaid family workers.
b. 1947 for Argentina and 1951 for Colombia.
c. 1963 for Mexico and 1961 for Peru and Venezuela.
d. Includes unpaid family workers.
e. 1968 for Peru and 1971 for Venezuela.
f. Includes employers.
SOURCES: Same as Table 14.

TABLE 23 Relative Wages by Occupation in Selected Years,
1961–1968 (ratio to average wage of entire work force)

Occupation	Argentina 1967	Brazil 1966/68	Colombia 1967	Peru 1963	Venezuela 1961
Employers	1.49	1.68	2.38	5.98	1.91
Employees	0.90	0.95	1.05	0.57	1.19
Own-account workers	1.25	n.a.	0.88	1.44	1.75
Unpaid family workers	n.a.	0.32	n.a.	0.38	0.54
Others	n.a.	n.a.	n.a.	0.94	0.86

n.a. = not available.
NOTE: No data are available for Mexico.
SOURCES: Same as Table 14 and CONADE (1968); Brady (1967); World Bank country studies.

TABLE 24 Average Annual Change of the Quality Component of Labor Based on
Occupation, 1940–1970 (percentage)

Period	Argentina	Brazil	Chile	Colombia	Mexico	Peru	Venezuela
1940–1950	n.a.	0.027	−0.101	n.a.	n.a.	n.a.	n.a.
1950–1960	−0.022	−0.082	0.078	n.a.	n.a.	−0.088	0.529
1960–1970	−0.494	0.714	0.001	0.017	−0.262	0.831	−0.322

n.a. = not available.
SOURCES: Tables 22 and 23.

TABLE 25 Labor Force Composition by Economic Sector in Selected Years, 1940–
1980 (percentage)

Year/economic sector	Argentina	Brazil	Chile	Colombia	Mexico	Peru	Venezuela
1940[a]							
Primary	25.3	64.2	39.8	n.a.	65.4	n.a.	n.a.
Secondary	32.2	10.1	n.a.	n.a.	12.7	n.a.	n.a.
Tertiary	42.5	25.7	n.a.	n.a.	21.9	n.a.	n.a.
1950							
Primary	19.9	60.1	34.2	55.5	59.0	64.2	44.0
Secondary	35.0	13.6	23.4	15.8	14.4	17.5	15.4
Tertiary	45.1	26.3	42.4	28.7	26.6	18.3	40.6
1960							
Primary	18.1	46.6	31.5	48.8	55.5	59.6	34.1
Secondary	34.7	15.2	23.7	17.1	17.3	19.5	17.6
Tertiary	47.2	38.2	44.8	34.1	27.2	20.9	48.3

(continued on following page)

TABLE 25   (continued)

Year/economic sector	Argentina	Brazil	Chile	Colombia	Mexico	Peru	Venezuela
1970[b]							
Primary	17.2	40.1	24.0	48.9	40.8	50.2	35.0
Secondary	35.4	19.7	22.4	17.3	21.6	20.0	21.0
Tertiary	47.4	40.2	53.6	33.8	37.6	29.8	44.0
1980							
Primary	13.0	31.2	16.5	34.3	36.5	40.1	17.1
Secondary	33.9	26.6	25.2	23.5	29.0	18.2	30.3
Tertiary	53.1	42.2	58.4	42.2	34.5	41.7	52.6

n.a. = not available.
a. 1943 for Argentina.
b. 1969 for Argentina, 1968 for Peru, and 1965 for Venezuela.
NOTE: Primary sector = agriculture and mining; secondary sector = manufacturing; tertiary sector = services and the public sector.
SOURCES: Same as Table 14.

TABLE 26   Relative Wages by Economic Sector in Selected Years, 1940–1970 (ratio to average wage of total labor force)

Year/economic sector	Argentina	Brazil	Chile	Colombia	Mexico	Peru	Venezuela
1940							
Primary	n.a.	n.a.	n.a.	n.a.	0.402	n.a.	n.a.
Secondary	n.a.	n.a.	n.a.	n.a.	2.111[a]	n.a.	n.a.
Tertiary	n.a.	n.a.	n.a.	n.a.	n.a.	n.a.	n.a.
1950							
Primary	0.560	n.a.	n.a.	n.a.	0.691	n.a.	n.a.
Secondary	1.180	n.a.	n.a.	n.a.	1.539[a]	n.a.	n.a.
Tertiary	1.060	n.a.	n.a.	n.a.	n.a.	n.a.	n.a.
1960[b]							
Primary	0.620	0.620	0.517	0.668	n.a.	0.623	0.469
Secondary	1.110	1.220	1.141	1.058	n.a.	1.160	1.048
Tertiary	1.070	1.370	1.301	1.325	n.a.	1.519	1.482
1970[c]							
Primary	0.570	0.490	0.492	0.433	n.a.	n.a.	0.630
Secondary	1.140	1.270	1.116	1.567[a]	n.a.	n.a.	1.070
Tertiary	1.030	1.370	1.183	n.a.	n.a.	n.a.	1.043

n.a. = not available.
a. Includes the tertiary sector.
b. 1961 for Colombia and 1959 for Peru.
c. 1969 for Argentina, 1967 for Colombia, and 1969 for Venezuela.
SOURCES: Same as Table 15.

TABLE 27 Average Annual Change of the Quality Component of Labor Based on Economic Sector, 1940–1980 (percentage)

Period	Argentina	Brazil	Chile	Colombia	Mexico	Peru	Venezuela
1940–1950	0.254	0.255	0.348	n.a.	0.544	n.a.	n.a.
1950–1960	0.080	0.991	0.208	0.403	0.297	0.342	0.904
1960–1970	0.043	0.421	0.905	−0.009	1.245	0.831	−0.322
1970–1980	0.177	0.714	0.500	0.794	0.365	0.970	0.764

n.a. = not available.
SOURCES: Tables 25 and 26.

TABLE 28 Average Annual Change of the Quality Component of Labor Based on Regional Reallocation, 1940–1980 (percentage)

Period	Argentina	Brazil	Mexico
1940–1950	n.a.	0.114	0.245
1950–1960	n.a.	−0.033	0.298
1960–1970	0.040	0.083	0.327
1970–1980	n.a.	0.150	−0.048

n.a. = not available.
SOURCES: Cuca-Tolosa (1972); Fundação Instituto Brasileiro de Geografía e Estatística (1974); Instituto Nacional de Estadísticas y Censos (Argentina, 1947, 1960, 1970, 1980); Langoni (1970); Reynolds and Alejo (1987).

CHAPTER 7

Capital Input

The sources-of-growth method analyzes capital input, as it did labor input, in terms of the gross component and the quality component. Figure 15 (page 108) gives a schematic representation of the different elements that enter into the definition of capital input. It also provides a general picture of the contents of this chapter.

For this methodology, it would be optimal to express each capital component in terms of services provided per unit of time, such as machine hours in the production process. However, the available information does not allow for this measurement at the aggregate level, so a different approach must be pursued.

To overcome this difficulty, I will represent each capital component by the value of its stock, a certain amount at a given time. In this way, the flow of capital services can be estimated by calculating the product of the stock value times its rate of return or, as an alternative, by establishing a fixed proportionality between the amount of services provided per period and the value of the stock at a given time.

Another difficulty is that the value of the capital stock of each component of capital input, in general, is not provided by the national accounts, so it must be estimated indirectly from the investment flow toward each capital component.[1] This can be done by using the inventory method, which relies on the process of the accumulation of capital, and not on the actual value of the stock, in a given time period. This method can be applied to either the aggregate capital stock or its components.

The value of each component of capital stock in a given year, following the inventory method, will be equal to the value of the capital stock of the previous year, plus the real gross investment during that year, minus the depreciation of the initial capital during that year. This calculation could also be expressed in terms of all past values of real gross investment minus depreciation (that is, real net investment), since previous capital stock can be defined in the same way as current capital stock.

The information available for the flow of investments covers only real gross investment for the recent past, so this study, which begins in 1940, requires an accurate estimation of initial capital stock for that year. Depending on the information available for different countries, I used diverse methods to calculate initial capital stock. In some cases, I used census estimates of capital stock for some economic sectors around 1940. For others, I estimated initial capital stock for 1940 by establishing the ratio between the annual average of real gross investment, for the year 1940 (using data for the three or four years around 1940, depending on the quality of the data available), and the sum of an assumed rate of capital growth and rate of depreciation. The figures for real gross investment come from national accounts.

Finally, since there are no direct estimates of capital depreciation, I need an indirect method. In this case, I used the simple geometric method for calculating depreciation, which for each year is a fixed percentage of the previous year's capital stock.[2] According to this method, the capital stock for a given period is equal to the sum of the percentage of surviving capital stock from the previous period plus the real gross investment for that period. And the rate of the survival of capital is calculated as one minus the rate of depreciation calculated for each case. The specific value for this rate will be presented in the discussion of the estimates of each component of capital stock.[3]

Estimate of Gross Capital Input

The estimates of the aggregate capital stock for selected years are presented here in Table 29 (page 111; see Appendix E for complete series).

Before analyzing these findings, I will discuss the specific method followed in the estimation of the aggregate capital stock. The real gross investment was derived from the gross nominal investment divided by the price index for investment goods (in a few cases, these indexes were corrected by taking into account quality changes in capital goods in order to avoid underestimating real investment). Both series came from national accounts estimates. The rate of depreciation varies from 2 percent to 20 percent, depending on the kind of capital good in question. Taking into account the composition of the aggregate capital stock, I used an average rate of depreciation that varied across countries from 4 percent to 6 percent per year. Finally, the initial capital stock, as mentioned in the previous section, was estimated by different methods, depending on the availability of information for each country. In some cases (Argentina, for example), I used investment series before 1940 based on the importation of capital goods, which allowed me to establish figures for 1940. In the period 1900–1930, imported capital goods represented a large part of total investment goods in Latin America, thus recommending this method for establishing initial values for capital stock. In other cases, I used the alternative indirect method discussed above (that is, the ratio of gross investment to the sum of capital growth and depreciation). For some of the components, I used the information coming from the corporate sector (balance sheet data), national accounts (for housing, for example), and other previous studies (Langoni 1970 and Elías 1985, and others).

To advance the analysis of the findings displayed in Table 29, Figure 16 (page 109) presents the average annual rate of growth of the total capital stock, by country and decade. The behavior of capital stock is variable across countries and through time. The highest value observed, 12.3 percent in Brazil in the 1970s, is comparable to the highest rate observed in the rapidly growing Pacific Rim countries. Another interesting fact observed in this figure is the acceleration of the rate of growth of capital in the period 1940–1980 in Argentina, Brazil, and Mexico, and in Chile until 1970.[4]

The Quality Component of Capital Input

The estimation of the quality component of capital input requires estimates of capital stock composition, with rates of return for each constitutive element: the net rate of return, the depreciation rate, capital gains, taxes on capital income and capital value, and tax deduction allowances (see the schematic representation of capital input in Figure 15). So the gross rate of return could differ on the various components of the capital stock, because of differences in their elements. Also, if the net rates of return on two kinds of capital are equal, the gross rate could differ because of their other elements.

Differences in the gross rate of return on diverse kinds of capital should reflect the differences in the services provided by each unit of capital. The sources-of-growth methodology uses these facts in order to weight changing capital composition in its definition of the quality component of capital input.[5]

Capital input can be classified by many criteria useful for the measurement of its quality component. Classifications are created in terms of the different gross rates of return on the components, as defined. Our classifications, for this section, are the following: (1) corporate and noncorporate sectors; (2) private and public sectors; (3) goods composition, such as residential structures, nonresidential structures, and equipment; (4) domestic and imported capital goods; and (5) economic sector, such as agriculture and manufacturing.

The first classification, corporate and noncorporate sectors, deals mainly with the different tax treatments of capital income in these two sectors. This is to say, different tax treatments of capital income will produce differences in the gross rate of return on capital in these two sectors. Nevertheless, the net rates of return are still equal (produced by capital mobility). Differences in taxes on capital income and tax deduction allowances are one of the more important factors that create gross rate of return disparities among different sectors.

I establish the private-public distinction in my treatment of the composition of capital in order to allow for the diverse investment criteria at play in these two sectors as they pursue different objectives. In general, the private sector will be more interested in private returns, while the public sector will pay attention to social returns and income distribution objectives. Some differences in production efficiency could also exist.

The classification of capital-in-goods tries to capture differences in the gross rate of return coming from disparities in the rate of depreciation and tax treatment of diverse kinds of capital. There also may be differences in the adjustment produced by differences between desired and actual capital stock composition.

Finally, the classification of the import/domestic composition of capital stock is based on the theory of embodied technology through new investment goods. This theory argues that since the countries from which Latin American countries import investment goods (to be incorporated into their capital stock) have technological advantages, an increase in the share of imported investment goods in total capital will imply a larger increase in the technology embodied in capital in the importing countries.[6]

Table 30 (page 111) presents the composition of fixed capital according to all of these criteria. The five kinds of capital composition presented in this table differ greatly across countries and show important changes over time. First, in the corporate/noncorporate classification, the noncorporate element is more important in terms of total capital for the countries for which there are data. Its share for all countries and periods was around 85 percent, with a small decreasing trend in recent years. This trend can be associated with the fall in the share of some economic sectors in which the noncorporate organization is common.

In the second classification, private and public, the private sector varies in importance from 86 percent in Colombia to 64 percent in Mexico. In addition, the private sector share of total capital followed a negative trend in five of the seven countries.

The third classification, housing and nonhousing, shows that the housing share in total capital was around 15 percent and remained more or less stable for the whole period. In the cases of Mexico and Peru, the housing component probably includes other components besides housing, such as nonhousing structures.

The import/domestic classification of capital seems to be particularly relevant for our analysis. Except for the case of Peru (which was exceptionally low), the share of the import component varies from 14 percent for Argentina to 34 percent for Chile and is extremely variable over time. This variability could come from changes in trade policies and in the terms of trade.

The shares of agriculture (not including rural land value) and manufacturing in total capital stock vary greatly across countries. Agriculture runs from 7 percent for Argentina to 33 percent for Colombia, and manufacturing runs from 7 percent for Venezuela to 29 percent for Mexico. In general, the share of agriculture decreased through time, while the share of manufacturing has been increasing.

The estimate of the quality component of the capital input requires the calculation of the gross rate of return on each component of capital, along with the basic information on capital composition.

Table E18 (page 229) gives the complete data for the annual series of the gross rates of return on total capital for the period 1940–1985. This chapter will present data that show that the average annual gross rate of return on fixed capital was, for selected years, around 25 percent (see Table 31, page 113).

Compared with previous empirical estimates for other countries, this average seems very high. An overestimation of the rate of return may be due to several factors: capital stock does not include the value of rural land;

capital income includes some labor income (income of independent workers); and the stock of capital may have been underestimated because of underestimations of real investment and an overestimated rate of depreciation.

If the value of land were incorporated into the capital stock, assuming a share of 20 percent for land in total capital, the rate of return would be around 21 percent. This same calculation could be performed for the other factors mentioned above.

With respect to the rates of return on each capital element, Table 32 (page 114) suggests that the rate of return on the corporate element is much lower than the average on total capital in the cases of Colombia and Mexico. This result is the opposite of what is found in developed countries.

In the case of Colombia, the table shows that the rate of return on private capital is much larger than that on public capital. The figures for public capital seem very low and could be explained by underestimates of the benefits of public investment. In fact, some estimates of rates of return on public investment projects give much higher values than those presented in the table for these countries.

As expected, the gross rate of return on the housing component is generally much lower than that for total capital, except in Venezuela. In the case of economic sector composition, agriculture reports the highest rate of return, and the manufacturing component shows a similar rate across countries.

Over time, it is not possible to detect a definite trend in the rates of return, although the relative values of the rate of return on each component with respect to the average value of total capital are relatively stable.

The annual average rate of change of the quality component of the capital input is presented in Table 33 (page 114). In most periods and countries, the quality of capital either declined or did not grow at all, because of shifts in the capital composition in favor of components with a lower gross rate of return. The values of the annual rate of growth of the quality components were, in general, only 10 percent of the rate of growth of the gross capital input.

Notes

1. The values of capital and investment each have price and quantity components, and, according to capital theory, these prices are connected in equilibrium. The discounted value of the future services that will be provided by

the capital should also be equal to its current price. All these relations will be discussed in detail whenever necessary in the measurement of capital input.

2. Other methods for calculating depreciation used in the literature are the arithmetic, the double-geometric, and the sudden-death method (also called "one-hoss-shay"). After using diverse methods for this calculation and finding similar results, I opted for the simplest one.

3. The expression for capital stock, at year t, according to the method followed in this work will be:

$$K(t) = K(t - 1) + A(t) - d\, K(t - 1) = (1 - d)\, K(t - 1) + A(t)$$

where $K(t)$ is the value of capital stock for year t, $A(t)$ is the real gross investment for year t, and d is the rate of depreciation.

For a detailed discussion of the problems involved in the calculation of capital stock, see Jorgenson, Gollop, and Fraumeni (1987).

4. An explanation for this acceleration in the growth of capital is necessary because it would have important implications for future policy decisions and for a better understanding of the forces underlying growth process. For initial explorations, see Denison (1985), Helliwell, Sturm, and Salow (1985), and Abramovitz (1988). Also, since 1980, there has been a slowdown in the growth of capital in Latin America. (The output growth slowdown began in the mid-1970s, as I will discuss in Chapter 11). Both phenomena also occur in developed economies at the same time. See Maddison (1987).

The estimates of total capital stock do not include the land element in the agriculture sector. Even though this omission is not very important for estimating the rate of growth of capital (except in countries like Brazil, where extensive land expansion for agriculture has occurred), it becomes relevant for estimates of the rate of return on capital. Some preliminary estimates suggest that including the value of land could increase the total value of the stock of capital from 20 to 30 percent.

5. However, these differences could be due to other causes, such as differences in risks or market imperfections. Insofar as this occurs, my estimates will be biased.

6. International trade theory provides a mechanism for evaluating the contribution of foreign trade to national income through the theory of "gains of trade." (This was discussed in Chapter 4.) The production function approach has also been used to evaluate the role of the composition of capital in terms of imported and domestic goods. This approach considers the capital stock coming from imported goods and that coming from domestic capital goods as separate inputs. The production function will then determine whether these two kinds of capital should be considered separately or aggregated as a perfect substitute.

FIGURE 15 Schematic Presentation of the Capital Input

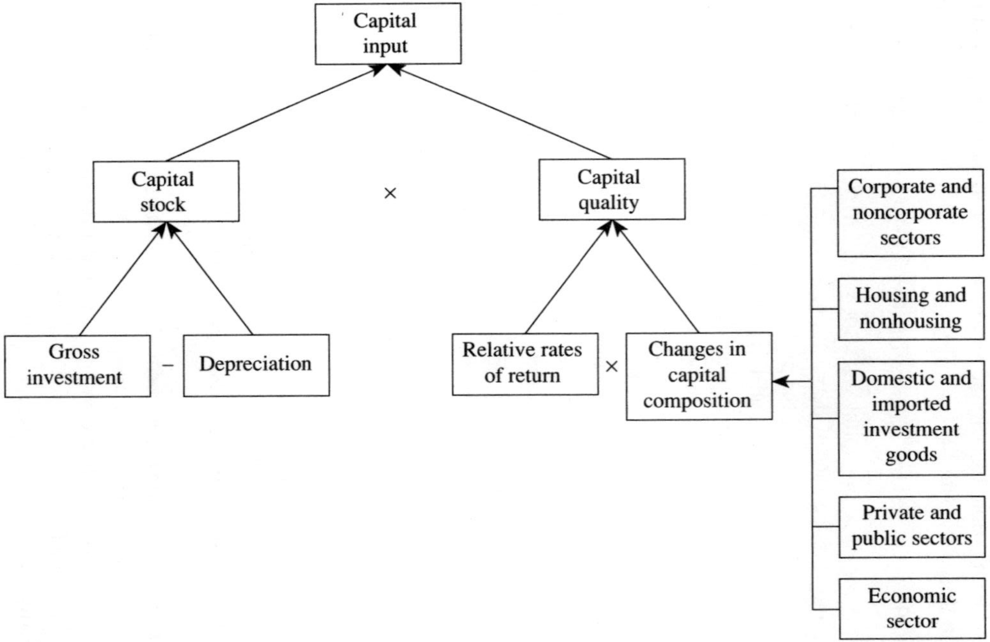

SOURCE: Author.

FIGURE 16 Average Annual Rate of Growth of Capital Stock by Decade, 1940–1985 (percentage)

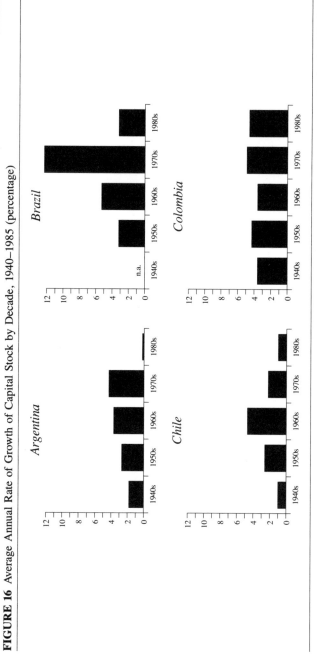

(continued on following page)

109

FIGURE 16 (continued)

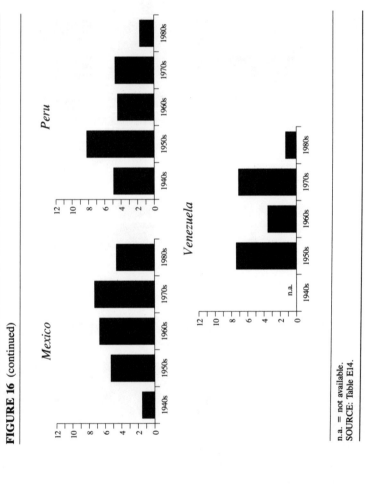

n.a. = not available.
SOURCE: Table E14.

110

TABLE 29 Stock of Fixed Capital in Selected Years, 1940–1985 (millions of 1960 U.S. dollars)

Year	1940	1950	1960	1970	1980	1985
Argentina	14,960	17,866	23,309	33,749	51,795	52,326
Brazil	n.a.	25,485	34,788	58,388	196,662	234,889
Chile	4,437	4,878	6,320	10,000	12,461	13,076
Colombia	3,743	5,396	8,246	11,710	19,095	24,044
Mexico	9,718	11,287	18,962	36,404	75,714	95,365
Peru	n.a.	1,897	4,156	6,388	10,220	11,148
Venezuela	n.a.	8,238	16,939	24,047	48,742	51,893

n.a. = not available.
SOURCE: Table E14.

TABLE 30 Composition of the Fixed Capital Stock according to Various Criteria in Selected Years, 1940–1980 (percentage)

Year/capital component	Argentina	Brazil	Chile	Colombia	Mexico	Peru	Venezuela
1940							
1. Corporate	n.a.	n.a.	n.a.	12.6	n.a.	n.a.	n.a.
Noncorporate	n.a.	n.a.	n.a.	87.4	n.a.	n.a.	n.a.
2. Private	n.a.	n.a.	n.a.	n.a.	54.2	n.a.	n.a.
Public	n.a.	n.a.	n.a.	n.a.	45.8	n.a.	n.a.
3. Housing	12.0	n.a.	n.a.	n.a.	n.a.	n.a.	n.a.
Nonhousing	88.0	n.a.	n.a.	n.a.	n.a.	n.a.	n.a.
4. Domestic	85.3	n.a.	n.a.	n.a.	74.9	n.a.	n.a.
Imported	14.7	n.a.	n.a.	n.a.	25.1	n.a.	n.a.
5. Agriculture	n.a.	n.a.	n.a.	n.a.	11.6	n.a.	n.a.
Manufacturing	10.0	n.a.	n.a.	n.a.	n.a.	n.a.	n.a.
Others	n.a.	n.a.	n.a.	n.a.	n.a.	n.a.	n.a.

(*continued on following page*)

TABLE 30 (continued)

Year/capital component	Argentina	Brazil	Chile	Colombia	Mexico	Peru	Venezuela
1950							
1.Corporate	10.3[a]	n.a.	n.a.	23.5	n.a.	n.a.	n.a.
Noncorporate	89.7[a]	n.a.	n.a.	76.5	n.a.	n.a.	n.a.
2.Private	74.2	82.8	n.a.	90.0	56.2	79.5	72.0
Public	25.8	17.2	n.a.	10.0	43.8	20.5	28.0
3.Housing	13.4	n.a.	n.a.	26.7	38.7	40.8	14.0
Nonhousing	86.6	n.a.	n.a.	73.3	61.3	59.2	86.0
4.Domestic	91.1	73.1	n.a.	70.0	73.1	96.1	82.3
Imported	8.9	26.9	n.a.	30.0	26.9	3.9	17.7
5.Agriculture	n.a.	10.7	16.0	44.7	17.9	31.2	18.6
Manufacturing	12.6	n.a.	n.a.	n.a.	24.4	7.6[a]	5.8
Others	n.a.	n.a.	n.a.	n.a.	57.7	n.a.	75.6
1960							
1.Corporate	14.4	n.a.	n.a.	18.9	n.a.	n.a.	n.a.
Noncorporate	85.6	n.a.	n.a.	81.1	n.a.	n.a.	n.a.
2.Private	76.9	78.8	60.8	86.6	63.4	81.6	64.1
Public	23.1	21.2	39.2	13.4	36.6	18.4	35.9
3.Housing	12.7	n.a.	18.0	27.2	50.7	40.7	15.6
Nonhousing	87.3	n.a.	82.0	72.8	49.3	59.3	84.4
4.Domestic	86.3	76.2	65.7	74.6	73.9	96.3	78.1
Imported	13.7	23.8	34.3	25.4	26.1	3.7	21.9
5.Agriculture	6.9	9.4	16.3	33.0	16.8	14.6	14.0
Manufacturing	15.8	n.a.	n.a.	18.5	28.9	9.8	7.4
Others	77.3	n.a.	n.a.	48.5	54.3	n.a.	78.6
1970							
1.Corporate	18.0[b]	n.a.	n.a.	n.a.	n.a.	n.a.	n.a.
Noncorporate	82.0[b]	n.a.	n.a.	n.a.	n.a.	n.a.	n.a.
2.Private	69.2	75.8	45.5	84.0	60.9	82.4	62.7
Public	30.8	24.2	54.5	16.0	39.1	17.6	37.3
3.Housing	11.0	7.4	23.3	28.7	53.5[b]	40.4	21.1
Nonhousing	89.0	92.6	76.7	71.3	46.5[b]	59.6	78.9
4.Domestic	83.9	85.0	62.8	75.8[b]	81.2	96.8	75.4
Imported	16.1	15.0	37.2	24.2[b]	18.8	3.2	24.6
5.Agriculture	6.5[b]	7.6	19.7	29.6[b]	15.4[b]	9.7	16.1
Manufacturing	19.3[b]	21.7	n.a.	18.1[b]	30.0[b]	n.a.	9.7
Others	74.2[b]	70.7	n.a.	52.3[b]	54.6[b]	n.a.	74.2

(*continued on following page*)

TABLE 30 (continued)

Year/capital component	Argentina	Brazil	Chile	Colombia	Mexico	Peru	Venezuela
1980							
1.Corporate	n.a.	n.a.	n.a.	n.a.	n.a.	n.a.	n.a.
Noncorporate	n.a.	n.a.	n.a.	n.a.	n.a.	n.a.	n.a.
2.Private	60.4	n.a.	n.a.	n.a.	n.a.	70.4	n.a.
Public	39.6	14.7	n.a.	19.2	47.2	29.6	44.5
3.Housing	n.a.	n.a.	n.a.	n.a.	n.a.	n.a.	n.a.
Nonhousing	n.a.	n.a.	n.a.	n.a.	n.a.	n.a.	n.a.
4.Domestic	n.a.	n.a.	n.a.	n.a.	n.a.	n.a.	n.a.
Imported	n.a.	n.a.	n.a.	n.a.	n.a.	n.a.	n.a.
5.Agriculture	15.4	3.3	20.0	9.2	10.9c	7.7	8.2
Manufacturing	17.4	23.0	14.1	n.a.	n.a.	n.a.	n.a.
Others	n.a.	73.7	n.a.	n.a.	n.a.	n.a.	n.a.

a. 1955.
b. 1965.
c. 1975.
SOURCE: Table E14.

TABLE 31 Real Gross Rate of Return to Fixed Capital in Selected Years, 1940–1985

Year	Argentina	Brazil	Chile	Colombia	Mexico	Peru	Venezuela
1940	22.62	n.a.	24.33	n.a.	n.a.	n.a.	n.a.
1950	25.55	20.13	30.90	31.30	45.50	48.30	23.40
1960	32.52	24.75	35.58	31.90	42.86	34.40	22.93
1970	29.97	36.79	32.71	34.81	42.64	34.25	28.28
1980	29.85	24.64	42.23	34.18	32.99	33.45	20.57
1985	n.a.	n.a.	n.a.	30.94	32.32	32.18	18.02

n.a. = not available.
NOTE: The gross rate of return is computed by dividing the capital income on the capital stock at the end of the year.
SOURCE: Table E14.

TABLE 32 Gross Rate of Return to Total Fixed Capital and Some of Its Components, 1960 and 1970 (percentage per year)

Year/capital component	Argentina	Brazil	Chile	Colombia	Mexico	Peru	Venezuela
1960							
Total capital	29.7	15.5	31.1	23.9	22.9	10.5	13.4
1. Corporate	n.a.	16.8	n.a.	6.7	7.7	n.a.	n.a.
2. Private	n.a.	n.a.	n.a.	33.4	n.a.	n.a.	n.a.
Public	n.a.	n.a.	n.a.	3.5	n.a.	n.a.	n.a.
3. Housing	n.a.	12.3	17.3	6.0	n.a.	7.6	33.6
4. Agriculture	n.a.	34.8	n.a.	n.a.	n.a.	n.a.	n.a.
Manufacturing	27.3	n.a.	n.a.	n.a.	26.0	n.a.	n.a.
1970							
Total capital	22.0	18.5	17.6	22.8	34.6	26.9	18.4

n.a. = not available.
SOURCES: Elías (1975b); Petrei (1971); Langoni (1970); Harberger (1969); World Bank (1973); Reynolds (1970); Banco de México (1969); Inter-American Development Bank (1968).

TABLE 33 Average Annual Growth Rate of the Quality of Capital Based on Capital Composition, 1940–1970 (percentage)

Period/composition	Argentina	Brazil	Chile	Colombia	Mexico	Peru	Venezuela
1940–1950							
Corporate/noncorporate	n.a.	n.a.	n.a.	−0.4	n.a.	n.a.	n.a.
Private/public	n.a.	n.a.	n.a.	n.a.	n.a.	n.a.	n.a.
Housing/nonhousing	n.a.	n.a.	n.a.	n.a.	n.a.	n.a.	n.a.
Economic sector	n.a.	n.a.	n.a.	n.a.	n.a.	n.a.	n.a.
1950–1960							
Corporate/noncorporate	n.a.	n.a.	n.a.	n.a.	n.a.	n.a.	n.a.
Private/public	n.a.	n.a.	n.a.	−0.4	n.a.	n.a.	n.a.
Housing/nonhousing	n.a.	n.a.	n.a.	n.a.	n.a.	0.0	0.1
Economic sector	n.a.	−0.2	n.a.	n.a.	0.0	n.a.	n.a.
1960–1970							
Corporate/noncorporate	0.4	n.a.	n.a.	n.a.	n.a.	n.a.	n.a.
Private/public	−0.2	n.a.	n.a.	−0.2	n.a.	n.a.	n.a.
Housing/nonhousing	n.a.	n.a.	−0.3	n.a.	n.a.	0.0	0.9
Economic sector	n.a.	−0.3	n.a.	n.a.	0.0	n.a.	n.a.

n.a. = not available.
SOURCES: Tables 30 and 32.

CHAPTER 8

Agriculture, Manufacturing, and the Public Sector

The analysis of the output composition of GDP is an important contribution to the study of the determinants of the sources of growth of GDP. In Chapters 6 and 7, the emphasis was on the study of inputs. This chapter, following the same method (explained in Chapter 4), will discuss three important economic sectors: agriculture, manufacturing, and the public sector.

These three sectors are mentioned in any major discussion of growth strategies. Agriculture is considered a dynamic sector, producing important linkages with the growth of other sectors. The manufacturing sector is important in export-oriented analysis, which generally perceives it as crucial for increasing the rate of growth of the whole economy. And the so-called public sector is usually mentioned as a handicap for achieving high rates of growth.

The study of the sources of growth of these sectors highlights the relevance of each of them in the performance of the whole economy. The total productivity analysis of each sector gives a precise idea of the contribution of each of them to the growth of the whole economy.[1]

The Agricultural Sector

Just as for the whole economy, the sources of growth of agriculture output are land, labor, and capital. Each of these basic inputs has two components: gross and quality. Traditional analyses of the sources of growth of agriculture considered a detailed list of inputs, such as the number of hectares of gross land, irrigation, fertilizers, construction, tractors, plantation, employment, research, extension, and so on. The weight of each of these inputs was derived from production function estimates and, in some cases, from farm expense accounts.

With production functions, it is possible to achieve more appropriate definitions of the gross and quality components of each input. In the case of land, for example, the gross component can be measured by the number of hectares under cultivation, and the quality component can be measured by an index of variables, such as irrigation and fertilizers. The equivalence of both approaches will depend on the kind of production function underlying farm production analysis.[2]

Because of the data available and my interest in an aggregate approach, I will initially estimate the sources of growth only for the gross part of each input. In the case of land, it is represented by the number of hectares under cultivation and dedicated to pasture; in the case of labor, the number of workers employed in agriculture; and in the case of capital, the investment made in construction, machinery, and plantation. Later, I will consider the quality component.

Table 34 (page 127) presents the contribution of each input to agricultural output growth. For most countries, high values for the growth rate of output are matched by high values for the growth rate of total input. In other words, countries with higher rates of output growth have much higher rates of individual input growth. There is some substitution between the different inputs, which is reflected in the variability of the capital-land, capital-labor, and land-labor ratios. Lastly, changes in the growth rate of output and changes in the growth rate of total input follow similar patterns.

The growth of agricultural output for the whole period from 1950 to 1980 was moderate in comparison with growth in other developing countries. The annual rate of growth ranged from 1.9 percent in Chile to 4.9 percent in Venezuela and averaged more than 3 percent for all seven. The amount of crop land used in agricultural production grew at an annual rate of about 2 percent in most Latin American countries. It grew faster in Brazil, more than 3 percent, and more slowly in Argentina and Peru. Only in Chile did it not grow at all. Most countries added land to agricultural production at a faster rate during the 1950s than later, but Mexico added it at a faster rate in the 1960s and Colombia at a faster rate in the 1970s.

The agricultural labor force grew at an average rate of 1 percent in most countries during the whole period. It grew about 2 percent annually in Brazil and Venezuela, but not at all in Argentina and Chile. The growth rate was positive for all countries during the 1950s, but negative for two of them in the 1960s and for three in the 1970s. These rates reflect the pattern of migration from rural to urban areas observed in most of these countries.

Capital input in agriculture increased at an average rate of between 2 percent and 4 percent a year in all but one of the study countries (Peru) between 1950 and 1980. It grew at a faster rate in Mexico and Chile and at a slower rate in Peru. But the range of variation of the growth rates of the three basic inputs was within the rate of variation of the growth rate of total output (between 1.9 and 4.9 percent). Figure 17 (page 122) shows how important each input was in the growth of agriculture for the whole period 1950–1980.

Land contributed from 0 percent in Chile to 8.2 percent in Mexico; labor contributed from −18.4 percent in Chile (because the rate of growth of labor was negative) to 35.0 percent in Peru; and capital contributed from 11.7 percent in Brazil to 124.2 percent in Chile. Capital made the largest contribution to agricultural growth in all countries except Peru and Brazil.

In six of the countries the share of TFP (the residual) in the share of the growth of output was high, between 21.0 percent and 56.8 percent. Also, the TFP contribution to agricultural growth was larger in the countries with higher rates of growth of agriculture. The contribution of land to agricultural growth was low. The contribution of labor was highly variable among countries and was negative only for Chile.[3]

These results leave several questions unanswered. Two of the more important are: what is total factor productivity made up of, and why is the rate of capital growth so high? Some components of TFP were described in earlier chapters, so in the remainder of this chapter, I will measure the contribution of the quality components of the inputs.[4]

TFP in the sources-of-growth equation can be accounted for by inputs that were omitted in the earlier analysis or by changes in the quality of the basic inputs (land, labor, and capital). Table 35 (page 128) presents the growth rates of some omitted inputs and some indicators of quality changes in those inputs. All the elements in this table seem important in explaining the residual left in the previous calculations. Fertilizer, research, and public inputs (such as infrastructure and marketing services) have especially high rates of growth, suggesting that agricultural policy may have been an important positive factor in growth during the years under consideration.

It is also useful to consider these omitted inputs in the aggregate, because most of them are modern inputs and are adopted by agriculture together. This hypothesis and the weights necessary to compute this aggregate input can be analyzed through estimates from production functions.

Using the figures for each input presented above and estimates of weights found in other studies (Reca and Verstraeten 1977), it can be shown that aggregate inputs will account for less TFP than separate estimates of the contribution of each input. It may be that modern inputs were included with basic inputs in the determination of the contribution of the inputs to agricultural growth. Moreover, there is no specific error in following the method used in the two stages, because calculating the contribution of basic inputs alone emphasizes the value of TFP; the measurements of modern inputs are less reliable than the measurements of the basic inputs; measuring the two sets of inputs separately gives a better idea of the relative importance of measuring the effects of government expenditure policies on agriculture; and the contributions of the inputs can be added directly, without weights.

Table 36 (page 128) shows the value of the net residual (or net TFP), when the contribution of the omitted and modern inputs and the public inputs have been accounted for.

The net residual is low in Argentina, Chile, Colombia, and Peru, but it maintains a high value in Brazil, Mexico, and Venezuela. It is interesting to observe from this table that, looking across countries, the contribution of public input in many cases is equal to or even more important than the contribution of the omitted and modern inputs.

The Manufacturing Sector

In most of the study countries, manufacturing grew much faster than the rest of the economy. This was especially true for Brazil and Colombia.

Many growth theorists believe manufacturing is a source of growth for the rest of the economy. They attribute to this sector the influence of external economies, economies of scale, or a high degree of elasticity due to price incentives. Others explain manufacturing growth as a demand phenomenon, without giving it a sizable interaction effect.

Good accounting is important for the analysis of the growth of manufacturing, especially in terms of the importance of each input. Based on the available data, I will comment on the proposals mentioned above.

Table 37 (page 129) presents the sources of growth for manufacturing. The 1940s and 1960s were the decades with the highest output growth, while the 1970s were the decade with the lowest output growth. Argentina and Peru show irregular variation in output growth across decades, while Venezuela presents a declining trend in its rate of growth. Brazil and Mexico also report some variability, but around a high mean.

Similar fluctuations occur for the various sources of growth: labor, capital, and the residual. Therefore, there seems to be a high positive association between output and total input growth in the period under consideration.

The capital input is the largest source of growth in almost all decades for the seven countries. TFP (the residual) had an important share in the 1960s, a decade of high growth, with values of from 2 percent to 3.5 percent, which represented almost 40 percent of the growth of output. In other decades, it was important for only a few countries.

Almost all of the countries with complete data show a large increase in the capital-labor ratio. In Mexico, this ratio grew at an average annual rate of almost 4 percent; in Argentina, at 2 percent. Insofar as the available data allow for tentative conclusions, I can say that the increase of capital per unit of worker ("capital deepening") seemed more intensive in this sector than in the rest of the economy.

The size of TFP seems positively associated with the growth of output, showing a high coincidence for most countries and decades. Moreover, it has a positive association with the growth of the capital-labor ratio.

Figure 18 (page 123) summarizes the share of the contribution of labor to output growth from 1940 to 1980. The contributions of the labor input across countries are surprisingly similar. Part of this similarity could be due to the similar labor income share used to weight labor growth in estimating its contribution to output growth.

In four out of seven cases, the labor contribution to output growth seems to be related to the level of output growth. The cases of Brazil and Peru are exceptions (see Table 37).

The Public Sector

The public sector is composed of the administrative and public-enterprise sectors at the federal, state, and local levels. It is not possible to use the sources-of-growth technique for the administrative component, because accounts usually cannot specify the value of its output in terms of quantity and price. In fact, most of the accounts do not discriminate between the value of its output and that of its inputs.

There are various approaches to the study of the economics of the public sector. The sources-of-growth technique focuses on its role as a producer of public goods and on its interaction with the private sector (external economies effect). Other approaches consider its role as regulator and analyze the cost and benefits of different regulations.[5]

Table 38 (page 130) presents the growth and the sources of growth of public output. The table does not show the public sector growing relative to the whole economy. The data show only that in the cases of Argentina and Colombia, public output grew at a higher rate than GDP (see GDP in Table 2). However, if public enterprises are included in the estimate of public output, most countries report an overall increase in the share of public output.

The different countries do not exhibit common behavior across decades. In four countries, the public sector grew at a higher rate in the 1960s than in other decades (Brazil, Chile, Colombia, and Peru). In Argentina, the highest rate occurred in the 1940s; in Mexico and Venezuela, it occurred in the 1950s.

The growth of the capital-labor ratio for the public sector presents extremely high variability across countries and decades. The same is observed for the value of TFP, with a high proportion of negative values. Interestingly, the negative TFP values correspond, in general, to cases with high rates of growth of the public sector capital-labor ratio, and positive TFP values correspond to very low rates of growth of the capital-labor ratio. In the case of agriculture and manufacturing, as was observed, the opposite was the case.

Figure 19 (page 124) presents the contribution share of each input to the growth of the public output.

A Comparison of the Agricultural, Manufacturing, and Public Sectors

Figure 20 (page 125) presents a summary of the results discussed above. It shows that the manufacturing sector had the highest overall rate of growth and agriculture had the lowest. Argentina and Venezuela present exceptions for some of these conclusions.

The contribution of labor to output growth was irregular for agriculture and stable for manufacturing, while the contribution of capital to output growth was important for all three sectors.

Notes

1. Another potentially worthwhile way of analyzing output is based on international trade theory and focuses on tradables and nontradables sectors. However, since national account data are not organized according to these criteria, it is very difficult to obtain reliable measurements for these sectors. With the data that are available, it is possible to approximate the tradable sector by integrating agriculture and manufacturing. This method, however, could be considered an oversimplification, even though it would constitute a first approximation to accurate estimates.

2. This analysis can be performed on the basis of the data included in this chapter.

3. The value of the TFP contribution to agricultural growth can be explained in part by errors in measuring the inputs. Changes in the quality of labor through education were not considered. Estimates of the changes in labor quality require data concerning years of schooling for the agricultural labor force and with respect to the wages earned by laborers with different amounts of education, but the data were not available. In Latin America, labor quality made up almost one-fourth of labor's contribution to the growth of the entire economy. The education of the labor force seems to be particularly important in agriculture because many technological changes depend heavily on worker education.

Errors in measuring capital can also be important. Alternative estimates for Chile, where the contribution of capital was extraordinarily large, show a lower rate of growth for the period 1950–1960, indicating an increase for the contribution of TFP and a decrease for that of capital (see Garcés Voisenat 1983).

4. As Mundlak (1984) suggests, there is a positive association between the rate of growth of capital and the contribution of TFP to agricultural growth (which represents, in part, the rate of technological change). The high rate of TFP growth can be explained in part by a labor-saving bias in technological change, by rural-urban migration, and by differences in the rates of return on physical capital.

5. The importance of the size of the public sector in the development of the whole economy will depend on the approach used to analyze its performance. The sources-of-growth technique could serve as a way of integrating the different approaches, although, for that purpose, information other than that which is currently available must be supplied. Stigler (1982) provides a good summary of the different views suggested in the literature with respect to the importance of the size of the public sector and suggests the usefulness of a quantitative approach, adding some methodological considerations that could be followed to attack the problem.

FIGURE 17 Contribution of Land, Labor, and Capital to the Growth of Agricultural Output, 1950–1980 (annual percentage)

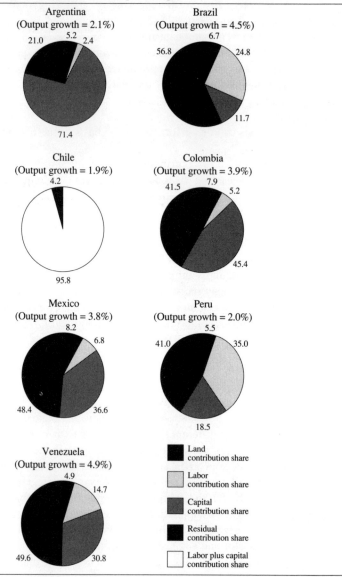

Argentina
(Output growth = 2.1%)
21.0   5.2   2.4
71.4

Brazil
(Output growth = 4.5%)
6.7
56.8   24.8
11.7

Chile
(Output growth = 1.9%)
4.2
95.8

Colombia
(Output growth = 3.9%)
41.5   7.9   5.2
45.4

Mexico
(Output growth = 3.8%)
8.2   6.8
48.4   36.6

Peru
(Output growth = 2.0%)
5.5
41.0   35.0
18.5

Venezuela
(Output growth = 4.9%)
4.9   14.7
49.6   30.8

■ Land contribution share

▨ Labor contribution share

▨ Capital contribution share

■ Residual contribution share

□ Labor plus capital contribution share

SOURCE: Table 34.

FIGURE 18 Labor Contribution Share in Manufacturing, 1940–1980 (percentage)

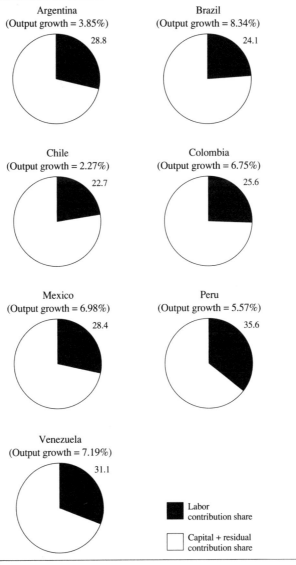

Argentina
(Output growth = 3.85%)
28.8

Brazil
(Output growth = 8.34%)
24.1

Chile
(Output growth = 2.27%)
22.7

Colombia
(Output growth = 6.75%)
25.6

Mexico
(Output growth = 6.98%)
28.4

Peru
(Output growth = 5.57%)
35.6

Venezuela
(Output growth = 7.19%)
31.1

■ Labor
contribution share

□ Capital + residual
contribution share

SOURCE: Table 37.

FIGURE 19 Contribution of Labor, Capital, and Total Factor Productivity to Public Output Growth, 1940–1980 (percentage)

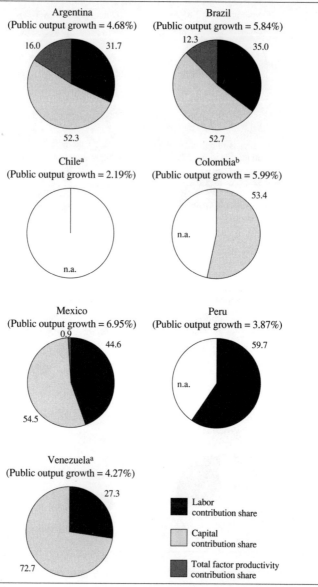

n.a. = not available
a. 1960–1980.
b. 1950–1980.
SOURCE: Table 38.

FIGURE 20 Growth of Output, Labor Contribution, and Capital Contribution by Sector, 1940–1980 (average annual percentage)

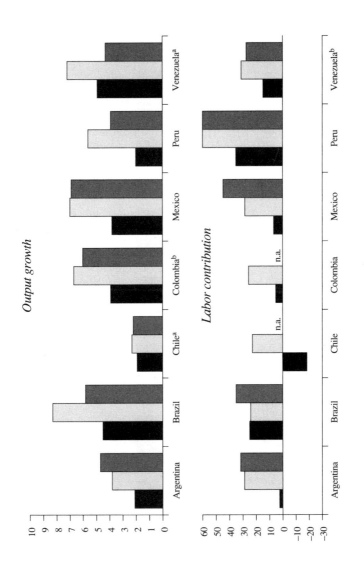

Output growth

Labor contribution

(continued on following page)

125

FIGURE 20 (continued)

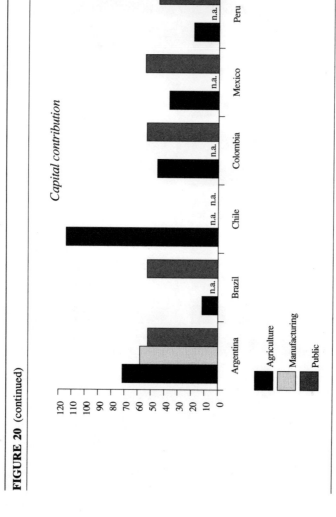

Capital contribution

n.a. = not available
a. 1960–1980.
b. 1950–1980. SOURCES: Tables 34, 37, and 38.

126

TABLE 34 Sources of Growth of Agriculture, 1950–1980 (average annual percentage)

Output and source	Argentina	Brazil	Chile	Colombia	Mexico	Peru	Venezuela
1950–1960							
Output	1.60	4.40	1.80	3.30	4.40	2.00	5.40
Total input	1.94	1.91	4.33	1.00	1.20	0.96	3.00
Land	0.26	0.35	0.12	0.36	0.35	0.22	0.36
Labor	0.18	1.01	0.36	0.35	0.85	0.61	0.80
Capital	1.50	0.55	3.85	0.29	2.00	0.13	1.84
Residual	−0.34	2.49	−2.53	2.30	3.20	1.04	2.40
1960–1970							
Output	2.30	4.40	2.10	3.60	3.80	3.20	5.30
Total input	1.81	1.53	1.04	2.48	0.54	1.07	3.20
Land	0.12	0.32	−0.13	0.16	0.40	0.11	0.28
Labor	0.19	0.70	−0.54	0.35	−0.63	0.93	0.95
Capital	1.50	0.51	1.71	1.97	0.77	0.03	1.97
Residual	0.49	2.87	1.06	1.02	3.26	2.13	2.10
1970–1980							
Output	2.50	4.90	1.90	5.10	3.00	0.90	4.00
Total input	1.41	6.07	1.15	3.26	n.a.	1.49	3.00
Land	−0.05	0.23	0.00	0.41	0.19	0.00	0.08
Labor	−0.04	2.16	−0.78	−0.20	0.29	0.56	0.42
Capital	1.50	3.68	1.93	3.05	n.a.	0.93	0.52
Residual	1.09	−1.17	0.75	1.84	n.a.	−0.59	1.00
1950–1980							
Output	2.10	4.50	1.90	3.90	3.80	2.00	4.90
Total input	1.66	1.95	2.01	2.28	1.96	1.18	2.47
Land	0.11	0.30	0.00	0.31	0.31	0.11	0.24
Labor	0.05	1.12	−0.35	0.20	0.26	0.70	0.72
Capital	1.50	0.53	2.36	1.77	1.39	0.37	1.51
Residual	0.44	2.55	−0.11	1.62	1.84	0.82	2.43

n.a. = not available.
NOTE: The contribution of each input—land, labor, and capital—to the output growth presented in this table is equal to its rate of growth times its share in total output. The shares used in the computations for land, labor, and capital for each country were the following percentages: Argentina: 15, 35, and 50; Brazil: 9, 60, and 31; Chile: 14, 40, and 46; Colombia: 16, 30, and 54; Mexico: 15, 35, and 60; Peru: 12, 50, and 38; Venezuela: 13, 43, and 42.
SOURCE: Elías (1985).

TABLE 35 Average Compound Rates of Change of the Residual, Some Omitted Inputs, and Quality Change Indicators, 1950–1980 (annual percentage)

Country	Residual	Draft animals	Tractors	Fertilizer	Irrigation	Research and extension	Public inputs
Argentina	0.44	1.21	9.26	10.25	n.a.	6.2	1.45
Brazil	2.55	2.94	12.56	12.82	n.a.	11.7	3.20
Chile	0.09	1.55	4.77	3.16	1.28	5.0	4.86
Colombia	1.62	2.30	5.03	10.16	4.43	3.8	7.15
Mexico	1.84	2.63	4.49	16.60	4.43	10.4	4.08
Peru	0.82	1.01	5.21	3.77	0.84	3.9	4.31
Venezuela	2.43	2.03	7.89	5.86	5.70	n.a.	5.66

n.a. = not available.
SOURCE: Elías (1985).

TABLE 36 Average Compound Growth Rates of the Residual and the Contributions of Modern Inputs, Public Inputs, and the Net Residual, 1950–1980 (annual percentage)

Country	Residual	Modern inputs	Public inputs	Net residual
Argentina	0.44	0.14	0.07	0.23
Brazil	2.55	0.67	0.16	1.72
Chile	0.09	0.21	0.07	−0.19
Colombia	1.62	0.42	0.36	0.84
Mexico	1.84	0.24	0.20	1.40
Peru	0.82	0.05	0.22	0.55
Venezuela	2.43	0.10	0.28	2.05

NOTE: The net residual is equal to the difference between the residual and the contribution of modern and public inputs.
SOURCE: Elías (1985).

TABLE 37 Sources of Growth of Manufacturing, 1940–1980 (average annual percentage)

Output and source	Argentina	Brazil	Chile	Colombia	Mexico	Peru	Venezuela
1940–1950							
Output	4.85	9.31	2.99	8.14	7.45	5.83	n.a.
Total input	4.71	n.a.	3.46	n.a.	6.99	n.a.	n.a.
Labor	2.66	1.55	1.45	n.a.	1.90	n.a.	n.a.
Capital	2.05	n.a.	2.01	6.28	5.09	n.a.	n.a.
Residual	0.14	n.a.	−0.47	n.a.	0.46	n.a.	n.a.
1950–1960							
Output	2.78	8.56	2.12	6.39	5.88	6.44	9.62
Total input	3.35	n.a.	n.a.	n.a.	5.35	n.a.	6.29
Labor	0.92	1.65	0.30	2.41	2.40	n.a.	1.48
Capital	2.43	n.a.	n.a.	n.a.	2.95	5.16	4.81
Residual	−0.57	n.a.	n.a.	n.a.	0.53	n.a.	3.33
1960–1970							
Output	5.48	6.71	2.60	5.84	8.70	6.71	7.01
Total input	2.84	5.96	n.a.	2.38	5.69	n.a.	5.09
Labor	0.55	1.70	−0.16	1.04	1.64	2.06	2.25
Capital	2.29	4.26	2.43	1.34	4.05	n.a.	2.84
Residual	2.64	0.75	0.33	3.46	3.01	n.a.	1.92
1970–1980							
Output	2.20	8.76	1.35	6.04	5.90	3.29	4.04
Total input	2.49	7.47	n.a.	n.a.	n.a.	n.a.	n.a.
Labor	0.29	2.67	0.47	3.97	n.a.	1.91	2.98
Capital	2.20	4.80	−0.24	n.a.	n.a.	n.a.	n.a.
Residual	−0.29	1.29	1.12	n.a.	n.a.	n.a.	n.a.
1940–1980							
Output	3.85	8.34	2.27	6.75	6.98	5.57	n.a.
Total input	3.35	n.a.	n.a.	n.a.	n.a.	n.a.	n.a.
Labor	1.11	1.89	0.52	n.a.	n.a.	n.a.	n.a.
Capital	2.24	n.a.	n.a.	n.a.	n.a.	n.a.	n.a.
Residual	0.50	n.a.	n.a.	n.a.	n.a.	n.a.	n.a.

n.a. = not available.
SOURCES: *Argentina*: Elías (1986); *Brazil*: Fundação Instituto Brasileiro de Geografía e Estatística (1970), Fundação Getúlio Vargas (1973, 1984); *Chile*: Meller and Rahilly (1974), Coeymans (1989); *Colombia*: ECLA (1967), World Bank (1984), DANE (1985); *Mexico*: Banco de México (1969), Nacional Financiera (1969), Banco Nacional de México (1981); *Peru*: Banco Central de la Reserva (1961, 1968); *Venezuela*: Inter-American Development Bank (1968), Banco Central de Venezuela (1986).

TABLE 38 Sources of Growth of Public Output, 1940–1980 (percentage)

Output and source	Argentina	Brazil	Chile	Colombia	Mexico	Peru	Venezuela
1940–1950							
Public output	6.87	3.16	n.a.	n.a.	2.18	1.79	n.a.
Total input	n.a.	n.a.	n.a.	n.a.	9.85	n.a.	n.a.
Labor	n.a.	1.20	1.30	n.a.	4.60	n.a.	n.a.
Capital	2.32	n.a.	n.a.	n.a.	5.25	n.a.	n.a.
Total factor productivity	n.a.	n.a.	n.a.	n.a.	−7.67	n.a.	n.a.
1950–1960							
Public output	4.48	7.09	n.a.	5.28	8.75	2.62	6.28
Total input	1.74	4.20	n.a.	n.a.	2.78	n.a.	7.75
Labor	0.96	1.60	0.80	n.a.	1.08	n.a.	2.90
Capital	0.78	2.60	n.a.	3.58	1.70	1.53	4.85
Total factor productivity	2.74	2.89	n.a.	n.a.	5.97	n.a.	−1.47
1960–1970							
Public output	3.27	8.50	2.51	6.61	8.38	6.90	3.70
Total input	3.95	5.70	4.76	n.a.	7.21	4.53	4.08
Labor	0.66	2.45	0.82	n.a.	3.62	2.60	2.14
Capital	3.29	3.25	3.94	2.64	3.59	1.93	1.94
Total factor productivity	−0.68	2.80	−2.25	n.a.	1.11	2.37	−0.38
1970–1980							
Public output	4.10	4.60	1.86	6.54	8.49	4.18	2.82
Total input	4.09	5.89	n.a.	n.a.	8.65	6.99	n.a.
Labor	0.69	2.50	n.a.	n.a.	4.25	2.02	n.a.
Capital	3.40	3.39	n.a.	3.38	4.60	4.97	4.44
Total factor productivity	0.01	−1.29	n.a.	n.a.	−0.16	−2.81	n.a.

n.a. = not available.
SOURCES: Same as Tables E1–E7, E10–E13, and E14.

CHAPTER 9

Complementary Approaches to the Analysis of Latin American Economic Growth

This chapter will apply diverse econometric techniques to the available data in order to broaden the analysis of the growth behavior of the seven Latin American countries. These exercises should help explain the growth processes experienced by these countries in a way useful for the design of economic policies.

The first exercise will be an analysis of the growth rate of GDP on a one-year, two-year, and three-year basis for selected countries. The objective will be to identify the shape of the GDP growth curve as it varies over time, considered as a statistical time series in itself. For this purpose, I will extend the time period to 1900–1986, a convenient adjustment for this type of analysis.

The second exercise will use a technology transmission model to help explain the growth rate of TFP. The objective will be to estimate the influence of external factors in the behavior of the so-called technological changes. These changes play an important role in explaining GDP growth in the countries analyzed in this study.

The third exercise will be to attempt an estimate of an econometric growth model as an extension of the sources-of-growth method. This model includes formulas for explaining the sources of input growth. It includes some external sector variables that explain the growth slowdown phenomenon experienced by most Latin American countries in the period 1978–1985.

The last exercise uses profile analysis to detect similarities and differences across countries in the behavior of variables that are generally understood to be important dynamic elements in growth processes and, therefore, important factors to be considered in an optimum policy for growth.

Growth Behavior

My analysis of growth behavior is described in Figure 21 (page 138), which presents the relevant GDP growth rate time-series data. This figure presents the growth rates for each country on a one-year, two-year, and three-year basis (annual averages, compounded). The second two calculations help smooth the series and allow for better comparisons across countries.

Table 39 (page 148) reports statistically qualitative information about the behavior of the annual growth rate, for the five countries studied, as a summary and guide for the study of the figure. This table shows that Argentina and Chile had extremely variable behavior in their rates of growth, while Colombia was more stable, followed by Mexico and then by Brazil. Part of the variability in the cases of Argentina, Brazil, and Chile may be due to measurement errors. These countries have experienced very high and unstable inflationary processes, with the result that the national accounts, in real terms, could be less reliable than the ones for countries with more stable economic processes.

Figure 21 shows that, except for Colombia, even the three-year rates of growth are not smooth. They may reflect growth cycles, which, on the average, last from four to five years in Latin America, closely synchronized with global cycles.

Technology Transmission

TFP is important as a source of economic growth in Latin American countries. Therefore, it is important to search for its determinants, instead of considering it an exogenous factor in the growth process.

Figure 22 (page 143) presents estimates of the annual rate of growth of TFP for the seven Latin American countries and the United States and an average for some Western European countries for the period 1948–1973.

An interesting approach toward the explanation of the behavior of TFP is provided by technology transmission models, developed in the international trade theory literature (Arrow 1969; Berglas and Jones 1977; Findlay 1978; Rodríguez 1978; Teubal 1979; McCulloch 1977). According to these models, the rate of growth of domestic technological change depends mainly on the gap between the levels of technology in developed and developing countries, and the coefficient of adjustment of developing countries to this gap.[1]

This coefficient, when assumed to be flexible, can be treated as dependent on certain variables related to technological creation or adoption. Some variables proposed to explain fluctuations in the adjustment coefficient are the following: (1) the ratio of foreign-owned to domestically owned capital in the country, (2) the cost of communication, (3) average firm size, (4) input prices, (5) the share of human capital in total capital, and (6) labor income share in the GDP.[2]

Table 40 (page 148) presents simple correlation coefficients between the annual growth rates of TFP in different Latin American countries and those observed in the United States and some Western European countries, showing comparative technological change over time, which will help explain the analysis performed by the technological transmission model.

Some observations can be made on the basis of the data presented in this table: most of the coefficients are low; there are high correlations between Argentina and Western Europe and between Mexico and the United States, as would be expected. The high correlation between Peru and Western Europe and the negative correlation between Brazil and the United States, however, are surprising. So is the fact that in five out of seven cases, the correlation is higher between Latin American countries and Western Europe than that between Latin America and the United States.

I present here the results of the regression estimates generated by the technology transmission model for Venezuela and Brazil. The variables used to explain the change in domestic technology for these two countries were the index of total factor productivity of the United States; the index of total factor productivity of Western European countries; the level of trade protection in the domestic economy (measured by the import tariff revenues divided by the value of imports); import composition by country of origin (U.S. and non-U.S.); import composition by kind of good (capital and noncapital); and import share of the GDP. Of these variables, the import composition by country of origin seems relevant for Venezuela and import composition by kind of good seems relevant for Brazil.[3]

Some of the interpretations coming from estimates for Venezuela are that, given the explanatory variables, the rate of change of Venezuela's total factor productivity is a weighted average of the rates of change of total factor productivity in the United States and Europe, with weights that, in this case, add up to much more than one, which seems to indicate that Venezuela reacts faster than other Latin American countries to technological change in the United States and Europe.[4]

An Econometric Growth Model

Latin American countries, as well as many developed economies, have had a declining and variable rate of growth since 1974. Another interesting phenomenon is the substantial discrepancy in growth performances (measured by the size and duration of periods of growth) observed for Latin American and some East Asian countries.

The dependent variables used in the econometric growth model are the growth rates, in a given period, of

1. GDP

2. labor input

3. capital input

4. technology

The exogenous variables are the growth rates of

1. the size of the gap between actual and potential GDP

2. population

3. the real price of energy

4. the real exchange rate

5. real wages

6. the real world interest rate

7. the GDP of developed countries

8. foreign debt service

9. the government share in total capital stock

10. the labor income share in GDP

Table 41 (page 149), which shows the actual behavior of these variables for Argentina, Colombia, and Mexico from 1940 to 1983, reports the growth slowdown that occurred after 1974. Most of the variables display substantial variability in the subperiod 1965–1983. The real exchange rate shows marked variability in Argentina and much greater stability in Colombia and Mexico.

The GDP gap also fluctuates considerably in Argentina and occasionally in Colombia. It is interesting to observe, as well, the fluctuations of the real wage rate for those countries. These data also reveal close synchronization of Latin American fluctuations with global growth cycle estimates for the industrialized economies (Moore 1989; Maddison 1987).

This econometric model was applied to explain the rates of growth of the GDP and of capital input for some Latin American countries. The estimates seem to reveal that the variables were much more relevant for capital than for the GDP, suggesting that they could affect GDP growth through capital accumulation and, consequently, that their effects occur with some lag.

The importance of these variables in growth processes is diverse across countries. For example, real wages are relevant for Argentina and Colombia but not for Mexico. And the GDP gap between actual and potential performance is relevant for Argentina and Mexico but not for Colombia. The real interest rate is relevant only for Argentina and the real exchange rate, only for Mexico. (See the regression results in Appendix F.)

Profile Analysis

The selection of the main variables that explain differences in the growth performance between countries could be performed with the graphic and statistical tools provided by profile analysis.[5] This method performs three kinds of hypothesis testing: a test of mean equality across the variables for each country; a test of parallelism; and, finally, under the assumptions of parallelism, a test for the differences in levels of the profile curves between countries.

Obviously, the selection of variables is an important part of this method and is crucial in explaining growth disparities. I suggest selecting those variables that are mainly influenced by economic policies. Then, it will be possible to derive policy implications from the analytical exercise. A complementary possibility for the selection of the variables is to derive suggestions from the empirical and theoretical literature.

Combining these possibilities, I have defined the following variables: consumption-GDP ratio; public sector share of capital stock; the share of high inflation periods in the whole period analyzed; and some policy indicators for financial markets and the foreign trade sector, such as trade protection and the productivity gap.

Figures 23, 24, and 25 (pages 146–147) present two-country profile analyses for Argentina-Brazil, Argentina-Colombia, and Brazil-Colombia. All the variables relevant for this analysis were defined in such a way that a lower value for them will indicate a higher potential for GDP growth.

Figure 23 shows that Brazil reports a much better growth performance than Argentina in terms of both higher and more stable growth rates. The figure indicates a similar profile curve for both, except in the productivity gap variable. There are also some differences in the government share of capital stock.

For Argentina-Colombia and Brazil-Colombia, Figures 24 and 25 show some crossing of the profiles, which indicates that the variables do not show clearly what policy behavior could explain differences in these countries' growth performance.

Notes

1. The technology transmission model, in a simple form, proposes the following:

$$\frac{dTD}{dt} \cdot \frac{1}{TD} = q \cdot (TF - TD)$$

where TD is the level of domestic technology; TF, the level of the advanced countries' (here called foreign) technology; and q, the adjustment coefficient.

In this way, various alternatives can be considered, depending on assumptions about the adjustment coefficient.

2. An extension of the formula includes the addition of the domestic production of technology and a model to explain the gap $(TF - TD)$ (see Jorgenson and Nishimizu 1977). The aim is to create a model that explains the different paths observed in the behavior of TD and to cover situations in which a country originally importing technology is transformed into an exporter.

3. Following the basic proposal of note 1, two similar specifications were estimated for Venezuela and Brazil. Applying the ordinary least squares method, the following results were obtained:

Venezuela

$$\dot{T}^D/T^D = -0.2 - 0.2X_1 + 0.3X_2 + 0.9\dot{T}_1^F/T_1^F + 0.7\dot{T}_2^F/T_2^F$$
$$(2.7)(0.5)(2.1)(2.0)(1.2)$$

$$\overline{R}^2 = 0.52;\ n = 12$$

Brazil

$$(\dot{T}^D/T^D)/(T^F/T^D - 1) = 0.5 + 4.5X_3 + 3.5X_1 - 19.8X_4$$
$$(0.2)(1.9)(0.3)(1.7)$$
$$\overline{R}^2 = 0.35;\ n = 23$$

where T_1^F: index of TFP of the United States

T_2^F: index of TFP of Western European countries

X_1: level of trade protection in the domestic economy (measured by the import tariff revenues divided by imports)

X_2: import composition by country of origin (U.S. and non-U.S.)

X_3: import composition by kind of good (capital and noncapital)

X_4: import share of the GDP.

The values under the equations in parentheses are the absolute values of the t-statistics.

4. The factor price equalization theorem from international trade theory, which states that product mobility could be a perfect substitute for factor mobility depending on the connection of technology transmission to either one of them, establishes the possible association between the rate of growth of total factor productivity and product mobility.

5. The chi-square test, based on the differences between expected and observed values of the variables, is an interesting alternative to this method and was used in many comparative studies. In the case of time-series data, it could have an advantage over profile analysis.

FIGURE 21 Annual, Biannual, and Triannual Growth Rate of GDP in Argentina, Brazil, Chile, Colombia, and Mexico, 1900–1986 (percentage)

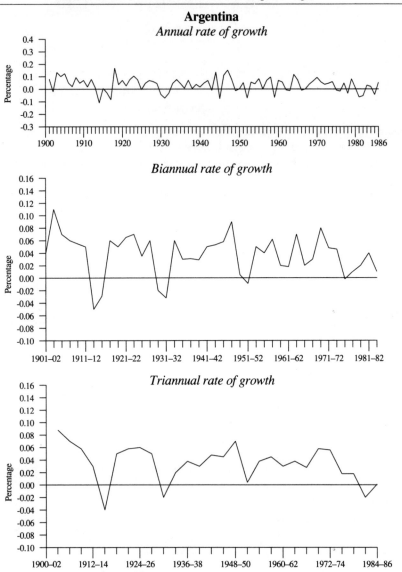

(*continued on following page*)

FIGURE 21   (continued)

Brazil

Annual rate of growth

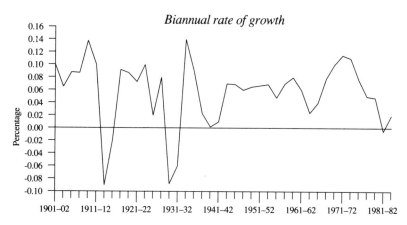

Biannual rate of growth

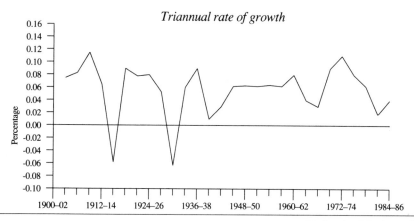

Triannual rate of growth

(*continued on following page*)

FIGURE 21 (continued)

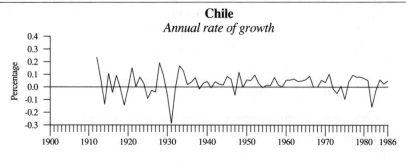

Chile
Annual rate of growth

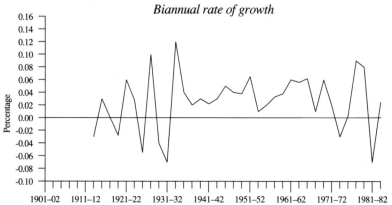

Biannual rate of growth

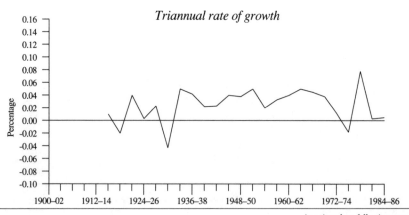

Triannual rate of growth

(*continued on following page*)

FIGURE 21 (continued)

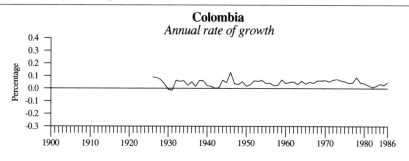

Colombia
Annual rate of growth

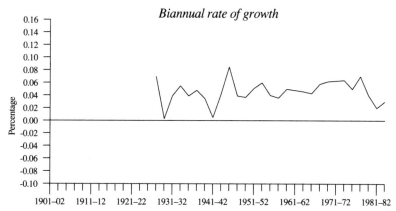

Biannual rate of growth

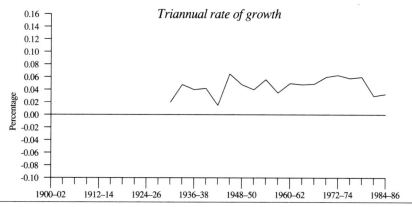

Triannual rate of growth

(*continued on following page*)

FIGURE 21 (continued)

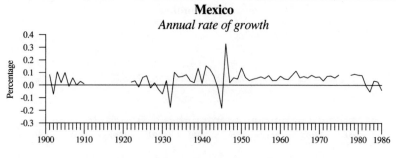

Mexico
Annual rate of growth

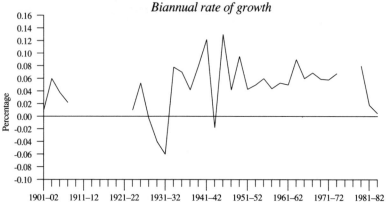

Biannual rate of growth

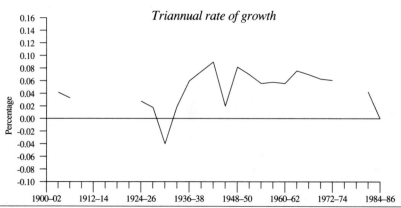

Triannual rate of growth

SOURCE: Same as Figure 2.

FIGURE 22 Annual Rate of Change of Total Factor Productivity in Latin American Countries, the United States, and Western Europe, 1948–1973 (percentage)

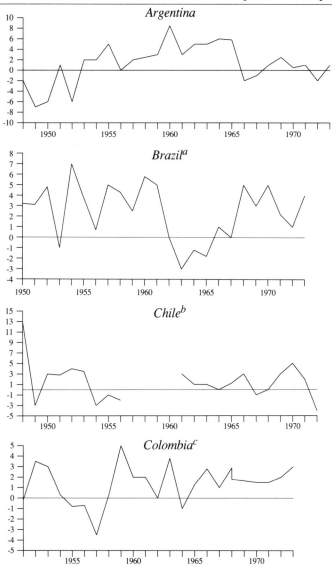

a. 1948 and 1949 not available.
b. 1957–1960 and 1973 not available.
c. 1948–1950 not available.

(continued on following page)

FIGURE 22 (continued)

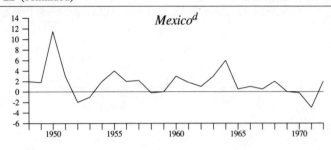

Mexico[d]

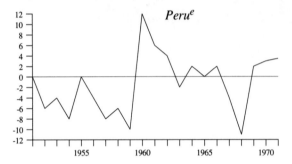

Peru[e]

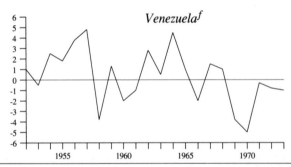

Venezuela[f]

d. 1973 not available.
e. 1948–1950, 1972, and 1973 not available.
f. 1948–1951 not available.

(*continued on following page*)

FIGURE 22 (continued)

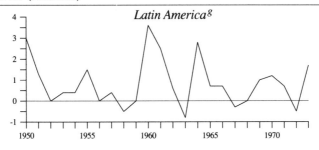

Latin America[g]

United States

Europe[h]

g. 1948 and 1949 not available.
h. 1948–1950 not available.
SOURCES: Tables E1–E7, E10–E14; Christensen, Cummings, and Jorgenson (1980).

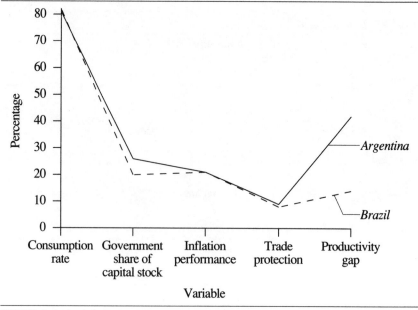

FIGURE 23 Profile Analysis: Argentina and Brazil, 1940–1980

SOURCE: Author's calculations.

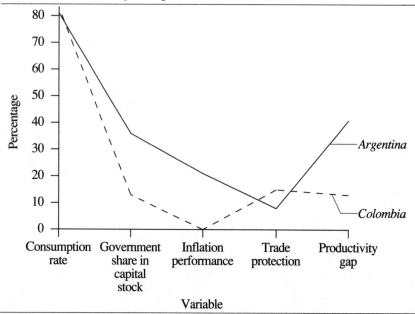

FIGURE 24 Profile Analysis: Argentina and Colombia, 1940–1980

SOURCE: Author's calculations.

FIGURE 25 Profile Analysis: Brazil and Colombia, 1940–1980

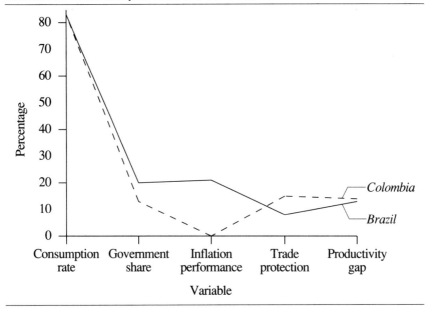

SOURCE: Author's calculations.

TABLE 39 Signs Behavior of the Annual Rate of Growth of the GDP, 1900–1986 (number of years)

Signs characteristic	Argentina	Brazil	Chile	Colombia	Mexico
Negative signs	22	10	22	2	12
Maximum consecutive years with positive signs	11	38	13	55	34
Number of runs of two consecutive negative signs	7	4	8	1	2
Total number of years	86	86	75	61	73

SOURCE: Figure 21.

TABLE 40 Simple Correlation Coefficients between the Annual Rate of Change of TFP of Latin American Countries and the United States and Western European Countries, 1948–1973

Countries	Argentina	Brazil	Chile	Colombia	Mexico	Peru	Venezuela
United States	−0.16	−0.36	0.03	0.27	0.50	0.05	0.30
Western European countries[a]	0.46	0.00	0.12	0.31	0.31	0.75	0.13

a. France, West Germany, Italy, the Netherlands, and the United Kingdom.
SOURCE: Figure 22.

TABLE 41 Average Annual Values for Variables in the Econometric Growth Model, 1940–1983 (percentage growth rate)

Period	GDP	Labor	Capital	Technology	Population	Real energy price	Real exchange rate	Real wages
Argentina								
1940–1970	4.1	2.2	3.0	1.5	1.7	−4.2	−4.3	1.3
1965–1970	4.2	2.8	4.1	−0.6	1.4	−2.9	2.4	4.6
1970–1975	3.6	3.0	4.2	1.0	1.3	27.2	13.7	3.4
1975–1980	1.8	−0.2	3.8	−1.0	1.8	9.3	−15.0	−0.1
1980–1983	−3.1	n.a.	n.a.	n.a.	n.a.	6.9	32.5	n.a.
Colombia								
1940–1970	4.8	2.9	3.9	1.3	2.8	−4.2	3.0	4.5
1965–1970	5.7	3.2	3.9	2.1	2.9	−2.9	2.1	1.8
1970–1975	6.6	2.1	4.9	2.9	2.3	27.2	−4.5	−1.4
1975–1980	5.0	4.9	n.a.	n.a.	2.3	9.3	−3.2	4.6
1980–1983	1.3	n.a.	n.a.	n.a.	n.a.	6.9	n.a.	n.a.
Mexico								
1940–1970	6.2	2.7	4.4	2.3	3.1	−4.2	−0.4	0.8
1965–1970	7.6	2.8	7.3	1.8	3.2	−2.9	−0.1	2.0
1970–1975	5.9	3.5	7.0	0.1	3.3	27.2	−1.3	1.9
1975–1980	6.5	3.0	n.a.	n.a.	2.7	9.3	−0.9	−0.3
1980–1983	1.1	n.a.	n.a.	n.a.	n.a.	6.9	8.7	n.a.

(*continued on following page*)

Table 41 (continued)

Period	Labor income share in GDP	Public sector share of total capital stock	Real world interest rate	GDP gap
Argentina				
1940–1970	46.4	25.7	−4.4	0.7
1965–1970	47.2	28.5	3.5	2.8
1970–1975	47.6	33.5	−0.7	11.0
1975–1980	n.a.	36.6	0.9	3.2
1980–1983	n.a.	n.a.	8.2	−11.5
Colombia				
1940–1970	37.7	17.4	−4.4	−1.3
1965–1970	40.0	19.6	3.5	−4.1
1970–1975	39.3	24.0	−0.7	1.4
1975–1980	43.3	n.a.	0.9	4.2
1980–1983	n.a.	n.a.	8.2	n.a.
Mexico				
1940–1970	n.a.	41.2	−4.4	0.3
1965–1970	n.a.	41.6	3.5	2.0
1970–1975	40.0	n.a.	−0.7	1.7
1975–1980	41.2	n.a.	0.9	−0.2
1980–1983	40.1	n.a.	8.2	n.a.

n.a. = not available.
NOTE: The real price of energy is defined by the ratio of the price of Saudi Arabian oil to the wholesale price index of the United States. The real exchange rate for each country is defined by the product of the nominal official exchange rate with the ratio of the wholesale price index of the United States to the wholesale price index of the country. The real interest rate is defined by the difference between the nominal U.S. prime rate and the rate of change of the wholesale price index of the United States. The gap is the percentage of the difference between actual and potential GDP, to the potential GDP; and the potential GDP is the estimate of the GDP coming from a regression between the natural log of GDP in the time variable for the period 1940–1983. SOURCES: Tables E1–E7, E10–E13, E14, and *International Financial Statistics* (IMF, many issues).

CHAPTER 10

A Comparative Growth Analysis of Latin American and Other Countries

In this chapter I will begin by discussing the main "rules" and hypotheses established for developed economies in previous comparative studies of sources of economic growth. I will also make reference to the convergency hypothesis for labor productivity (developed by Abramovitz 1986 and Baumol 1985). These hypotheses will serve as a framework for my comparison of Latin American countries among each other and with developed economies. Then, I will determine whether or not Latin American economies have followed Maddison's stages of growth of developed economies.

The sources-of-growth method used in comparative country studies has already produced many important conclusions, which will be useful for organizing the findings presented in Chapter 4.

Christensen, Cummings, and Jorgenson (1980) offered the following "rules":

1. Variations in average growth rates of output among countries are associated with variations in growth rates of total factor inputs.

2. Increases and decreases in average growth rates of total factor

inputs are strongly associated with increases and decreases in average output growth rates.

3. Very high average output growth rates are associated with high average growth rates for both capital and labor inputs, and low average output growth rates are associated with low average rates of growth of both inputs.

4. A rise or fall in the average rate of growth of the labor input is associated with a fall or rise in the rate of growth of capital input.

These rules offer general support for the usefulness of the growth-accounting method because both sides of the accounts seem to behave consistently.

They also have interesting implications for economic policies that seek to increase the growth rate of output because they show the minimum conditions that must be established to achieve certain growth targets.[1]

Moreover, Denison (1967) provides interesting conclusions about the role of each of the various sources of growth in studies of developed economies. He discovered that:

1. The contribution of labor has been much more important than the contribution of capital.

2. The growth of labor *quality* was a very important component of the total growth of the labor input.

3. Increasing returns to scale, through the labor specialization effect (due to the increase of market size), has an important contribution share in output growth.

However, some of Denison's conclusions contrast with those obtained for Latin American countries. For example, in Latin America, the capital contribution share in output growth has been much more important than that of labor in recent decades.

Other comparative studies based on observations of labor productivity, performed for developed economies and taking into account long periods of time, allow for the detection of some convergency in productivity among those economies, implying a decrease in the so-called productivity gap among them. This is also known as the "convergency phenomenon" (see Baumol 1985; Maddison 1987; and Abramovitz 1988).

Most of the lessons derived from comparative sources-of-growth studies refer to the direct determinants of output growth only. The studies generally mention causes of input changes only marginally and do not examine them in a systematic way. Therefore, those lessons fail to consider many policy variables explicitly.

A Comparative Analysis of Labor Productivity

This section will compare trends of labor productivity among Latin American countries and Australia, Italy, Japan, and the United States.

As mentioned in Chapter 4, trends in labor productivity are explained by many determinants. The most important of them are the capital-labor ratio and technology. In this sense, labor productivity is an indicator of trends in those important variables.

This comparative analysis also gives an idea of the degree of convergence among the countries compared. This degree of convergence allows us to discuss the relative position of Latin American countries with respect to more developed countries.

Figure 26 (page 157) presents the labor productivity for selected years of the period 1940–1984.[2] The United States reports the highest value of labor productivity for the whole period. The second highest value belongs to Australia, although toward the end of the period, Italy and Japan come close to Australia's values. Latin American countries show very different values among themselves, with some of them achieving high values in comparative terms internationally (Argentina and Venezuela).

Brazil and Japan registered the fastest growth in labor productivity for the whole period. In these countries, labor productivity increased more than three times, thus closing part of the productivity gap with the United States. Mexico and Italy also register good performances. The other Latin American countries report a performance almost similar to that of Australia and the United States, without, therefore, significantly changing the gap.

In the cases of Argentina, Chile, Colombia, Mexico, and the United States, technological change alone explains most of the increase in labor productivity. On the other hand, the growth of the capital-labor ratio alone explains most of the increase in labor productivity in the cases of Peru and Venezuela. However, for the fastest growers, Brazil and Japan, changes in technology and the capital-labor ratio have an almost equal share in explaining the growth of labor productivity, which gives some support to the hypothesis mentioned in Chapter 4 concerning the importance of the interaction effect between technology and capital accumulation for high economic growth.

A Comparative Analysis of the Sources of Growth

From a long-run perspective, the period 1940–1980 provides a good framework for comparing sources of growth among Latin American countries and between them and those of Japan and the United States (as representatives of developed economies). Some observed periods of rapid growth will provide additional insights.

Table 42 (page 160) presents data for the sources of growth that will allow comparative analysis. It is clear that TFP plays a much larger role in Japan and the United States than in Latin America. Its contribution share in Japan and the United States is around 40 percent, while the average for all of Latin America is only 28 percent.

Comparing the contribution of capital and labor, we see that capital has the larger share in Japan and Latin America, while labor has a much larger share in the United States. This difference between Japan and the United States is mainly due to differences in their rates of capital growth. And, in the case of Latin America, the higher capital income share, which weights the rate of capital growth to measure its growth contribution, was decisive for the difference.[3]

This means that across countries the differences in the contribution share of these inputs will depend on differences in wages, rates of return to capital, and growth of inputs. In the case of the labor input, it is possible to observe substantial differences in real wages across countries. In the case of capital, differences in the rates of return across countries are much less important (see Harberger 1978). According to these results, differences in the labor contribution should be attributed to differences in real wages and, in the capital contribution, to differences in the growth of capital.

The differences in the contribution of each input (labor and capital) to GDP growth among Latin American countries are mainly due to differences in the rates of growth of each input. The differences with respect to Japan and the United States are also due to differences in the income shares of both inputs.[4]

Many economists favor the hypothesis that the size of the contribution of TFP to output growth is associated positively with capital accumulation. However, Abramovitz (1988) suggests that this is not the case for Latin

America. I find that, in fact, for Latin America his conjecture is correct. I must add, however, that this contribution is not related to labor growth either, as one could expect. The data show that it is more directly related to output growth.

Finally, countries with high output growth also have high capital accumulation, as reflected in the data for the contribution share of capital.

Stages of Economic Growth

Identifying the stages of growth that are common to many countries reveals some of the underlying growth forces. Maddison (1987) has investigated the growth acceleration and slowdown in developed economies (France, Germany, Japan, the Netherlands, the United Kingdom, and the United States) and proposed three stages of growth: 1913–1950 (low growth), 1950–1973 (growth acceleration), and 1973–1984 (growth slowdown).

Using his framework to study the growth of Latin American countries is very helpful. Table 43 (page 161) provides the average annual rate of growth of GDP, arranged according to Maddison's stages of growth, of our seven Latin American study countries and the countries analyzed by Maddison.

The Latin American countries follow the same pattern as the developed economies. Differences between the countries of these two groups stem from the degree of intensity of the stages of acceleration and slowdown. In the period of growth acceleration, the Latin American countries experienced only a little more than half of that experienced by the developed countries (an average of 1.8 percent compared with 3.5 percent for the developed countries). In the period of growth slowdown, the decrease of the growth of the Latin American countries was nearly the same as that experienced by the developed countries (-2.5 percent compared with -3.2 percent for the developed countries).

Some of the underlying forces that can help explain this phenomenon are found in the behavior of the inputs (capital and labor). As discussed in Chapter 4, fluctuations in output growth are mainly associated with fluctuations in capital accumulation and its associated factors.

Notes

1. They also lend support to aggregate production function analysis, which relates output to inputs.

2. A weighted average of the seven Latin American countries is also presented. The weights used were the 1960 percentage of the labor force for each country with respect to the total labor force of the seven countries. In this weighted average, 45 percent of the weights correspond to Brazil.

3. The contribution shares of each input have two components: the output-input elasticities and their corresponding rates of growth. They can also be expressed in terms of input services' prices and absolute input changes, according to which real wages and capital rates of return play an important role.

4. Production function estimates support, in part, this result.

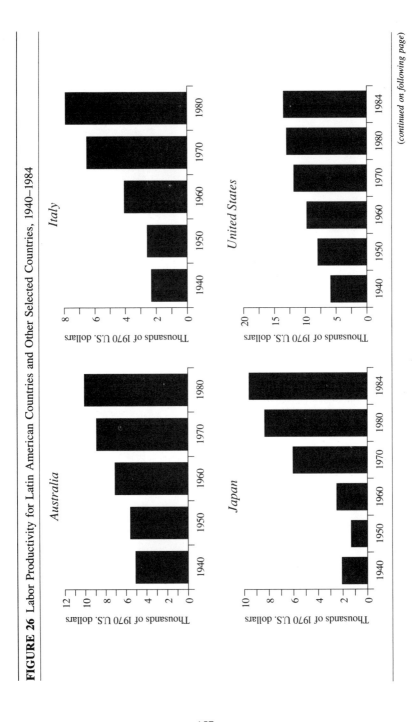

FIGURE 26 Labor Productivity for Latin American Countries and Other Selected Countries, 1940–1984

(continued on following page)

157

FIGURE 26 (continued)

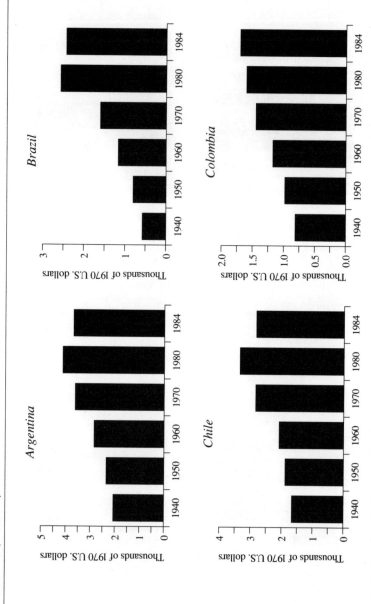

(continued on following page)

158

FIGURE 26 (continued)

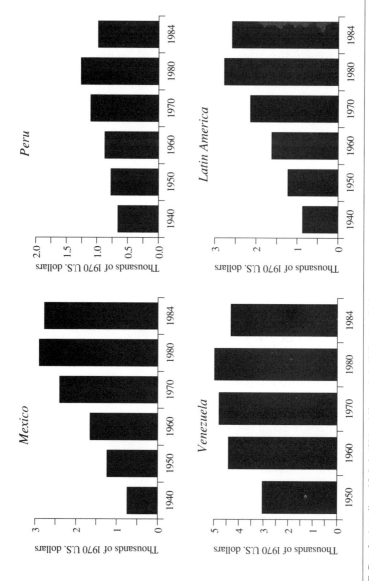

NOTE: Data for Australia and Italy in 1984 and Venezuela in 1940 not available.
SOURCE: Table E15; Maddison (1987).

TABLE 42 Sources of Growth, Input Contribution Shares, and Input Rate of Growth for Latin American Countries, Japan, and the United States, 1940–1980 (percentage)

Variable	Argentina	Brazil	Chile	Colombia	Mexico	Peru	Venezuela	Latin America	Japan	United States
Sources of growth										
Output	3.60	6.40	3.80	4.80	6.30	4.20	5.20	5.34	5.20	3.62
Total input	2.50	4.55	2.30	3.60	4.00	4.20	4.70	3.85	3.26	2.07
Labor	0.95	1.30	1.00	1.55	1.45	1.35	1.75	1.32	0.90	1.28
Capital	1.55	3.25	1.30	2.05	2.55	2.85	2.95	2.53	2.36	0.79
Total factor productivity	1.10	1.85	1.50	1.20	2.30	0.00	0.50	1.49	1.94	1.55
Input contribution shares										
Labor	26.4	20.3	26.3	32.3	23.0	32.1	33.7	24.7	17.3	35.4
Capital	43.1	50.8	34.2	42.7	40.5	67.9	56.7	47.4	45.4	21.8
Total factor productivity	30.5	28.9	39.5	25.0	36.5	0.0	9.6	27.9	37.3	42.8
Total	100.0	100.0	100.0	100.0	100.0	100.0	100.0	100.0	100.0	100.0
Rate of growth of inputs										
Labor	1.9	2.6	2.0	3.1	2.9	2.7	3.5	2.6	1.3	1.7
Capital	3.1	6.5	2.6	4.1	5.1	5.7	5.9	5.1	7.9	3.2
Capital-labor ratio	1.2	3.9	0.6	1.0	2.2	3.0	2.4	2.4	6.6	1.5

SOURCES: Latin American countries: Tables 2 and 3; other countries: Maddison (1987); Denison (1985).

TABLE 43 Average Annual GDP Growth in Selected Countries and Periods and Its Acceleration (percentage)

Country	1913–1950 I	1950–1973 II	1973–1984 III	Changes from I to II	Changes from II to III
Latin America					
Argentina	3.2	3.7	0.6	0.5	−3.1
Brazil	4.0	6.8	4.2	2.8	−2.6
Chile	1.9	3.9	2.1	2.0	−1.8
Colombia	4.3	5.0	4.2	0.7	−0.8
Mexico	3.1	6.1	4.0	3.0	−1.9
Peru	n.a.	4.7	1.4	n.a.	−3.3
Venezuela	n.a.	5.6	1.8	n.a.	−3.8
Average	3.3	5.1	2.6	1.8	−2.5
Selected countries					
France	1.1	5.1	2.2	4.0	−2.9
Germany	1.3	5.9	1.7	4.6	−4.2
Japan	2.2	9.4	3.8	7.2	−5.6
Netherlands	2.4	4.7	1.6	2.3	−3.1
United Kingdom	1.3	3.0	1.1	1.7	−1.9
United States	2.8	3.7	2.3	0.9	−1.4
Average	1.8	5.3	2.1	3.5	−3.2

n.a. = not available.
SOURCES: Same as Table 42.

CHAPTER 11

Predictions and Policy Implications for Latin American Economic Growth

This chapter presents some predictions and policy implications for Latin American economic growth, derived mainly from the analyses and findings presented in the previous chapters.

In this chapter I will make predictions for the 1990s in terms of input growth, based on its determinants (component sources of growth), so as to predict output growth. My comparative analysis also provides a framework for determining policy measures that could encourage improved performance in the near future.

The principal sources of uncertainty in this analysis are introduced by the behavior of capital input and the adoption of new technologies (TFP). Both are highly variable factors, and both make important contributions to economic growth rates.

The economic predictions are based not only on past behavior, but also on the possible effects of future economic policies (as mentioned in Chapter 9). I make my predictions on the basis of national accounts, analyzed according to the sources-of-growth method, and derive from them some policy recommendations. At the same time, I recognize certain limitations both in the data, commented on above, and in the method, such as the uncertain behavior of capital input and of TFP. I also presuppose the implementation of those economic policies derived from the comparative analysis. In other words, this section of the chapter is an exercise in the use of the method for economic policy design. Because my analysis is aggregate, it is useful for the design of general policies and permits the ongoing evaluation of those policies.

Predictions for the Period 1990–2000

My prediction for the rate of GDP growth is based on predictions of the rates of growth of the inputs—labor and capital—along with some assumptions about the growth of technology.

The growth slowdown observed for the period 1973–1984 creates some problems for predictions for the 1990s, because such predictions must take into account or "weight" the periods of growth acceleration (1950–1973) and growth slowdown (1973–1984).

Because labor input can be expressed as the product of the labor force participation rate multiplied by the population, its prediction has been based on separate estimates for these two components. Population growth is determined by fertility, mortality, and international migration rates, so separate predictions have been made for each of these components as well (Gayer 1986).

In the case of capital output, I have explored various methods of prediction. The first ones were based on savings and investment function estimates, which are the main sources for the growth of gross capital.[1] I complemented this method with the study of the behavior of the growth rate of capital input during the period 1940–1985. In this way, I can derive predictions for capital input growth trends for the near future.

In order to predict the rate of GDP growth, I had to make some assumptions with regard to TFP. Again, I worked with two alternatives. The first assumes zero technological change, and the second a value similar to that observed in the study period (1940–1980). On the basis of these two pairs of analytical tools, Figure 27 (page 168) gives my predictions for the rate of GDP growth for the 1990s.

Most of the differences in the predictions of the annual GDP growth rate are due to differences in the growth rate of *capital* as predicted for the different countries. In this kind of short-run prediction, the estimates made for capital input and technology play a very important role (see Chapter 4).

The differences between the upper and lower estimates of the GDP growth rate across countries average around 1.2 percent. The minimum difference is 0.5 percent (Chile) and the maximum difference is 2.0

percent (Brazil and Mexico). This range of differences represents more than 30 percent of the predicted average GDP rate of growth, computed at the lower level.

In the predictions presented in Figure 27, the past growth-acceleration period acquires greater influence in the estimations than the slowdown period because it was longer. These predictions are the annual *average* rate anticipated for the decade 1990–1999. For some countries, such as Chile, the predictions show a lower performance than that registered recently.

Economic Policy Analysis

My findings, discussed in Chapters 4 and 8, and my comparative analysis in Chapter 10 explore the growth dynamics of seven Latin American countries for nearly half a century. This effort has led to useful conclusions for the formulation of policy for these countries.

Among these growth dynamics, I would like to highlight the following:

1. There have been phases of growth acceleration and slowdown. The accelerations were not as pronounced as those of developed countries, but they were somewhat smoother. The phases were synchronized with those of the developed countries and had similar durations.

2. The quality of labor has played an important role as a source of growth. However, its role was more varied in Latin America than in the developed countries, making its role in the future more difficult to predict.

3. Capital input has been an important factor in GDP growth, mainly because of its gross component. This phenomenon is different from that observed in developed countries, where both components of capital (gross and quality) were important.

4. In the agricultural, manufacturing, and public sectors, capital input was, again, an important growth factor. At the same time, the labor contribution to growth was irregular across these sectors, both among countries and over time.

5. The rate of technological change is less closely tied to capital accumulation in Latin American countries than it is in developed economies.

6. Important productivity gaps exist among Latin American countries and between those countries and more developed countries.

7. Policy variables, such as those related to government expenditure, the size of the fiscal deficit, and foreign trade, are significant elements in explaining the diverse rates of growth observed among Latin American countries.

8. Some Latin American countries, in the fifty-year period studied, report greater growth stability than others, notably Colombia and Mexico.

Given the overall targets of growth acceleration and stability, my analysis suggests that specific policies should be designed on the basis of careful attention to the behavior of the main sources of growth, especially in the public, agricultural, and manufacturing sectors.

Although the lessons of the growth acceleration period and the existence of substantial productivity gaps suggest interesting lessons from which Latin American countries could benefit, some of these countries have found it difficult to maintain their old standards of growth.

The exploitation of these lessons requires well-defined economic policies. My message is that the policy options exist and have not yet been exhausted. What are the optimum economic policies? In what sense are these findings helpful for the formulation of those policies? The sources-of-growth method, as applied in this study, offers general clues and provides a framework to guide the formulation of specific policies.

For example, my method reveals that the quality of labor has been an important source of labor input growth, and, within it, the education component has been its main source of growth. Therefore, educational investment would seem to be a useful tool for future economic policies. More detailed analyses will define the level of education most relevant for growth acceleration (primary, secondary, or superior).

Another example concerns the role of capital. The gross component of capital was the main determinant of its growth. The role of the quality component has been very minor. This makes clear the inefficiency of the Latin American capital markets because, in this situation, a small change in the composition of capital should make its quality component important, which has not occurred. This suggests that policies that make the markets more efficient should greatly improve the quality of capital, thereby accelerating growth.

The productivity analysis of the public sector reveals misallocations of both inputs, labor and capital, suggesting that future policies could stimulate growth by promoting the transfer of part of these inputs to the private sector.

At the aggregate level, technological change in Latin America has not been as associated with capital accumulation as in developed countries. However, in the case of the agricultural sector, such change has been associated with capital accumulation, suggesting that some additional contribution from technological change could be stimulated.[2]

Notes

1. In the case of investment functions, I studied the interaction between private and public investment. The crowding-out effect of public investment was identified as a problem only in cases in which substantial acceleration in public investment was observed.

2. Detailed analysis of economic policies contributing to capital accumulation will require an analysis of their relevance at the level of investment and savings decisions. In general, investment demand fluctuates more than the savings supply. This requires in-depth study of investment demand determinants, which will contribute to the understanding of the effects of economic policies on investment.

FIGURE 27 Predicted Growth Rates of Labor, Capital, and GDP for the 1990s (annual percentage)

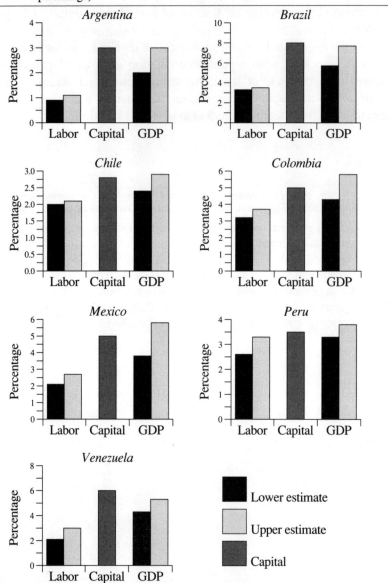

NOTE: The upper estimates of GDP growth are based on the upper estimates of labor input growth plus TFP. The weights used to combine the growth of both inputs are the same as those established in Chapter 4.
SOURCE: Author's estimates.

The Sources-of-Growth Methodology

The sources-of-growth method is mainly an accounting approach. Here I will present, first, my version of the national accounts approach, based on the procedures suggested by Jorgenson and Griliches (1967).

There are two kinds of outputs, consumption (C) and investment goods (I); m kinds of labor inputs ($L_1, L_2, \ldots L_m$); and n kinds of capital inputs ($K_1, K_2, \ldots K_n$). The value of the total output of a given period is equal to the sum paid for all the inputs used during the same period. This is expressed by the following relationship, which explicitly expresses these two forms of defining the GDP of a given economy:

$$p_C \cdot C + p_I \cdot I = \sum_{i=1}^{m} w_i L_i + \sum_{j=1}^{n} r_j K_j \tag{A1}$$

where p is the price of consumption investment goods, and w and r are the prices of services of each kind of labor and capital, respectively. This relation is defined for a given period t, which in this case is one year.

Relationship (A1) is the basic equation for organizing the information concerning outputs and identifying the role of each variable in the growth of the GDP. In this way, we work with two accounts simultaneously: one explains changes in the GDP by the changes occurring in the two kinds of output: consumption and investment goods. The other, on the right-hand side of the equation, explains the sources of these changes. Thus, the output level is explained by the inputs used in the process of production.

As we are interested in rates of growth, we derive a suitable equation from (A1). The rate of economic growth of a variable X is defined by $(dX/dt)\cdot(1/X)$, where the first part is the derivative of X with respect to the time period t, and will be expressed as $\dot{X}$.

Then, if we take the derivative of (A1) with respect to the time period t (each variable should be indexed by t and defined for a given period), we will have the following:

$$p_C\dot{C} + p_I\dot{I} + C\dot{p}_C + I\dot{p}_I \\ = \Sigma_i\, w_i\dot{L}_i + \Sigma_i L_i\dot{w}_i + \Sigma_j\, r_j\dot{K}_j + \Sigma_j K_j\dot{r}_j \tag{A2}$$

We can rearrange the terms of expression (A2) in order to leave all the derivatives of output and input quantities for a given period on the left-hand side, and the derivatives of output and input prices for the same period on the right-hand side. Then, we will have the following:

$$p_C\dot{C} + p_I\dot{I} - \sum_i w_i\dot{L}_i - \sum_j r_j\dot{K}_j \\ = \Sigma_i\, L_i\dot{w}_i + \Sigma_j\, K_j\dot{r}_j - C\dot{p}_C - I\dot{p}_I \tag{A3}$$

Expression (A3) presents the so-called duality between prices and quantities, a term used in production and cost-function theory. This expression states that the difference between the changes in output and input values for given output and input prices is equal to the difference between the input and output price changes for given inputs and products.

Under conditions of cost minimization, both sides will be equal to zero. Therefore, we could pursue either side of the relationship or both if we were interested in checking results and interpreting them in different ways.

The left-hand side states that output changes are due to input changes, and the right-hand side states that the price of inputs corresponds to price of outputs.

Both sides of this relationship can be useful, depending on the kind of information available. The relationship with respect to prices is useful for income distribution analysis, which, in this way, is integrated into the accounting of economic growth.

We will now consider only the quantity side of relationship (A3). Under conditions of cost minimization, we had:

$$p_C\dot{C} + p_I\dot{I} = \sum_i w_i\dot{L}_i + \sum_j r_j\dot{K}_j \tag{A4}^1$$

We can express this relationship in terms of rates of change by dividing and multiplying each derivative by the corresponding variable:

$$p_C C(\dot{C}/C) + P_I I(\dot{I}/I) = \sum_i w_i L_i(\dot{L}_i/L_i) + \sum_j r_j K_j(\dot{K}_j/K_j) \quad (A5)$$

Now, if we divide both sides by the GDP, which is expressed by each side of expression (A1), and define

$$\alpha_C = (p_C C/\text{GDP})$$
$$\alpha_I = (p_I I/\text{GDP})$$
$$\beta_i = (w_i L_i/\text{GDP})$$
$$\beta_j = (r_j K_j/\text{GDP})$$
$$\beta_L = \sum_i \beta_i$$
$$\beta_K = \sum_j \beta_j$$

as the shares of consumption and investment goods in total output, and the share of each kind of labor and capital in total output (the last two shares being the total share of all kinds of labor and all kinds of capital), we then have the following expression:

$$\alpha_C(\dot{C}/C) + \alpha_I(\dot{I}/I) = \sum_i \beta_i(\dot{L}_i/L_i) + \sum_j \beta_j(\dot{K}_j/K_j) \quad (A6)$$

Expression (A6) states that the weighted average of the rates of change of consumption and investment goods is equal to the weighted average of the rates of change of all kinds of labor and capital inputs. The weights represent the share of these factors in the GDP. All the components of expression (A6), the rates of change and the weights, depend on the time period t, which is not included as a subindex for the sake of simplicity.

Now, I will state expression (A6) in a different way, which will be useful for my work. First, I define the gross concept of each input, which is simply the sum of all kinds of labor and capital:

$$L = \sum_i L_i$$
$$K = \sum_j K_j$$

and the weighted average of the unit price of labor and capital by:

$$w = \sum_i w_i L_i/L$$
$$r = \sum_j r_j K_j/K$$

If we add and subtract from the right-hand side of expression (A6) the terms $\sum_i \beta_i (\dot{L}/L)$ and $\sum_j \beta_j (\dot{K}/K)$ and make some rearrangements of terms, we find:

$$
\alpha_C(\dot{C}/C) + \alpha_I (\dot{I}/I) = \sum_i \beta_i(\dot{L_i}/L_i - \dot{L}/L) + \sum_j \beta_j(\dot{K_j}/K_j - \dot{K}/K)
$$
$$
+ \beta_L(\dot{L}/L) + \beta_K(\dot{K}/K)
$$
$$
= \beta_L(\dot{L}/L) + \beta_L \sum_i w_i/w(\dot{L_i}/L) + \beta_K(\dot{K}/K) + \beta_K \sum_j r_j/r(\dot{K_j}/K) \quad \text{(A7)}
$$

(See schematic representation in Chapter 4.)

On the right-hand side of expression (A7), we can observe that the weighted sum of the rates of change of all kinds of labor and capital have been decomposed into two terms for each kind of input. The first one is what we call the rate of growth of the gross components of labor and capital (L and K), weighted by the total income share of each kind of input. The second component for each kind of input is what we call the rate of change of the quality of labor and capital.

The approach I am presenting considers changes in technology as changes in the quality of the inputs. The best way to capture these changes is through a definition of input price indexes that take into account changes in quality. (There are also other approaches that consider technology as an additional input, measured by the so-called investment in research and development or by some other explicit indicator.)

Continuing with the dual approach, I can now apply to the price side of the expression (A3) the same kind of derivation I applied to the quantity side. This will produce the following expression:

$$
\alpha_C(\dot{p_C}/p_C) + \alpha_I(\dot{p_I}/p) = \beta_L(\dot{w}/w) + \beta_K(\dot{r}/r)
$$
$$
+ \beta_L \sum_i L_i/L(\dot{w_i}/w) + \beta_K \sum_j K_j/K(\dot{r_j}/r) \quad \text{(A8)}
$$

Expression (A8) states that the weighted average of the rates of changes in output prices is equal to the weighted average of the rates of change in the average unit prices of labor and capital, plus the changes in the relative prices between each kind of input.

The third and fourth components of the right-hand side of expression (A8) tell us about the change in personal income distribution, which is a good complement to the previous decomposition.

In the production function approach, we begin by presenting a multiple product production function for the whole economy. This is defined by:

$$
G(C, I) = F(L_1, L_2, \ldots L_m, K_1, K_2, \ldots K_n) \quad \text{(A9)}
$$

This function could be of any shape at this stage. Later on, some assumptions have to be made in order to relate it to the previous national account approach. And, because it is defined for a period of time, all the variables should have the subindex t. Next, we will differentiate the function with respect to time, and then we will multiply and divide each derivative by its corresponding variable.

In this way, we have:

$$
\begin{aligned}
&(G_C C/G)(\dot{C}/C) + (G_I I/G)(\dot{I}/I) \\
&= \Sigma_i \, [(F_{L_i} L_i/F)(\dot{L}_i/L_i)] + \Sigma_j \, [(F_{K_j} K_j/F)(\dot{K}_j/K_j)]
\end{aligned}
\tag{A10}
$$

where the terms G_C, G_I, F_{L_i}, F_{K_j} are the partial derivatives of the functions G and F with respect to the corresponding variables.

Expression (A10) shows that the weighted average of the rates of change in each kind of output is equal to the weighted average of the rates of change in each kind of labor and capital input. The weight, here, is given by output-input elasticities.

If we assume that there are constant returns to scale, that each input is paid the value of its marginal product, and that the prices of the products correspond to their rate of substitution, we can connect the weights of expression (A10) with the weights of expression (A6) of the national accounts approach.

The characteristics of the weights in this approach will depend on certain assumptions. First, they are going to add up to one if we assume constant returns to scale. If there are increasing returns to scale, the sum of weights will add up to more than one and we will not have correspondence with the national accounts approach.

For example, in the case of increasing returns to scale, the possibility of including a variable that measures the change in firm-size distribution could be considered. For this approach, we would have to define the aggregate production function from the firm level.

In general, the weights can be constant or variable over time. This will depend on the kind of elasticity of substitution between inputs and outputs we are assuming. If we assume constant elasticity of substitution and make it equal to one (as in the case of the Cobb-Douglas multiple production function), we will have a constant share through time.

Working with expression (A10) and applying the same procedure followed for expression (A6), we will obtain an expression equivalent to (A7), which will operate with the same assumptions referred to above (in order to make the weights equal). Now, we have expressions for both components of each input: gross and quality changes.

The production function approach allows a very elastic treatment of the technological factor, either as a new variable or as embodied in the different inputs already defined. The shape of the production function and the possibility of its empirical verification are closely related, depending on assumptions with respect to technology or the elasticities of input substitution.

Identifying the effects of the quality component of each input through econometric estimates of the production function produces underestimates, owing to cases in which the quality variable contributes, in part, to maintain the quality level of the labor force. In these cases, the contribution share of the gross component of labor will be overstated.

An empirical application of relationships (A7) and (A10) will not always give a complete identity between both sides of the equation. In general, some discrepancies will arise as a result of mistakes made in the observation of the variables included in the account or misspecifications with respect to all kinds of outputs and inputs (including technology).

Notes

1. A useful new version of equation (A4) was provided by Harberger (1983), considering the case of distortion in the labor and capital markets. Defining as D_i and D_j, the distortions in the labor and capital markets respectively, equation (A4) can be expressed as:

$$p_C \dot{C} + p_I I = \Sigma_i \, (w_i + D_i) \dot{L}_i + \Sigma_j \, (r_j + D_j) \dot{K}_j \qquad \text{(A4a)}$$

This expression could become useful for aggregate cost-benefit analysis, according to Harberger's suggestion.

Production Function Estimates

Equation (A9) provides a general expression of a multiple production function, which is an alternative to national accounts for the sources-of-growth method:

$$G(C, I) = F(L_1, L_2, \ldots L_m, K_1, K_2, \ldots K_n) \qquad \text{(B1)}$$

This appendix will discuss some of the characteristics of this production function, adjusted to the aggregate data for Latin American economies. These characteristics, which have important implications for the method I followed in my accounting estimates of growth, are (1) the degree of return to scale; (2) the constancy of the output-input elasticities, which depend on the elasticity of substitution; and (3) the kind of technology.

The degree of return to scale is difficult to capture in an aggregate function because it is basically a concept for use at the firm or even at the plant level, making its meaning difficult to interpret at the aggregate level. However, one possibility is to interpret the return to scale as the measurement of the effect of increases in market size, which produces benefits through labor specialization (the so-called Adam Smith effect).

In terms of the growth-accounting equation, the return to scale will determine whether or not the sum of the weights will be equal to, less than, or greater than one. In the latter case, the calculation of sources of growth presented in Chapter 4 will underestimate the contribution of total inputs.

The traditional Cobb-Douglas production function implies constant output-input elasticity and, consequently, constant input weights in the sources-of-growth equation. Other production functions, either with constant or variable elasticities of substitution, allow for variations in the output-input elasticities.

The translog production function is very flexible and has been used in many econometric models (see Jorgenson, Gollop, and Fraumeni 1987). For one output (GDP) and two inputs (L and K), the translog production function takes the following logarithmic form:

$$\ln \text{GDP} = \alpha + \beta_L \ln L + \beta_K \ln K + \beta_{LL}(\ln L)^2$$
$$+ \beta_{KK}(\ln K)^2 + \beta_{LK} \ln K \ln L \qquad (B2)$$

This production function allows for variable output-input elasticities and non-homotheticity. The output-input elasticities are obtained from the partial derivation of equation (A10), with respect to the corresponding inputs. In the case of labor, this will be:

$$\frac{\partial \ln \text{GDP}}{\partial \ln L} = \beta_L + 2\beta_{LL} \ln L + \beta_{LK} \ln K \qquad (B3)$$

The econometric estimation of this production function could be obtained either directly by estimating equation (B2) or indirectly through the equations for the output-input elasticities. For the second method, the partial derivative of $\ln \text{GDP}$ with respect to each input is replaced by the input income share. The estimation is done with restrictions on homotheticity and on the sum of the output-input elasticities. Without restrictions, estimates can be used to test this kind of restriction, which in general is implicitly imposed under other kinds of production functions.

Technology enters into the production function in different forms. The simple form is in a Hicks neutral way, as a variable multiplying the function F. If technology is assumed to increase in an exponential form, at the rate g, then, in the log version of the translog production function, we will only need to add to equation (B2) the component $g.t$.

If technology is considered in the same way as any other input variable, the production function will now have three inputs: labor, capital, and technology, T. In this case, it is necessary to separate the cases where T is measured from cases that are considered as a function of time. In the latter case, technology can be neutral or non-neutral, depending on how it is defined.

Many approaches for the measurement of T have been developed. The most convenient approach, empirically, is constructed from the flow of expenditures on research and development made by the private and public sectors. The main problem here is how to add up past expenditures (as not all expenditures produce successful results and the adoption of new technology is not instantaneous). Other possibilities considered in the literature were patents of inventions, payments of royalties, and research publications.

The approach followed for growth accounting has been to identify changes in quality that represent embodied technology for each input. A related method is the hedonic price index approach, which has been applied to human and physical capital and provides an index of technological change based on changes in the characteristics of the corresponding inputs. In the case of physical capital, the hedonic price index literature provides the weights that should be given to each product characteristic, allowing for the construction of a time series from the evolution of the characteristics of each capital good. In a sense, this methodology is based on a view of technology distinct from the previous one, which considers the inputs involved in the production of technology.

The previous discussion was developed in terms of one aggregate output, the GDP. Expression (B1) considers the possibility of a multiple production function, with two kinds of output, consumption and investment goods. The econometric estimation of multiple production functions becomes more difficult. This function provides information about the degree of substitution between outputs, that is, the shape of the transformation curve.

An indirect approach to the treatment of multiple outputs is to add to the input side of the production function an indicator of the output composition. This methodology gives some information about the relevance of output composition for estimates of the parameters related to the output-input and input-input relationships.

Here, I will provide only an initial econometric approximation to the production function approach. My main objective is to complement the sources-of-growth methodology and provide a check for the relevant results presented above.

Table B1 presents the econometric estimation of Cobb-Douglas production functions for each country, and Table B2 is a Cobb-Douglas production estimation, pooling the time series of the seven countries. These tables show that separate production function estimates for each country do not give reasonable results, while the pooling of all the country data gives estimates comparable to those obtained by the sources-of-growth method.

In Table B2, we see that the output-capital input elasticity was around 0.40 and constant economy of scale cannot be rejected (because the coefficient of the variable $\ln L$ was not statistically significantly different from zero). The rate of technological change is estimated at around 1.5 percent.

TABLE B1 OLS Estimations of Cobb-Douglas Production Function, with the Form
$\ln(GDP/L)_t = a + bt + c\ln(K/L)_t + d\ln L_t + u_t$

Parameter	Argentina 1944–1985	Brazil 1950–1983	Chile 1940–1982	Colombia 1950–1985	Mexico 1940–1985	Peru 1942–1980	Venezuela 1950–1985
a	−1.64	1.44	0.51	5.08	9.09	23.06	−4.59
	(0.58)	(0.73)	(0.24)	(4.00)	(6.83)	(5.29)	(1.06)
b	0.005	0.035	0.016	0.040	0.066	0.114	−0.018
	(0.50)	(4.92)	(2.56)	(6.85)	(13.42)	(6.32)	(0.92)
c	0.40	0.24	0.34	−0.28	−0.13	−0.38	0.06
	(1.33)	(4.71)	(2.94)	(1.71)	(1.56)	(4.45)	(0.20)
d	0.20	−0.21	−0.08	−0.65	−1.10	−3.16	0.75
	(0.65)	(1.03)	(0.31)	(4.24)	(7.12)	(5.44)	(1.23)
$\bar{R}^2$	0.88	0.98	0.96	0.97	0.98	0.95	0.45
DW	0.35	0.31	1.28	0.59	0.44	0.81	0.19

NOTE: The absolute values of the t-test are in parentheses.
SOURCE: Author's computation.

TABLE B2 OLS Estimation of Cobb-Douglas Production Function, Pooling Time Series with Cross-Country Data, with the Form $\ln(GDP/L)_t = a + bt + c \ln(K/L)_t + d \ln L_t + \text{dummies} + u_t$

Parameter	Estimate	t-test
a	0.715	1.218
b	0.014	6.137
c	0.385	9.886
d	−0.067	−0.868
Constant dummies		
Argentina	−0.163	−2.725
Brazil	−0.467	−2.589
Chile	−0.346	−6.505
Colombia	−0.598	−7.400
Mexico	−0.454	−4.380
Peru	−0.837	−10.697
$\bar{R}^2$	0.961	

SOURCE: Author.

The Stock of
Educational Capital

Another estimate of the stock of educational capital computes the investment flow on the basis of the amount spent on education by public and private institutions, plus the income forgone by people going to school. Then, applying the inventory approach, and assuming a determined depreciation rate, the stock of educational capital is built. This is the capital stock for the country as a whole and therefore is larger than that incorporated in the labor force. Under certain assumptions, it is possible to demonstrate that this method is equivalent to that presented in Chapter 6. Table C1 presents the findings obtained for the stock of educational capital, following this second approach. The results show a very high growth rate for the stock of educational capital, even though it was computed in terms of per unit labor. These results are much higher than the growth rate of labor quality as presented in Table 16.

Some factors that could explain, in part, this high rate of growth are the price index used to deflate the investment flow in nominal terms, the question of how much of the measured investment should be considered as consumption rather than investment, and the analytical treatment of students who abandon school before graduating.

TABLE C1 Stock of Educational Capital in Selected Years and Its Average Annual Growth Rate by Decade, 1940–1970

Year	Stock of educational capital				
	Argentina (millions of 1960 pesos)	Chile (millions of 1961 escudos)	Colombia (millions of 1958 pesos)	Mexico (millions of 1960 pesos)	Peru (millions of 1960 soles)
1940	n.a.	1,090	n.a.	14,468	8,737
1945	n.a.	1,402	n.a.	13,666	9,630
1950	480	1,882	3,472	13,884	12,616
1955	613	2,657	3,960	14,797	16,252
1960	767	3,509	4,914	17,267	20,773
1965	994	n.a.	6,744	23,067	29,384
1970	1,368	n.a.	10,671	38,598	40,818
Period	Average annual growth rate of educational capital stock (percentage)				
1940–1950	n.a.	7.23	n.a.	−0.41	4.44
1950–1960	5.98	8.65	4.15	2.44	6.47
1960–1970	7.84	n.a.	11.72	12.35	9.65

n.a. = not available.
SOURCE: Elías (1975a).

Occupation Classification II

The second alternative for the classification of labor is presented in this appendix. Table D1 shows disparities in labor composition by occupation. Here, the larger disparities across countries appear in occupations related to the primary and industrial sectors.

Occupation classification II also reports some similarities across countries: administrative, executive, and managerial workers; and service, sport, and recreation workers. The similarity detected within this first group contradicts the disparities reported for the same group by classification I (Table 22). This suggests that the criteria employed in these alternative kinds of classification could be very different.

With respect to relative wages, classification II also reports differences within countries, as seen in Table D2. In Venezuela the range of variation in relative wages is smaller than that observed in Table 23, classification I, and is mainly due to the kind of classification of the labor force used in occupation classification II. Under classification II, classification of the other labor characteristics differs less across occupations.

TABLE D1 Labor Force Composition by Occupation Classification II in Selected Years, 1960–1980 (percentage)

Year/occupation	Argentina	Brazil	Chile	Colombia	Mexico	Peru	Venezuela
1960[a]							
Professional, technical, and related workers	6.1	n.a.	n.a.	3.9	4.2	3.4	6.1
Administrative, executive, and managerial workers	2.5	n.a.	n.a.	2.6	0.8	1.5	1.7
Clerical workers	11.0	n.a.	n.a.	4.6	9.2	4.5	7.7
Sales workers	9.4	n.a.	n.a.	5.6	13.9	7.6	10.6
Farmers, fishermen, hunters, loggers, and related workers	17.9	n.a.	n.a.	47.4	36.1	51.6	28.5
Miners, quarrymen, and related workers	0.3	n.a.	n.a.	0.8	n.a.	1.2	0.9
Transport and communication workers	4.2	n.a.	n.a.	3.0	n.a.	2.4	7.0
Craftsmen, manufacturing workers, and others	30.8	n.a.	n.a.	17.4	25.3[b]	18.4	20.8
Service, sport, and recreation workers	9.2	n.a.	n.a.	11.2	9.4	9.4	12.5
Others	8.6	n.a.	n.a.	3.5	1.4	0.0	4.2
1970[c]							
Professional, technical, and related workers	7.5	4.7	7.1	3.9	5.7	4.7	8.5
Administrative, executive, and managerial workers	1.5	5.3	1.9	2.6	2.5	1.8	2.2
Clerical workers	11.4	4.8	9.5	4.6	7.5	5.8	10.0
Sales workers	11.9	4.6	8.2	5.6	7.5	9.4	13.8
Farmers, fishermen, hunters, loggers, and related workers	14.4	43.5	21.1	47.3	38.2	46.9	19.6
Miners, quarrymen, and related workers	n.a.	0.4	n.a.	0.8	n.a.	0.2	0.7
Transport and communication workers	n.a.	3.9	n.a.	3.0	n.a.	3.0	6.8
Craftsmen, manufacturing workers, and others	34.3[b]	15.0	33.4[b]	17.5	26.6[b]	19.4	24.5
Service, sport, and recreation workers	12.6	7.7	11.7	11.2	12.0	8.8	12.7
Others	6.4	10.1	7.1	3.5	0.0	0.0	1.2

(continued on following page)

TABLE D1 (continued)

Year/occupation	Argentina	Brazil	Chile	Colombia	Mexico	Peru	Venezuela
1980							
Professional, technical, and related workers	10.0	n.a.	n.a.	n.a.	n.a.	8.0	10.9
Administrative, executive, and managerial workers	0.5	n.a.	n.a.	n.a.	n.a.	0.5	1.7
Clerical workers	14.6	n.a.	n.a.	n.a.	n.a.	10.4	11.4
Sales workers	13.4	n.a.	n.a.	n.a.	n.a.	10.6	10.9
Farmers, fishermen, hunters, loggers, and related workers	11.2	n.a.	n.a.	n.a.	n.a.	36.9	11.5
Miners, quarrymen, and related workers	n.a.	n.a.	n.a.	n.a.	n.a.		
Transport and communication workers	n.a.	n.a.	n.a.	n.a.	n.a.		
Craftsmen, manufacturing workers, and others	35.2[b]	n.a.	n.a.	n.a.	n.a.	20.2[b]	41.4[b]
Service, sport, and recreation workers	12.2	n.a.	n.a.	n.a.	n.a.	7.6	12.2
Others	2.9	n.a.	n.a.	n.a.	n.a.	5.8	0.0

n.a. = not available.
a. 1956 for Mexico; 1961 for Peru and Venezuela.
b. Covers miners, quarrymen, and related workers, and transport and communication workers.
c. 1971 for Venezuela.
SOURCES: Same as Table 14.

185

TABLE D2 Venezuela's Relative Wages by Occupation Classification II, 1961

Occupation	Ratio to average wage of entire work force
Professional, technical, and related workers	1.75
Administrative, executive, and managerial workers	1.95
Clerical workers	1.59
Sales workers	1.20
Farmers, fishermen, hunters, loggers, and related workers	0.54
Miners, quarrymen, and related workers	1.50
Transport and communication workers	1.26
Craftsmen, manufacturing workers, and others	1.15
Service, sport, and recreation workers	0.71
Others	0.86

SOURCES: Same as Table 15.

APPENDIX E

Basic Data

TABLE E1 Output, Consumption Goods, and Investment Goods in Argentina, 1940–1980

Year	Nominal GDP (millions of current pesos ley[a])	$p_C C$ (millions of current pesos ley[a])	$p_I I$ (millions of current pesos ley[a])	P_{GDP} (%)	Constant GDP (millions of 1960 pesos ley)	P_C (%)	C (millions of 1960 pesos ley)	P_I (%)	I (millions of 1960 pesos ley)
1940	125.7	n.a.	n.a.	2.6	4,835	n.a.	n.a.	2.2	n.a.
1941	135.2	119.8	15.4	2.7	5,007	2.7	4,391	2.5	616
1942	152.6	n.a.	n.a.	2.9	5,262	n.a.	n.a.	2.7	n.a.
1943	162.0	141.0	21.0	3.1	5,226	3.1	4,550	3.1	676
1944	184.2	161.2	23.0	3.1	5,942	3.1	5,223	3.2	719
1945	205.4	175.3	30.1	3.5	5,869	3.4	5,099	3.9	770
1946	278.7	238.7	40.0	4.3	6,481	4.3	5,591	4.5	890
1947	387.2	327.7	59.5	5.1	7,592	5.0	6,510	5.5	1,082
1948	475.6	384.3	91.3	6.1	7,797	5.8	6,596	7.6	1,201
1949	571.0	456.2	114.8	7.5	7,613	7.1	6,464	10.0	1,149
1950	676.8	558.1	118.7	9.0	7,520	8.5	6,547	12.2	973
1951	969.8	807.3	162.5	12.4	7,821	12.2	6,643	13.8	1,178

(continued on following page)

TABLE E1 (continued)

Year	Nominal GDP (millions of current pesos ley[a])	$p_C C$ (millions of current pesos ley[a])	$p_I I$ (millions of current pesos ley[a])	P_{GDP} (%)	Constant GDP (millions of 1960 pesos ley)	P_C (%)	C (millions of 1960 pesos ley)	P_I (%)	I (millions of 1960 pesos ley)
1952	1,122.2	932.0	190.2	15.1	7,432	14.8	6,300	16.8	1,132
1953	1,295.4	1,088.8	206.6	16.5	7,851	16.2	6,716	18.2	1,135
1954	1,435.2	1,205.4	229.8	17.6	8,155	17.2	7,000	19.9	1,155
1955	1,696.2	1,415.3	280.9	19.4	8,743	19.1	7,405	21.0	1,338
1956	2,220.7	1,862.8	357.9	24.7	8,991	24.1	7,722	28.2	1,269
1957	2,847.7	2,403.0	444.7	30.1	9,461	29.3	8,208	35.5	1,253
1958	4,019.4	3,349.7	669.7	40.1	10,023	39.0	8,595	46.9	1,428
1959	7,674.3	6,598.1	1,076.2	81.8	9,382	80.5	8,193	90.5	1,189
1960	10,124.0	8,445.1	1,678.9	100.0	10,124	100.0	8,445	100.0	1,679
1961	12,071.8	9,925.1	2,146.7	111.3	10,846	111.7	8,889	109.7	1,957
1962	14,928.7	12,548.2	2,380.5	139.9	10,671	138.8	9,039	145.9	1,632
1963	18,670.9	16,141.2	2,529.7	179.2	10,419	179.7	8,984	176.3	1,435

(continued on following page)

TABLE E1 (continued)

Year	Nominal GDP (millions of current pesos ley[a])	$p_C C$ (millions of current pesos ley[a])	$p_I I$ (millions of current pesos ley[a])	P_{GDP} (%)	Constant GDP (millions of 1960 pesos ley)	P_C (%)	C (millions of 1960 pesos ley)	P_I (%)	I (millions of 1960 pesos ley)
1964	26,021.1	22,561.3	3,459.8	226.5	11,488	229.5	9,832	208.8	1,656
1965	36,393.9	31,038.8	5,355.1	290.1	12,545	291.1	10,663	284.5	1,882
1966	45,410.7	38,692.3	6,718.4	359.7	12,625	360.9	10,720	352.7	1,905
1967	59,662.1	50,604.7	9,057.4	459.9	12,973	460.6	10,986	455.9	1,987
1968	68,727.5	57,672.4	11,055.1	508.5	13,516	511.5	11,276	493.6	2,240
1969	80,983.9	66,668.2	14,315.7	552.1	14,668	560.8	11,887	514.7	2,781
1970	94,793.4	77,513.2	17,280.2	613.2	15,459	622.2	12,458	575.9	3,001
1971	132,667.2	109,593.2	23,164.0	819.0	16,199	834.4	13,124	753.3	3,075
1972	219,938.4	183,327.2	36,611.2	1,316.6	16,705	1,352.3	13,557	1,163.0	3,148
1973	364,591.2	312,244.5	52,346.7	2,056.7	17,727	2,173.2	14,368	1,558.4	3,359
1974	514,902	421,621	93,281	2,850.0	18,067	2,918.8	14,445	2,536.2	3,678
1975	1,526	1,169	357	8,232.2	18,537	7,942.9	14,720	9,209.8	3,879
1976	7,660	5,604	2,056	43,716.5	17,522	42,225.2	13,272	49,410.7	4,162
1977	21,349	1,571	5,638	120,019.1	17,788	122,024.6	12,875	118,475.7	4,759
1978	52,799	40,011	12,788	313,347.2	16,850	322,796.2	12,395	298,223.2	4,288
1979	147,481	110,382	37,100	787,112.6	18,737	831,248.4	13,729	769,865.1	4,819
1980	294,120	223,400	70,720	1,517,020.8	19,388	1,542,178.6	14,486	1,505,000.1	4,699

n.a. = not available.

a. Since 1975, billions of pesos ley.

NOTE: $p_C C$ = consumption goods at nominal prices; $p_I I$ = investment goods at nominal prices; P_{GDP} = index of implicit GDP deflator; P_C = index of implicit consumption goods deflator; C = consumption goods in real terms; P_I = index of implicit investment goods deflator; and I = investment goods in real terms.

SOURCES: Banco Central de la República Argentina (1975, 1976); Díaz Alejandro (1970). *General sources for Tables E1–E7*: Economic Commission for Latin America (1951, 1989); Ruddle and Barrows (1974).

190

TABLE E2 Output, Consumption Goods, and Investment Goods in Brazil, 1940–1980

Year	Nominal GDP (millions of current NC$_r$)	$p_C C$ (millions of current NC$_r$)	$p_I I$ (millions of current NC$_r$)	P_{GDP} (%)	Constant GDP (millions of 1949 NC$_r$)	P_C (%)	C (millions of 1949 NC$_r$)	P_I (%)	I (millions of 1949 NC$_r$)
1940	39.3	n.a.	n.a.	27.5	142.8	n.a.	n.a.	n.a.	n.a.
1941	45.7	n.a.	n.a.	30.5	149.8	n.a.	n.a.	n.a.	n.a.
1942	50.2	n.a.	n.a.	34.4	145.8	n.a.	n.a.	n.a.	n.a.
1943	62.2	n.a.	n.a.	39.3	158.2	n.a.	n.a.	n.a.	n.a.
1944	85.1	n.a.	n.a.	50.0	170.2	n.a.	n.a.	n.a.	n.a.
1945	102.5	n.a.	n.a.	58.4	175.6	n.a.	n.a.	n.a.	n.a.
1946	133.7	n.a.	n.a.	68.2	196.1	n.a.	n.a.	n.a.	n.a.
1947	164.9	141.5	23.4	82.9	198.8	82.2	172.1	87.7	26.7
1948	194.6	171.4	23.2	90.3	215.6	89.8	190.8	93.6	24.8
1949	229.9	201.3	28.6	100.0	229.9	100.0	201.3	100.0	28.6
1950	272.1	238.9	33.2	111.2	244.8	111.9	213.4	105.5	31.4
1951	322.7	277.5	45.2	124.4	259.3	124.3	223.3	125.5	36.0
1952	397.3	346.9	50.4	140.9	281.9	142.6	243.2	130.3	38.7
1953	469.5	406.9	62.6	162.5	289.0	161.9	251.4	166.5	37.6
1954	627.4	541.6	85.8	197.2	318.2	193.4	280.1	225.2	38.1
1955	783.4	695.8	87.6	230.4	340.0	229.1	303.7	241.3	36.3

(continued on following page)

TABLE E2 (continued)

Year	Nominal GDP (millions of current NC_t^a)	$p_C C$ (millions of current NC_t^a)	$p_I I$ (millions of current NC_t^a)	P_{GDP} (%)	Constant GDP (millions of 1949 NC_t)	P_C (%)	C (millions of 1949 NC_t)	P_I (%)	I (millions of 1949 NC_t)
1956	995.9	876.4	119.5	283.9	350.8	282.3	310.5	296.3	40.3
1957	1,218.0	1,078.5	139.5	321.3	379.1	321.4	335.6	320.9	43.5
1958	1,457.5	1,260.5	197.0	357.0	408.3	349.4	360.8	415.1	47.5
1959	1,987.6	1,674.6	313.0	461.1	431.1	445.1	376.2	570.6	54.9
1960	2,750.7	2,343.6	407.1	581.7	472.9	565.5	414.4	695.4	58.5
1961	4,052.1	3,445.0	607.1	776.9	521.6	748.6	460.2	988.2	61.4
1962	6,601.4	5,616.1	985.3	1,202.4	549.0	1,150.1	488.3	1,624.2	60.7
1963	11,928.6	10,059.9	1,868.7	2,139.7	557.5	2,033.9	494.6	2,971.0	62.9
1964	23,055.0	19,553.7	3,501.3	4,017.9	573.8	3,855.2	507.2	5,255.6	66.6
1965	36,817.6	31,796.7	5,020.9	6,245.6	589.5	6,068.1	524.0	7,663.4	65.5
1966	53,724.1	46,283.3	7,440.8	8,670.8	619.6	8,528.3	542.7	9,680.5	76.9

(continued on following page)

TABLE E2 (continued)

Year	Nominal GDP (millions of current NC_r[a])	$p_C C$ (millions of current NC_r[a])	$p_I I$ (millions of current NC_r[a])	P_{GDP} (%)	Constant GDP (millions of 1949 NC_r)	P_C (%)	C (millions of 1949 NC_r)	P_I (%)	I (millions of 1949 NC_r)
1967	71,486.3	62,327.5	9,158.8	11,011.4	649.2	10,885.0	572.6	11,960.4	76.6
1968	99,879.8	83,396.5	16,483.3	14,073.5	709.7	13,786.8	604.9	15,734.0	104.8
1969	133,116.9	113,999.9	19,117.0	17,207.5	773.6	n.a.	n.a.	18,561.4	103.0
1970	175,526.2	135,960.2	39,566.0	20,718.4	847.2	20,460.5	664.5	21,656.3	182.7
1971	234,726.7	181,190.7	53,536.0	24,896.8	942.8	24,888.8	728.0	24,925.9	214.8
1972	306,987.9	237,523.9	69,464.0	29,495.4	1,040.8	29,668.2	800.6	28,914.0	240.2
1973	406,220.8	310,490.7	95,730.1	34,376.0	1,181.7	34,641.4	896.3	33,540.2	285.4
1974	614.6	438.2	176.4	48,083.2	1,278.2	47,974.6	913.4	49,205.0	358.5
1975	892.0	695.0	197.0	60,120.0	1,483.7	59,968.3	1,158.9	64,723.6	304.4
1976	1,430.0	1,033.9	396.1	84,435.5	1,693.6	86,583.8	1,194.1	87,596.3	452.2
1977	2,190.8	1,608.8	582.0	119,344.1	1,835.7	123,391.4	1,303.8	120,956.0	481.2
1978	3,347.0	2,492.0	855.0	167,887.2	1,993.6	176,820.0	1,409.3	161,476.2	529.5
1979	5,697.8	4,390.0	1,307.8	259,758.4	2,193.5	272,695.1	1,609.9	252,798.0	517.3
1980	11,929.7	9,296.3	2,633.4	536,045.8	2,225.5	555,878.6	1,672.4	545,390.5	482.8

n.a. = not available.

a. Since 1974, billions of NC_r.

NOTE: $p_C C$ = consumption goods at nominal prices; $p_I I$ = investment goods at nominal prices; P_{GDP} = index of implicit GDP deflator; P_C = index of implicit consumption goods deflator; C = consumption goods in real terms; P_I = index of implicit investment goods deflator; and I = investment goods in real terms.

SOURCES: Contador and Haddad (1975); Fundação Getúlio Vargas (1973); Fundação Instituto Brasileiro de Geografia e Estatística (1970, 1974); Haddad (1975); Langoni (1970). See also Table E1.

TABLE E3 Output, Consumption Goods, and Investment Goods in Chile, 1940–1980

Year	Nominal GDP (millions of current escudos[a])	$p_C C$ (millions of current escudos[a])	$p_I I$ (millions of current escudos[a])	P_{GDP} (%)	Constant GDP (millions of 1961 escudos)	P_C (%)	C (millions of 1961 escudos)	P_I (%)	I (millions of 1961 escudos)
1940	21.24	n.a.	n.a.	0.93	2,284	n.a.	n.a.	0.96	n.a.
1941	24.72	22.6	2.11	1.09	2,268	1.08	2,086	1.16	182
1942	34.99	33.4	1.57	1.48	2,364	1.48	2,256	1.45	108
1943	39.41	37.6	1.85	1.63	2,418	1.64	2,298	1.54	120
1944	41.47	39.2	2.25	1.69	2,454	1.69	2,324	1.73	130
1945	48.01	46.3	1.72	1.80	2,667	1.80	2,578	1.93	89
1946	58.64	54.5	4.17	2.07	2,833	2.06	2,645	2.22	188
1947	70.89	68.8	2.06	2.67	2,655	2.66	2,586	2.99	69
1948	91.73	82.4	9.30	3.07	2,988	3.03	2,720	3.47	268
1949	104.20	96.5	7.70	3.50	2,977	3.47	2,782	3.95	195
1950	129.11	119.3	9.79	4.10	3,149	4.07	2,928	4.43	221
1951	165.93	153.8	12.13	5.01	3,312	4.97	3,095	5.59	217
1952	235.23	222.0	13.20	6.66	3,532	6.65	3,339	6.84	193
1953	306.88	292.3	14.57	8.19	3,747	8.17	3,577	8.57	170
1954	479.18	452.9	26.27	12.85	3,729	12.83	3,530	13.20	199
1955	890.80	835.7	55.13	23.56	3,781	23.52	3,553	24.18	228

(continued on following page)

TABLE E3 (continued)

Year	Nominal GDP (millions of current escudos[a])	$p_C C$ (millions of current escudos[a])	$p_I I$ (millions of current escudos[a])	P_{GDP} (%)	Constant GDP (millions of 1961 escudos[a])	P_C (%)	C (millions of 1961 escudos[a])	P_I (%)	I (millions of 1961 escudos[a])
1956	1,455.41	1,380.9	74.53	38.03	3,827	37.98	3,636	39.02	191
1957	2,059.63	n.a.	n.a.	49.87	4,130	n.a.	n.a.	51.16	n.a.
1958	2,754.96	n.a.	n.a.	65.61	4,199	n.a.	n.a.	67.34	n.a.
1959	3,830.32	n.a.	n.a.	91.22	4,199	n.a.	n.a.	93.64	n.a.
1960	4,160	3,738	422	93.85	4,433	93.57	3,995	96.34	438
1961	4,707	4,222	485	100.00	4,707	100.00	4,222	100.00	485
1962	5,677	5,086	591	114.87	4,942	115.96	4,386	106.36	556
1963	8,410	7,399	1,011	162.51	5,175	162.37	4,557	163.58	618
1964	12,743	11,279	1,464	236.35	5,392	234.88	4,802	248.07	590
1965	17,956	15,903	2,053	317.16	5,661	316.60	5,023	321.77	638
1966	25,043	22,415	2,628	413.23	6,060	412.50	5,434	419.85	626

(continued on following page)

TABLE E3 (continued)

Year	Nominal GDP (millions of current escudos)[a]	$p_C C$ (millions of current escudos)[a]	$p_I I$ (millions of current escudos)[a]	P_{GDP} (%)	Constant GDP (millions of 1961 escudos)[a]	P_C (%)	C (millions of 1961 escudos)[a]	P_I (%)	I (millions of 1961 escudos)[a]
1967	32,881	29,752	3,129	530.16	6,202	531.29	5,600	519.85	602
1968	44,238	39,842	4,441	693.88	6,382	695.69	5,727	678.03	655
1969	64,551	58,562	5,989	956.51	6,749	961.61	6,090	908.77	659
1970	96,971	88,215	8,756	1,328.78	7,298	1,336.19	6,602	1,258.07	696
1971	129,041	118,354	10,678	1,678.77	7,687	1,689.56	7,005	1,567.05	682
1972	238,985	216,914	22,071	3,134.53	7,624	3,138.68	6,911	3,095.47	713
1973	1,246	1,131	115	16,330.3	7,630	16,353.4	6,916	16,220.0	709
1974	9,199	7,813	1,386	115,478.3	7,966	112,336.4	6,955	136,551.7	1,015
1975	35,447	31,386	4,061	580,907.9	6,102	572,946.3	5,478	592,846.7	685
1976	128,676	117,733	10,943	1,983,903.8	6,486	1,974,061.0	5,964	1,933,392.2	566
1977	287,770	264,035	23,735	4,040,578.5	7,122	4,012,080.2	6,581	4,016,074.5	591
1978	487,506	444,229	43,277	6,222,951.2	7,834	6,170,704.3	7,199	6,308,600.6	686
1979	762,129	687,790	74,339	8,756,077.7	8,704	8,694,096.8	7,911	8,945,728.0	831
1980	1,095,178	975,269	119,909	12,098,740.6	9,052	12,100,111.7	8,060	11,755,784.3	1,020

n.a. = not available.

a. Since 1973, billions of escudos.

NOTE: $p_C C$ = consumption goods at nominal prices; $p_I I$ = investment goods at nominal prices; P_{GDP} = index of implicit GDP deflator; P_C = index of implicit consumption goods deflator; C = consumption goods in real terms; P_I = index of implicit investment goods deflator; and I = investment goods in real terms.

SOURCES: Banco Central de Chile (1975); Harberger and Selowsky (1966); Mamalakis and Reynolds (1965); Oficina de Planificación Nacional (1973); Selowsky (1967). See also Table E1.

TABLE E4 Output, Consumption Goods, and Investment Goods in Colombia, 1940–1980

Year	Nominal GDP (millions of current pesos)	$p_C C$ (millions of current pesos)	$p_I I$ (millions of current pesos)	P_{GDP} (%)	Constant GDP (millions of 1958 pesos)	P_C (%)	C (millions of 1958 pesos)	P_I (%)	I (millions of 1958 pesos)
1940	1,421	n.a.	n.a.	14.5	9,802	n.a.	n.a.	n.a.	n.a.
1941	1,355	n.a.	n.a.	13.6	9,966	n.a.	n.a.	n.a.	n.a.
1942	1,698	n.a.	n.a.	17.0	9,986	n.a.	n.a.	n.a.	n.a.
1943	2,086	n.a.	n.a.	20.8	10,027	n.a.	n.a.	n.a.	n.a.
1944	2,666	n.a.	n.a.	24.9	10,705	n.a.	n.a.	n.a.	n.a.
1945	3,026	n.a.	n.a.	27.0	11,207	n.a.	n.a.	n.a.	n.a.
1946	3,801	n.a.	n.a.	29.8	12,756	n.a.	n.a.	n.a.	n.a.
1947	4,852	n.a.	n.a.	36.6	13,258	n.a.	n.a.	n.a.	n.a.
1948	5,823	n.a.	n.a.	42.6	13,669	n.a.	n.a.	n.a.	n.a.
1949	6,462	n.a.	n.a.	44.8	14,425	n.a.	n.a.	n.a.	n.a.
1950	7,861	6,998	863	53.5	14,689	55.8	12,536	40.1	2,153
1951	8,941	8,053	888	59.0	15,147	61.5	13,091	43.2	2,056
1952	9,655	8,700	951	59.9	16,102	62.2	13,989	45.0	2,113
1953	10,735	9,792	943	62.8	17,081	65.4	14,963	44.5	2,118
1954	12,759	11,420	1,339	69.9	18,262	74.3	15,371	46.3	2,891
1955	13,250	11,821	1,429	69.8	18,976	73.8	16,017	48.3	2,959

(continued on following page)

197

TABLE E4 (continued)

Year	Nominal GDP (millions of current pesos)	$p_C C$ (millions of current pesos)	$p_I I$ (millions of current pesos)	P_{GDP} (%)	Constant GDP (millions of 1958 pesos)	P_C (%)	C (millions of 1958 pesos)	P_I (%)	I (millions of 1958 pesos)
1956	14,863	13,195	1,668	75.3	19,746	79.2	16,651	53.9	3,095
1957	17,811	15,365	2,446	88.2	20,186	90.7	16,938	75.3	3,248
1958	20,683	17,874	2,809	100.0	20,683	100.0	17,874	100.0	2,809
1959	23,649	20,543	3,106	106.6	22,177	106.3	19,325	108.9	2,852
1960	26,747	23,197	3,550	115.7	23,123	115.8	20,028	114.7	3,095
1961	30,421	26,090	4,331	125.2	24,300	125.8	20,741	121.7	3,559
1962	34,199	29,992	4,207	133.5	25,615	133.5	22,461	133.4	3,154
1963	43,526	38,364	5,162	164.5	26,457	163.9	23,408	169.3	3,049
1964	53,760	48,003	5,757	191.4	28,089	192.6	24,919	181.6	3,170
1965	60,798	53,413	7,385	208.9	29,100	208.6	25,605	211.3	3,495
1966	73,612	63,097	10,515	240.1	30,658	238.1	26,505	253.2	4,153

(continued on following page)

TABLE E4 (continued)

Year	Nominal GDP (millions of current pesos)	$p_C C$ (millions of current pesos)	$p_I I$ (millions of current pesos)	P_{GDP} (%)	Constant GDP (millions of 1958 pesos)	P_C (%)	C (millions of 1958 pesos)	P_I (%)	I (millions of 1958 pesos)
1967	83,083	72,857	10,226	260.1	31,947	257.0	28,349	284.2	3,598
1968	96,422	82,944	13,478	284.4	33,902	279.9	29,634	315.8	4,268
1969	110,953	96,218	14,735	307.7	36,061	302.4	31,822	347.6	4,239
1970	130,591	120,849	9,742	339.3	38,492	336.7	35,888	374.1	2,604
1971	153,766	136,454	17,312	378.7	40,605	373.6	36,522	424.0	4,083
1972	185,535	168,911	16,624	426.9	43,463	423.3	39,901	466.7	3,562
1973	242,480	214,695	27,785	520.3	46,603	517.9	41,451	539.3	5,152
1974	327,786	287,657	40,129	665.7	49,242	660.5	43,554	705.5	5,688
1975	405,108	359,724	45,384	826.8	48,996	822.5	43,735	862.5	5,262
1976	532,270	470,320	61,950	998.5	53,307	989.5	47,531	1,072.0	5,779
1977	716,029	636,081	79,948	1,256.5	56,986	1,251.1	50,842	1,309.2	6,107
1978	909,487	803,678	105,809	1,501.4	60,576	1,489.6	53,953	1,610.2	6,571
1979	1,188,817	1,049,846	138,971	1,890.7	62,878	1,879.5	55,858	2,032.8	6,836
1980	1,579,130	1,386,811	192,319	2,391.9	66,021	2,375.5	58,380	2,595.2	7,410

n.a. = not available.
NOTE: $p_C C$ = consumption goods at nominal prices; $p_I I$ = investment goods at nominal prices; P_{GDP} = index of implicit GDP deflator; P_C = index of implicit consumption goods deflator; C = consumption goods in real terms; P_I = index of implicit investment goods deflator; and I = investment goods in real terms.
SOURCES: Banco de la República (1973); Economic Commission for Latin America (1967); Sarmiento (1972). See also Table E1.

TABLE E5 Output, Consumption Goods, and Investment Goods in Mexico, 1940–1974

Year	Nominal GDP (millions of current pesos)	$p_C C$ (millions of current pesos)	$p_I I$ (millions of current pesos)	P_{GDP} (%)	Constant GDP (millions of 1960 pesos)	P_C (%)	C (millions of 1960 pesos)	P_I (%)	I (millions of 1960 pesos)
1940	7,900	7,331	569	19.1	41,361	19.7	37,236	13.8	4,125
1941	8,800	8,140	660	18.2	48,352	18.6	43,862	14.7	4,490
1942	10,300	9,556	744	18.8	54,787	19.0	50,197	16.2	4,590
1943	12,600	11,689	911	21.4	58,879	21.6	54,207	19.5	4,672
1944	18,200	17,033	1,167	31.5	57,778	32.2	52,917	24.0	4,861
1945	19,900	18,613	1,287	30.8	64,610	31.1	59,789	26.7	4,821
1946	26,700	25,015	1,685	39.9	66,917	40.7	61,428	30.7	5,489
1947	29,800	27,605	2,195	43.7	68,192	44.9	61,439	32.5	6,753
1948	31,900	29,135	2,765	44.2	72,172	45.3	64,248	34.9	7,924
1949	35,200	31,717	3,483	46.5	75,699	47.6	66,580	38.2	9,119
1950	44,016	40,444	3,572	50.6	86,988	51.6	78,442	41.8	8,546
1951	54,220	49,062	5,158	58.3	93,002	60.0	81,740	45.8	11,262
1952	59,900	53,119	6,781	62.3	96,148	63.8	83,257	52.6	12,891
1953	62,091	55,324	6,767	61.6	100,797	62.5	88,449	54.8	12,348
1954	73,940	66,318	7,622	69.7	106,083	70.3	94,284	64.6	11,799
1955	88,269	79,260	9,009	77.4	114,043	77.9	101,702	73.0	12,341
1956	99,338	87,859	11,479	82.5	120,410	83.2	105,541	77.2	14,869

(continued on following page)

TABLE E5 (continued)

Year	Nominal GDP (millions of current pesos)	$p_C C$ (millions of current pesos)	$p_I I$ (millions of current pesos)	P_{GDP} (%)	Constant GDP (millions of 1960 pesos)	P_C (%)	C (millions of 1960 pesos)	P_I (%)	I (millions of 1960 pesos)
1957	114,718	101,335	13,383	88.8	129,187	89.2	113,661	86.2	15,526
1958	124,063	110,041	14,022	92.1	134,705	92.1	119,447	91.9	15,258
1959	134,222	118,485	15,737	95.9	139,960	96.3	123,057	93.1	16,903
1960	150,511	132,009	18,502	100.0	150,511	100.0	132,009	100.0	18,502
1961	163,265	144,310	18,955	103.4	157,897	104.1	138,614	98.3	19,283
1962	176,030	155,684	20,346	106.5	165,286	107.2	145,201	101.3	20,085
1963	195,983	170,203	25,780	109.8	178,491	110.3	154,375	106.9	24,116
1964	231,370	199,850	31,520	116.0	199,457	116.9	170,984	110.7	28,473
1965	252,028	216,683	35,345	118.7	212,323	119.1	181,906	116.2	30,417
1966	280,090	238,935	41,155	123.4	226,977	123.4	193,626	123.4	33,351
1967	306,317	257,697	48,620	127.0	241,194	126.6	203,475	128.9	37,719
1968	339,145	285,884	53,261	130.0	260,881	129.8	220,286	131.2	40,595
1969	374,900	314,550	60,350	135.1	277,498	135.2	232,695	134.7	44,803
1970	418,700	350,685	68,015	141.2	296,530	141.1	248,531	141.7	47,999
1971	452,400	380,984	71,416	147.5	306,712	147.3	258,653	148.6	48,059
1972	512,300	430,175	82,125	155.7	329,030	156.4	275,036	152.1	53,994
1973	619,600	n.a.	n.a.	175.0	354,057	n.a.	n.a.	n.a.	n.a.
1974	813,700	n.a.	n.a.	217.0	374,977	n.a.	n.a.	n.a.	n.a.

n.a. = not available.
NOTE: $p_C C$ = consumption goods at nominal prices; $p_I I$ = investment goods at nominal prices; P_{GDP} = index of implicit GDP deflator; P_C = index of implicit consumption goods deflator; C = consumption goods in real terms; P_I = index of implicit investment goods deflator; and I = investment goods in real terms.
SOURCES: Banco de México (1969, 1975); Banco Nacional de México (1981); Cossio and Izquierdo (1962); Davis (1967); Nacional Financiera (1969); Reynolds (1970); Solís (1967). See also Table E1.

TABLE E6 Output, Consumption Goods, and Investment Goods in Peru, 1940–1980

Year	Nominal GDP (millions of current soles)	$p_C C$ (millions of current soles)	$p_I I$ (millions of current soles)	P_{GDP} (%)	Constant GDP (millions of 1960 soles)	P_C (%)	C (millions of 1960 soles)	P_I (%)	I (millions of 1960 soles)
1940	n.a.	n.a.	n.a.	n.a.	n.a.	n.a.	n.a.	n.a.	n.a.
1941	n.a.	n.a.	n.a.	n.a.	n.a.	n.a.	n.a.	n.a.	n.a.
1942	3,034	n.a.	n.a.	11	27,582	n.a.	n.a.	11.6	n.a.
1943	3,330	n.a.	n.a.	12	28,462	n.a.	n.a.	n.a.	n.a.
1944	3,923	n.a.	n.a.	12	31,637	n.a.	n.a.	n.a.	n.a.
1945	4,515	n.a.	n.a.	13	34,731	n.a.	n.a.	16.0	n.a.
1946	5,433	n.a.	n.a.	14	38,807	n.a.	n.a.	17.5	n.a.
1947	7,056	n.a.	n.a.	19	37,137	n.a.	n.a.	22.6	n.a.
1948	8,871	n.a.	n.a.	24	36,963	n.a.	n.a.	29.6	n.a.
1949	12,495	n.a.	n.a.	34	36,750	n.a.	n.a.	34.2	n.a.
1950	15,528	13,747	1,781	40	38,820	40.2	34,158	38.2	4,662
1951	19,175	16,134	3,041	46	41,685	46.8	34,461	42.1	7,224
1952	21,490	18,312	3,178	49	43,857	49.8	36,794	45.0	7,063
1953	23,214	20,320	2,894	50	46,428	50.1	40,522	49.0	5,906
1954	25,711	22,408	3,303	55	46,747	55.5	40,346	51.6	6,401
1955	29,255	24,559	4,696	59	49,585	58.8	41,745	59.9	7,840

(continued on following page)

TABLE E6 (continued)

Year	Nominal GDP (millions of current soles)	$p_C C$ (millions of current soles)	$p_I I$ (millions of current soles)	P_{GDP} (%)	Constant GDP (millions of 1960 soles)	P_C (%)	C (millions of 1960 soles)	P_I (%)	I (millions of 1960 soles)
1956	32,418	27,674	4,744	63	51,457	63.0	43,951	63.2	7,506
1957	34,555	29,476	5,079	67	51,575	66.8	44,095	67.9	7,480
1958	37,861	33,413	4,448	72	52,585	71.8	46,508	73.2	6,077
1959	43,253	40,216	3,037	86	50,294	86.3	46,617	82.6	3,677
1960	56,909	51,462	5,447	100.0	56,909	100.0	51,462	100.0	5,447
1961	63,885	56,993	6,892	103.7	61,606	104.0	54,816	101.5	6,790
1962	73,376	64,932	8,444	109.2	67,194	109.4	59,346	107.6	7,848
1963	80,519	72,051	8,468	115.6	69,653	116.1	62,045	111.3	7,608
1964	96,741	87,673	9,068	130.6	74,074	132.1	66,363	117.6	7,711
1965	114,902	101,187	13,715	148.1	77,584	152.4	66,379	122.4	11,205
1966	136,783	122,451	14,332	166.2	82,300	172.0	71,181	128.9	11,119

(continued on following page)

TABLE E6 (continued)

Year	Nominal GDP (millions of current soles)	$p_C C$ (millions of current soles)	$p_I I$ (millions of current soles)	P_{GDP} (%)	Constant GDP (millions of 1960 soles)	P_C (%)	C (millions of 1960 soles)	P_I (%)	I (millions of 1960 soles)
1967	156,863	144,920	11,943	186.5	84,109	190.4	76,126	149.6	7,983
1968	190,426	174,338	16,088	219.8	86,636	225.1	77,448	175.1	9,188
1969	210,433	191,771	18,662	237.1	88,753	244.2	78,533	182.6	10,220
1970	242,105	219,835	22,270	253.9	95,354	262.5	83,743	191.8	11,611
1971	268,700	244,171	24,584	266.0	101,036	274.1	89,073	205.5	11,963
1972	311,334	283,583	27,751	290.7	107,098	300.2	94,455	219.5	12,643
1973	361,460	319,409	42,051	313.4	115,345	327.4	97,559	237.8	17,683
1974	452,163	394,057	58,106	371.2	121,804	391.2	100,730	272.3	21,339
1975	573,786	499,295	74,491	473.0	121,317	502.5	99,362	327.9	22,718
1976	759,491	654,590	104,901	606.6	125,199	632.5	103,492	473.2	22,082
1977	1,045,461	909,654	135,807	829.2	126,075	855.1	106,380	709.6	19,139
1978	1,695,843	1,515,079	180,764	1,335.8	126,958	1,373.0	110,348	1,200.7	15,055
1979	3,034,097	2,702,441	331,656	2,174.6	139,527	2,227.1	121,343	2,023.1	16,393
1980	5,146,655	4,580,608	566,047	3,536.6	145,526	3,626.7	126,302	3,258.5	17,371

n.a. = not available.

NOTE: $p_C C$ = consumption goods at nominal prices; $p_I I$ = investment goods at nominal prices; P_{GDP} = index of implicit GDP deflator; P_C = index of implicit consumption goods deflator; C = consumption goods in real terms; P_I = index of implicit investment goods deflator; and I = investment goods in real terms.

SOURCES: Banco Central de la Reserva (1961, 1968); Dirección General de Cuentas Nacionales (1980); Instituto Nacional de Planificación (1966, 1971); Oficina Nacional de Estadísticas y Censos (1971). See also Table E1.

204

TABLE E7 Output, Consumption Goods, and Investment Goods in Venezuela, 1940–1974

Year	Nominal GDP (millions of current bolivars)	$p_C C$ (millions of current bolivars)	$p_I I$ (millions of current bolivars)	P_{GDP} (%)	GDP (millions of 1957 bolivars)	P_C (%)	C (millions of 1957 bolivars)	P_I (%)	I (millions of 1957 bolivars)
1940	n.a.	n.a.	n.a.	n.a.	n.a.	n.a.	n.a.	n.a.	n.a.
1941	n.a.	n.a.	n.a.	n.a.	n.a.	n.a.	n.a.	n.a.	n.a.
1942	n.a.	n.a.	n.a.	n.a.	n.a.	n.a.	n.a.	n.a.	n.a.
1943	n.a.	n.a.	n.a.	n.a.	n.a.	n.a.	n.a.	n.a.	n.a.
1944	n.a.	n.a.	n.a.	n.a.	n.a.	n.a.	n.a.	n.a.	n.a.
1945	n.a.	n.a.	n.a.	n.a.	n.a.	n.a.	n.a.	n.a.	n.a.
1946	n.a.	n.a.	n.a.	n.a.	n.a.	n.a.	n.a.	n.a.	n.a.
1947	n.a.	n.a.	n.a.	n.a.	n.a.	n.a.	n.a.	n.a.	n.a.
1948	n.a.	n.a.	n.a.	n.a.	n.a.	n.a.	n.a.	n.a.	n.a.
1949	n.a.	n.a.	n.a.	n.a.	n.a.	n.a.	n.a.	n.a.	n.a.
1950	11,826	9,101	2,725	92.9	12,728	91.4	9,953	98.2	2,775
1951	13,007	10,268	2,739	91.5	14,212	90.3	11,377	96.6	2,835
1952	13,981	10,507	3,474	91.7	15,248	89.8	11,703	98.0	3,545
1953	14,806	11,115	3,691	91.5	16,190	90.5	12,288	94.6	3,902
1954	16,377	12,110	4,267	92.3	17,749	91.4	13,253	94.9	4,496
1955	17,893	14,018	3,875	92.6	19,325	91.9	15,259	95.3	4,066
1956	20,400	16,303	4,097	95.5	21,366	94.9	17,181	97.9	4,185

(continued on following page)

TABLE E7 (continued)

Year	Nominal GDP (millions of current bolivars)	$p_C C$ (millions of current bolivars)	$p_I I$ (millions of current bolivars)	P_{GDP} (%)	GDP (millions of 1957 bolivars)	P_C (%)	C (millions of 1957 bolivars)	P_I (%)	I (millions of 1957 bolivars)
1957	23,847	20,370	3,477	100.0	23,847	100.0	20,370	100.0	3,477
1958	24,585	20,233	4,352	101.7	24,164	101.4	19,951	103.3	4,213
1959	25,557	20,877	4,680	98.1	26,065	96.9	21,539	103.4	4,526
1960	25,620	21,804	3,816	96.2	26,643	95.1	22,920	102.5	3,723
1961	26,642	23,013	3,628	98.1	27,156	97.2	23,681	104.4	3,475
1962	28,524	24,799	3,725	99.3	28,736	98.2	25,245	106.7	3,491
1963	30,657	26,905	3,752	102.8	29,818	102.9	26,150	102.3	3,668
1964	35,749	30,386	5,363	110.6	32,326	109.0	27,883	120.7	4,443
1965	37,608	32,349	5,259	110.5	34,019	109.1	29,651	120.4	4,368
1966	39,144	34,629	4,515	112.5	34,786	111.0	31,200	125.9	3,586
1967	41,870	37,689	4,181	114.6	36,522	113.7	33,156	124.2	3,366
1968	44,848	37,820	7,028	116.6	38,458	115.1	32,858	125.5	5,600
1969	47,216	39,444	7,772	118.6	39,809	116.7	33,789	129.1	6,020
1970	51,991	44,368	7,623	127.9	40,649	127.0	34,939	133.5	5,710
1971	57,005	48,372	8,633	135.5	42,073	135.3	35,762	136.8	6,311
1972	63,305	52,904	10,401	144.9	43,680	146.1	36,219	139.4	7,461
1973	76,341	63,357	12,984	166.6	45,835	169.9	37,293	152.0	8,542
1974	126,699	112,875	13,824	264.4	47,917	281.3	40,120	177.3	7,797

n.a. = not available.

NOTE: $p_C C$ = consumption goods at nominal prices; $p_I I$ = investment goods at nominal prices; P_{GDP} = index of implicit GDP deflator; P_C = index of implicit consumption goods deflator; C = consumption goods in real terms; P_I = index of implicit investment goods deflator; and I = investment goods in real terms. I = investment goods in real terms.

SOURCES: Banco Central de Venezuela (1974, 1975); Inter-American Development Bank (1968). See also Table E1.

TABLE E8 Ratio of Investment Goods to Total GDP, 1940–1980

Year	Argentina	Brazil	Chile	Colombia	Mexico	Peru	Venezuela
1940	n.a.	n.a.	n.a.	n.a.	0.072	n.a.	n.a.
1941	0.114	n.a.	0.085	n.a.	0.075	n.a.	n.a.
1942	n.a.	n.a.	0.045	n.a.	0.072	n.a.	n.a.
1943	0.130	n.a.	0.047	n.a.	0.072	n.a.	n.a.
1944	0.125	n.a.	0.054	n.a.	0.064	n.a.	n.a.
1945	0.145	n.a.	0.036	n.a.	0.065	n.a.	n.a.
1946	0.144	n.a.	0.071	n.a.	0.063	n.a.	n.a.
1947	0.154	0.142	0.029	n.a.	0.074	n.a.	n.a.
1948	0.192	0.119	0.101	n.a.	0.087	n.a.	n.a.
1949	0.201	0.124	0.074	n.a.	0.099	n.a.	n.a.
1950	0.175	0.122	0.076	0.110	0.081	0.115	0.230
1951	0.168	0.140	0.073	0.099	0.095	0.159	0.211
1952	0.169	0.127	0.056	0.099	0.113	0.148	0.248
1953	0.159	0.133	0.047	0.088	0.109	0.125	0.249
1954	0.160	0.137	0.055	0.105	0.103	0.128	0.261
1955	0.166	0.112	0.062	0.108	0.102	0.161	0.217
1956	0.161	0.120	0.051	0.112	0.116	0.146	0.201
1957	0.156	0.115	n.a.	0.137	0.117	0.147	0.146
1958	0.167	0.135	n.a.	0.136	0.113	0.117	0.177
1959	0.140	0.157	n.a.	0.131	0.117	0.070	0.183
1960	0.166	0.148	0.101	0.133	0.123	0.096	0.149
1961	0.178	0.150	0.103	0.142	0.116	0.108	0.136
1962	0.159	0.149	0.104	0.123	0.116	0.115	0.131
1963	0.135	0.157	0.120	0.119	0.132	0.105	0.122
1964	0.133	0.152	0.115	0.107	0.136	0.094	0.150
1965	0.147	0.136	0.115	0.121	0.140	0.119	0.140
1966	0.148	0.139	0.114	0.143	0.147	0.105	0.115
1967	0.152	0.128	0.105	0.123	0.159	0.076	0.100
1968	0.161	0.165	0.095	0.140	0.157	0.084	0.157
1969	0.177	0.169	0.100	0.133	0.161	0.089	0.165
1970	0.182	0.225	0.093	0.075	0.162	0.092	0.147
1971	0.175	0.228	0.090	0.113	0.158	0.091	0.151
1972	0.166	0.226	0.083	0.090	0.160	0.089	0.164
1973	0.144	0.236	0.092	0.115	n.a.	0.116	0.170
1974	0.181	0.287	0.151	0.122	n.a.	0.128	n.a.
1975	0.234	0.221	0.115	0.112	n.a.	0.130	n.a.
1976	0.268	0.277	0.085	0.116	n.a.	0.138	n.a.
1977	0.264	0.266	0.082	0.112	n.a.	0.130	n.a.
1978	0.242	0.255	0.089	0.116	n.a.	0.107	n.a.
1979	0.252	0.230	0.098	0.117	n.a.	0.109	n.a.
1980	0.240	0.221	0.109	0.122	n.a.	0.110	n.a.

n.a. = not available.
SOURCES: Tables E1–E7.

TABLE E9 Share of Capital Income in GDP, 1940–1985 (percentage)

Year	Argentina	Brazil	Chile	Colombia	Mexico	Peru	Venezuela
1940	58.0	n.a.	52.9	n.a.	n.a.	n.a.	n.a.
1941	n.a.	n.a.	n.a.	n.a.	n.a.	n.a.	n.a.
1942	n.a.	n.a.	n.a.	n.a.	n.a.	n.a.	n.a.
1943	n.a.	n.a.	n.a.	n.a.	n.a.	n.a.	n.a.
1944	n.a.	n.a.	n.a.	n.a.	n.a.	n.a.	n.a.
1945	57.7	47.2	n.a.	n.a.	n.a.	n.a.	n.a.
1946	n.a.	n.a.	n.a.	n.a.	n.a.	n.a.	n.a.
1947	55.9	47.4	48.7	n.a.	74.9	n.a.	n.a.
1948	52.2	47.5	52.4	n.a.	73.3	n.a.	n.a.
1949	46.6	48.1	50.9	n.a.	72.4	n.a.	n.a.
1950	50.3	49.1	53.5	64.0	73.8	63.8	52.0
1951	52.6	49.2	47.9	63.8	75.7	n.a.	53.9
1952	50.2	45.8	40.8	64.5	73.9	n.a.	55.9
1953	50.3	45.6	n.a.	63.8	72.4	69.2	53.6
1954	49.2	45.3	n.a.	64.5	71.4	70.6	54.3
1955	52.3	44.3	n.a.	62.8	72.1	70.7	55.7
1956	54.7	42.6	n.a.	64.4	68.7	70.7	56.9
1957	56.2	42.2	n.a.	65.3	72.1	69.0	60.1
1958	55.6	43.6	n.a.	64.7	69.7	68.5	55.8
1959	62.3	44.2	n.a.	64.4	68.9	67.5	51.4
1960	62.0	42.6	56.7	63.3	67.5	67.9	50.0
1961	59.2	41.0	54.8	62.1	68.0	66.9	50.2
1962	60.2	41.4	55.8	60.5	67.0	67.6	52.0
1963	61.0	42.2	58.1	59.8	66.6	66.3	50.5
1964	61.1	42.1	58.4	61.7	67.9	66.1	54.7
1965	59.3	41.4	55.2	60.8	67.0	63.4	54.4
1966	56.3	43.5	54.2	60.6	66.2	66.4	53.9
1967	54.5	42.3	54.4	59.6	65.7	65.3	52.6
1968	55.6	42.8	51.1	60.5	66.0	65.7	58.8
1969	56.7	42.8	51.9	58.9	65.5	60.6	57.3
1970	54.2	59.2	50.1	58.9	65.5	62.1	57.4
1971	53.5	n.a.	n.a.	58.9	65.3	60.6	57.6
1972	57.3	n.a.	n.a.	60.0	65.9	58.0	58.0
1973	53.1	n.a.	n.a.	62.3	60.7	58.3	61.1
1974	55.3	n.a.	55.9	63.7	60.9	61.2	n.a.
1975	56.6	61.6	54.7	59.0	58.5	56.5	59.7
1976	72.1	n.a.	55.6	65.3	55.7	60.4	58.7
1977	73.2	n.a.	54.0	65.0	58.9	61.6	57.7
1978	70.4	n.a.	55.3	63.4	n.a.	65.1	54.5
1979	67.8	n.a.	56.8	n.a.	n.a.	68.2	58.1
1980	62.9	62.1	56.6	53.8	61.0	67.2	57.3
1981	n.a.	n.a.	52.8	n.a.	n.a.	65.9	56.8

(continued on following page)

TABLE E9 (continued)

Year	Argentina	Brazil	Chile	Colombia	Mexico	Peru	Venezuela
1982	n.a.	n.a.	52.0	52.8	n.a.	64.9	55.8
1983	n.a.	n.a.	n.a.	52.2	68.3	64.1	54.2
1984	n.a.	n.a.	n.a.	52.2	68.8	67.5	60.8
1985	n.a.	n.a.	n.a.	54.7	68.4	71.8	58.2

n.a. = not available.
SOURCES: *Argentina*: Banco Central de la República Argentina (1975); *Brazil*: Fundação Getúlio Vargas (1973); Fundação Instituto Brasileiro de Geografia e Estatística (1974); Langoni (1970, 1973); *Chile*: Oficina de Planficación Nacional (1973); *Colombia*: Banco de la República (1973); Berry (N.d., 1972); Economic Commission for Latin America (1967); *Mexico*: Banco de México (1969, 1975); Nacional Financiera (1969); *Peru*: Banco Central de la Reserva (1961); Figueroa (1972); Webb (1973).

TABLE E10 Employment, Population, and Labor Force Participation Rate in Argentina and Brazil, 1940–1985

	Argentina			Brazil		
Year	Employment (thousands of people)	Population (thousands of people)	Labor force participation rate (%)	Employment (thousands of people)	Population (thousands of people)	Labor force participation rate (%)
1940	n.a.	14,169	n.a.	13,969	41,114	34.0
1941	n.a.	14,401	n.a.	n.a.	42,069	n.a.
1942	n.a.	14,637	n.a.	n.a.	43,069	n.a.
1943	n.a.	14,877	n.a.	n.a.	44,093	n.a.
1944	3,969	15,130	26.2	n.a.	45,141	n.a.
1945	4,247	15,390	27.6	n.a.	46,215	n.a.
1946	4,659	15,654	29.8	n.a.	47,313	n.a.
1947	4,737	15,929	29.7	n.a.	48,411	n.a.
1948	4,861	16,264	29.9	n.a.	49,571	n.a.
1949	4,966	16,668	29.8	n.a.	50,758	n.a.
1950	5,066	17,093	29.6	17,117	51,973	32.9
1951	5,290	17,514	30.2	17,603	53,528	32.9
1952	5,080	17,893	28.4	18,103	55,129	32.8
1953	5,278	18,228	29.0	18,618	56,777	32.8
1954	5,327	19,559	28.7	19,147	58,475	32.7
1955	5,414	18,900	28.6	19,691	60,224	32.7

(continued on following page)

TABLE E10 (continued)

Year	Argentina Employment (thousands of people)	Argentina Population (thousands of people)	Argentina Labor force participation rate (%)	Brazil Employment (thousands of people)	Brazil Population (thousands of people)	Brazil Labor force participation rate (%)
1956	5,470	19,249	28.4	20,250	62,025	32.6
1957	5,605	19,606	28.6	20,852	63,880	32.6
1958	5,753	19,963	28.8	21,417	65,791	32.6
1959	5,624	20,317	27.7	22,025	67,810	32.5
1960	5,633	20,666	27.3	22,651	69,797	33.4
1961	5,676	21,020	27.0	23,593	71,811	32.9
1962	5,558	21,377	26.0	24,574	73,883	33.3
1963	5,469	21,737	25.2	25,596	76,015	33.7
1964	5,689	22,103	25.7	26,660	78,208	34.1
1965	5,889	22,475	26.2	27,768	80,465	34.5
1966	5,918	22,655	26.1	28,923	82,787	34.9
1967	6,144	22,836	26.9	30,125	85,176	35.4
1968	6,245	23,019	27.1	31,378	87,633	35.8
1969	6,557	23,203	28.3	30,437	90,162	33.8
1970	6,752	23,364	28.9	29,545	92,764	31.8
1971	6,855	23,569	29.1	31,429	95,435	32.9
1972	7,071	24,392	29.0	31,539	98,184	32.1

(continued on following page)

TABLE E10 (continued)

Year	Argentina Employment (thousands of people)	Argentina Population (thousands of people)	Argentina Labor force participation rate (%)	Brazil Employment (thousands of people)	Brazil Population (thousands of people)	Brazil Labor force participation rate (%)
1973	7,364	24,719	29.8	33,566	100,258	33.5
1974	7,644	25,050	30.5	35,303	102,749	34.4
1975	7,866	25,376	31.0	37,173	105,303	35.3
1976	7,858	25,706	30.6	40,237	107,920	37.3
1977	7,818	26,040	30.0	41,215	110,602	37.3
1978	7,670	26,378	29.1	42,587	113,351	37.6
1979	7,716	26,729	28.9	44,315	116,168	38.1
1980	7,806	27,900	28.0	45,459	119,056	38.2
1981	7,877	28,319	27.8	43,041	122,020	35.3
1982	7,950	28,743	27.7	40,929	125,059	32.7
1983	8,023	29,232	27.4	37,742	128,173	29.4
1984	8,151	29,700	27.4	n.a.	131,121	n.a.
1985	8,288	30,115	27.5	n.a.	134,268	n.a.

n.a. = not available.
SOURCES: *Argentina*: Ceballos (1985/1986); Gayer (1986); *Brazil*: Cuca-Tolosa (1972); Kogut (1972). *General sources for Tables E10–E13*: Gayer (1986); International Labor Organization (1971); United Nations (1972).

212

TABLE E11 Employment, Population, and Labor Force Participation Rate in Chile and Colombia, 1940–1985

Year	Chile			Colombia		
	Employment (thousands of people)	Population (thousands of people)	Labor force participation rate (%)	Employment (thousands of people)	Population (thousands of people)	Labor force participation rate (%)
1940	1,605	5,089	31.5	n.a.	9,094	n.a.
1941	1,637	5,178	31.6	n.a.	9,288	n.a.
1942	1,667	5,269	31.6	n.a.	9,486	n.a.
1943	1,703	5,361	31.8	n.a.	9,688	n.a.
1944	1,735	5,455	31.8	n.a.	9,895	n.a.
1945	1,771	5,556	31.9	n.a.	10,106	n.a.
1946	1,804	5,664	31.9	n.a.	10,542	n.a.
1947	1,842	5,774	31.9	n.a.	10,542	n.a.
1948	1,882	5,887	32.0	n.a.	10,767	n.a.
1949	1,916	6,001	31.9	n.a.	10,997	n.a.
1950	1,957	6,120	32.0	3,513	11,244	31.2
1951	1,994	6,242	31.9	3,630	11,615	31.3
1952	2,035	6,365	32.0	3,727	11,986	31.1
1953	2,086	6,511	32.0	3,829	12,369	31.0
1954	2,138	6,661	32.1	3,933	12,765	30.8
1955	2,198	6,823	32.2	4,040	13,172	30.7
1956	2,257	6,929	32.6	4,150	13,593	30.5

(continued on following page)

TABLE E11 (continued)

	Chile			Colombia		
Year	Employment (thousands of people)	Population (thousands of people)	Labor force participation rate (%)	Employment (thousands of people)	Population (thousands of people)	Labor force participation rate (%)
1957	2,321	7,037	33.0	4,262	14,028	30.4
1958	2,379	7,147	33.3	4,378	14,476	30.2
1959	2,440	7,258	33.6	4,496	14,938	30.1
1960	2,494	7,375	33.8	4,616	15,416	29.9
1961	2,549	7,602	33.5	4,739	15,908	29.8
1962	2,605	7,781	33.5	4,868	16,417	29.7
1963	2,663	7,834	34.0	4,999	16,941	29.5
1964	2,723	7,922	34.4	5,134	17,485	29.4
1965	2,783	7,987	34.8	5,337	17,975	29.7
1966	2,843	8,174	34.8	5,396	18,478	29.2
1967	2,888	8,340	34.6	5,611	18,995	29.5
1968	2,901	8,506	34.1	5,772	19,527	29.6
1969	2,961	8,672	34.1	6,000	20,074	29.9
1970	3,011	8,853	34.0	6,239	20,636	30.2
1971	2,967	9,012	32.9	6,438	21,214	30.3
1972	2,980	9,174	32.5	6,725	21,808	30.8

(continued on following page)

TABLE E11 (continued)

Year	Chile Employment (thousands of people)	Chile Population (thousands of people)	Chile Labor force participation rate (%)	Colombia Employment (thousands of people)	Colombia Population (thousands of people)	Colombia Labor force participation rate (%)
1973	n.a.	9,351	n.a.	7,032	22,571	31.2
1974	n.a.	9,510	n.a.	7,353	23,032	33.4
1975	3,115	9,672	32.2	7,675	23,502	32.7
1976	3,182	9,836	32.4	8,061	23,968	33.6
1977	3,199	10,003	32.0	8,448	24,434	34.6
1978	3,477	10,173	34.2	8,845	24,906	35.5
1979	3,478	10,346	33.6	9,431	25,376	37.2
1980	3,636	10,522	34.6	9,905	25,892	38.3
1981	3,688	10,701	34.5	10,054	26,426	38.0
1982	3,504	10,883	32.2	9,449	26,965	35.0
1983	3,598	11,068	32.5	10,163	27,503	37.0
1984	3,843	11,256	34.1	10,182	28,108	36.2
1985	4,061	11,448	35.5	11,481	28,726	40.0

n.a. = not available.
SOURCES: *Chile*: Ballesteros (1963); Centro Latinoamericano de Demografía (1969); Corbo (1974); Harberger and Selowsky (1966); Instituto de Organización y Racionalización Administrativa (1961); Meller and Rahilly (1974); Programa Regional del Empleo para América Latina y el Caribe (1982); Rosende (1988); Selowsky (1967); Valdés (1971); *Colombia*: Berry (1973). See also Table E10.

TABLE E12 Employment, Population, and Labor Force Participation Rate in Mexico and Peru, 1940–1985

	Mexico			Peru		
Year	Employment (thousands of people)	Population (thousands of people)	Labor force participation rate (%)	Employment (thousands of people)	Population (thousands of people)	Labor force participation rate (%)
1940	5,858	19,654	29.8	n.a.	7,033	n.a.
1941	5,954	20,332	29.2	n.a.	7,195	n.a.
1942	6,098	20,866	29.2	2,035	7,370	27.6
1943	6,246	21,418	29.2	2,070	7,509	27.6
1944	6,396	21,988	29.1	2,124	7,655	27.7
1945	6,492	22,576	28.8	2,161	7,802	27.7
1946	6,706	23,183	28.9	2,199	7,954	27.6
1947	6,870	23,811	28.9	2,258	8,111	27.8
1948	7,033	24,461	28.8	2,317	8,302	27.9
1949	7,200	25,132	28.6	2,372	8,486	28.0
1950	7,376	25,791	28.6	2,431	8,674	28.0
1951	7,593	26,544	28.6	2,478	8,838	28.0
1952	7,668	27,257	28.1	2,508	8,950	28.0
1953	8,024	28,956	28.6	2,558	9,126	28.0
1954	8,252	28,853	28.6	2,609	9,305	28.0
1955	8,310	29,679	28.0	2,668	9,519	28.0
1956	8,529	30,538	27.9	2,744	9,652	28.4
1957	8,738	31,426	27.8	2,862	9,787	29.2

(continued on following page)

TABLE E12 (continued)

Year	Mexico Employment (thousands of people)	Mexico Population (thousands of people)	Mexico Labor force participation rate (%)	Peru Employment (thousands of people)	Peru Population (thousands of people)	Peru Labor force participation rate (%)
1958	8,952	32,348	27.7	3,039	9,984	30.6
1959	9,171	33,304	27.5	3,147	10,063	31.3
1960	9,569	34,923	27.4	3,162	10,204	31.0
1961	9,527	36,091	26.4	3,227	10,320	31.3
1962	9,662	37,233	26.0	3,344	10,632	31.5
1963	10,334	39,642	26.1	3,443	10,958	31.4
1964	10,981	41,300	26.6	3,546	11,298	31.4
1965	11,746	42,700	27.5	3,655	11,650	31.4
1966	11,521	44,100	26.1	3,720	12,012	31.0
1967	11,540	45,700	25.3	3,886	12,385	31.4
1968	12,066	47,300	25.5	3,927	12,772	30.7
1969	12,297	48,900	25.1	4,057	13,172	30.8
1970	12,955	50,600	25.6	4,189	13,586	30.8
1971	13,338	52,371	25.5	4,291	14,015	30.6
1972	13,738	54,204	25.3	4,398	14,460	30.4
1973	15,924	55,218	28.8	4,529	14,628	31.0
1974	14,154	56,814	24.9	4,666	15,044	31.0

(continued on following page)

TABLE E12 (continued)

Year	Mexico			Peru		
	Employment (thousands of people)	Population (thousands of people)	Labor force participation rate (%)	Employment (thousands of people)	Population (thousands of people)	Labor force participation rate (%)
1975	15,448	58,456	26.4	4,809	15,470	31.1
1976	15,810	60,146	26.3	4,958	15,908	31.2
1977	14,341	61,883	23.2	5,113	16,358	31.3
1978	14,990	63,672	23.5	5,274	16,819	31.4
1979	16,318	65,512	24.9	5,441	17,293	31.5
1980	18,484	67,396	27.4	5,718	17,743	32.2
1981	21,505	69,057	31.1	n.a.	18,204	n.a.
1982	20,668	70,783	29.2	n.a.	18,677	n.a.
1983	19,118	72,553	26.4	n.a.	19,163	n.a.
1984	20,717	74,286	27.9	n.a.	19,661	n.a.
1985	21,601	76,025	28.4	6,676	20,172	33.1

n.a. = not available.
SOURCES: *Mexico*: García Rocha (1970); Morelos (1972); Selowsky (1967); *Peru*: Organization for Economic Cooperation and Development (1967); Oficina Nacional de Estadísticas y Censos (1971); Servicio del Empleo y Recursos Humanos (1965); Thorbecke and Stoutjesdijk (1971). See also Table E10.

TABLE E13 Employment, Population, and Labor Force Participation Rate in Venezuela, 1940–1985

	Venezuela		
Year	Employment (thousands of people)	Population (thousands of people)	Labor force participation rate (%)
1940	n.a.	3,710	n.a.
1941	n.a.	3,851	n.a.
1942	n.a.	3,932	n.a.
1943	n.a.	4,048	n.a.
1944	n.a.	4,167	n.a.
1945	n.a.	4,290	n.a.
1946	n.a.	4,417	n.a.
1947	n.a.	4,547	n.a.
1948	n.a.	4,681	n.a.
1949	n.a.	4,819	n.a.
1950	1,600	4,974	32.2
1951	1,651	5,179	31.9
1952	1,734	5,422	32.0
1953	1,796	5,665	31.7
1954	1,873	5,908	31.7
1955	1,924	6,150	31.3
1956	2,020	6,393	31.6
1957	2,108	6,636	31.8
1958	2,143	6,879	31.2
1959	2,273	7,122	31.9
1960	2,300	7,364	30.1
1961	2,344	7,612	30.8
1962	2,424	7,872	30.8
1963	2,507	8,144	30.8
1964	2,622	8,427	31.1
1965	2,719	8,725	31.2
1966	2,795	9,030	31.0
1967	2,852	9,352	30.5
1968	2,948	9,622	30.6
1969	3,081	9,944	31.0
1970	3,213	10,275	30.0
1971	3,307	10,612	31.2
1972	3,381	10,939	30.9
1973	3,500	11,280	31.0
1974	3,622	11,632	31.1
1975	3,831	n.a.	n.a.
1976	4,226	n.a.	n.a.
1977	4,373	n.a.	n.a.

(*continued on following page*)

TABLE E13 (continued)

| | Venezuela | | |
Year	Employment (thousands of people)	Population (thousands of people)	Labor force participation rate (%)
1978	4,383	n.a.	n.a.
1979	4,782	n.a.	n.a.
1980	4,601	n.a.	n.a.
1981	4,982	n.a.	n.a.
1982	4,968	16,060	30.9
1983	4,964	16,501	30.1
1984	4,953	16,966	29.2
1985	5,201	17,324	30.0

n.a. = not available.
SOURCES: International Labor Organization (1971); United Nations (1972). See also Table E10.

TABLE E14 Stock of Fixed Capital, 1940–1985

Year	Argentina (millions of 1960 pesos ley)	Brazil (millions of 1953 new C)	Chile (millions of 1960 E)	Colombia (millions of 1958 pesos)	Mexico (millions of 1960 pesos)	Peru (millions of 1960 soles)	Venezuela (millions of 1957 bolivars)
1940	12,387	n.a.	4,654	21,000	121,481	n.a.	n.a.
1941	12,336	n.a.	4,650	21,573	120,423	n.a.	n.a.
1942	12,218	n.a.	4,600	21,890	119,056	31,742	n.a.
1943	12,080	n.a.	4,565	22,285	118,079	31,889	n.a.
1944	12,044	n.a.	4,557	22,808	117,807	32,493	n.a.
1945	12,046	n.a.	4,561	23,759	118,794	33,525	n.a.
1946	12,338	n.a.	4,654	25,074	121,685	37,207	n.a.
1947	13,156	n.a.	4,637	26,877	126,304	41,271	n.a.
1948	13,950	803	4,808	28,498	131,049	42,840	n.a.
1949	14,487	814	4,964	29,257	135,823	46,617	n.a.
1950	14,793	830	5,117	30,274	141,083	51,256	26,523
1951	15,335	863	5,260	31,211	150,830	59,249	28,402
1952	15,690	896	5,366	32,303	160,098	67,010	31,055
1953	16,022	914	5,496	34,377	166,534	73,649	33,975
1954	16,274	937	5,607	36,984	173,905	79,601	37,402
1955	16,697	954	5,774	39,701	182,113	86,458	40,318
1956	17,116	976	5,911	42,003	193,749	94,198	43,495

(continued on following page)

221

TABLE E14 (continued)

Year	Argentina (millions of 1960 pesos ley)	Brazil (millions of 1953 new C)	Chile (millions of 1960 E)	Colombia (millions of 1958 pesos)	Mexico (millions of 1960 pesos)	Peru (millions of 1960 soles)	Venezuela (millions of 1957 bolivars)
1957	17,609	1,007	6,232	42,995	205,192	102,019	46,835
1958	18,217	1,042	6,337	43,754	215,130	107,706	49,920
1959	18,411	1,087	6,370	44,717	225,021	109,323	52,990
1960	19,300	1,133	6,630	46,260	237,026	112,305	54,535
1961	20,441	1,183	6,995	48,069	248,897	117,678	55,281
1962	21,273	1,233	7,362	49,787	260,661	124,689	56,160
1963	21,652	1,276	7,770	51,034	275,466	130,784	57,161
1964	22,099	1,320	8,124	52,736	295,378	136,023	58,909
1965	22,742	1,358	8,494	54,071	315,715	143,556	60,985
1966	23,390	1,418	8,853	55,687	337,642	152,447	63,007
1967	24,121	1,476	9,204	57,529	363,599	158,938	64,946
1968	25,113	1,563	9,602	60,035	391,847	163,162	69,207
1969	26,373	1,666	10,024	62,540	422,382	167,260	73,859
1970	27,944	1,900	10,490	65,698	455,049	172,605	77,420
1971	29,467	2,184	10,874	69,142	484,677	177,772	82,310
1972	30,999	2,508	11,211	72,270	520,553	183,641	88,542
1973	32,239	2,894	11,417	76,122	561,531	196,638	95,920
1974	33,705	3,373	11,735	80,019	609,825	215,916	101,839
1975	34,982	3,873	11,876	83,720	662,125	236,484	108,379
1976	36,283	4,403	11,930	87,454	707,178	250,497	116,615

(continued on following page)

222

TABLE E14 (continued)

Year	Argentina (millions of 1960 pesos ley)	Brazil (millions of 1953 new C)	Chile (millions of 1960 E)	Colombia (millions of 1958 pesos)	Mexico (millions of 1960 pesos)	Peru (millions of 1960 soles)	Venezuela (millions of 1957 bolivars)
1977	38,106	4,888	12,057	91,415	747,382	258,415	128,946
1978	39,420	5,386	12,277	96,273	798,047	261,281	142,582
1979	41,155	5,888	12,596	101,102	865,515	266,389	151,510
1980	42,886	6,505	13,072	107,129	946,426	276,156	156,924
1981	44,118	6,736	13,595	113,171	1,042,275	289,597	162,876
1982	44,334	7,055	13,656	119,101	1,106,795	301,343	168,297
1983	44,485	7,224	13,603	124,825	1,129,997	302,972	169,041
1984	44,288	7,406	13,609	130,365	1,157,805	303,086	167,695
1985	43,326	7,650	13,717	134,894	1,192,057	301,220	167,069

n.a. = not available.

SOURCES: *Argentina*: Banco Central de la República Argentina (1975, 1976); Dagnino Pastore (1966); Vázquez Presedo (1968); *Brazil*: Fundação Getúlio Vargas (1973); Gutiérrez (1981); Fundação Instituto Brasileiro de Geografia e Estatística (1970, 1984); Langoni (1970); *Chile*: Davis (1966); Garcés Voisenat (1983); Harberger and Selowsky (1966); Oficina de Planificación Nacional (1973, 1981); Selowsky (1967); Valdés (1971); *Colombia*: Banco de la República (1973); Departamento Administrativo Nacional de Estadística (1985); Harberger (1969); *Mexico*: Banco de México (1969); Banco Nacional de México (1981); Cossio and Izquierdo (1962); Davis (1967); Nacional Financiera (1969); Reynolds (1970); Selowsky (1967); *Peru*: Banco Central de la Reserva (1961); Instituto Nacional de Planificación (1980); *Venezuela*: Inter-American Development Bank (1968); Rodríguez (1984); *General source*: Elías (1975c).

TABLE E15 Partial Productivity of Labor, 1940–1985 (1960 U.S. dollars per worker per year)

Year	Argentina	Brazil	Chile	Colombia	Mexico	Peru	Venezuela
1940	1,573	437	1,273	621	565	n.a.	n.a.
1941	n.a.	n.a.	1,240	n.a.	650	n.a.	n.a.
1942	n.a.	n.a.	1,269	n.a.	719	502	n.a.
1943	n.a.	n.a.	1,270	n.a.	754	509	n.a.
1944	1,808	n.a.	1,265	n.a.	723	551	n.a.
1945	1,669	n.a.	1,347	n.a.	796	595	n.a.
1946	1,680	n.a.	1,405	n.a.	798	653	n.a.
1947	1,936	n.a.	1,290	n.a.	794	609	n.a.
1948	1,937	n.a.	1,420	n.a.	821	590	n.a.
1949	1,851	n.a.	1,390	n.a.	841	573	n.a.
1950	1,793	612	1,440	752	943	591	2,319
1951	1,786	630	1,486	750	980	622	2,509
1952	1,767	666	1,553	777	1,003	647	2,563
1953	1,796	664	1,607	802	1,005	672	2,628
1954	1,849	711	1,560	835	1,028	663	2,762
1955	1,950	739	1,540	845	1,098	688	2,928
1956	1,985	741	1,517	855	1,129	694	3,083
1957	2,039	778	1,592	852	1,183	667	3,298
1958	2,104	815	1,579	849	1,204	640	3,287
1959	2,015	837	1,540	887	1,221	591	3,343
1960	2,171	893	1,590	901	1,258	666	3,377
1961	2,308	946	1,652	922	1,326	707	3,377
1962	2,319	956	1,697	946	1,369	744	3,456
1963	2,301	932	1,739	952	1,382	749	3,467

(continued on following page)

TABLE E15 (continued)

Year	Argentina	Brazil	Chile	Colombia	Mexico	Peru	Venezuela
1964	2,439	921	1,772	984	1,453	773	3,594
1965	2,573	908	1,820	980	1,446	786	3,647
1966	2,576	916	1,907	1,022	1,576	819	3,628
1967	2,550	922	1,921	1,024	1,672	801	3,733
1968	2,595	967	1,968	1,056	1,730	816	3,803
1969	2,702	1,087	2,039	1,081	1,805	810	3,767
1970	2,765	1,226	2,168	1,109	1,831	842	3,688
1971	2,854	1,305	2,318	1,134	1,840	871	3,709
1972	2,853	1,459	2,289	1,162	1,916	901	3,766
1973	2,907	1,583	2,263	1,192	1,779	928	3,818
1974	2,972	1,636	2,509	1,204	2,119	960	3,857
1975	2,863	1,664	2,077	1,219	2,021	974	3,862
1976	2,817	1,715	2,120	1,209	2,017	963	3,795
1977	2,971	1,780	2,316	1,209	2,296	934	3,918
1978	2,925	1,818	2,306	1,261	2,357	899	4,033
1979	3,153	1,869	2,496	1,237	2,338	901	3,725
1980	3,150	1,966	2,555	1,225	2,217	890	3,808
1981	2,927	2,044	2,654	1,237	2,057	n.a.	3,506
1982	2,749	2,169	2,383	1,330	2,129	n.a.	3,540
1983	2,808	2,278	n.a.	1,260	2,219	n.a.	3,344
1984	2,820	n.a.	n.a.	1,303	2,121	n.a.	3,306
1985	2,652	1,865	2,157	1,185	2,034	749	3,157

n.a. = not available.
SOURCES: Tables E1–E7 and E10–E13.

225

TABLE E16 Partial Productivity of Capital, 1940–1985 (percentage per year)

Year	Argentina	Brazil	Chile	Colombia	Mexico	Peru	Venezuela
1940	39.03	n.a.	46.06	47.08	34.05	n.a.	n.a.
1941	40.59	n.a.	45.77	46.60	40.15	n.a.	n.a.
1942	43.07	n.a.	48.23	46.02	46.02	86.89	n.a.
1943	43.26	n.a.	49.71	45.39	49.86	89.25	n.a.
1944	49.34	n.a.	50.54	47.34	49.04	97.37	n.a.
1945	48.72	n.a.	54.88	47.59	54.39	103.60	n.a.
1946	52.53	n.a.	57.13	51.33	54.99	104.30	n.a.
1947	57.71	n.a.	53.74	49.76	53.99	89.98	n.a.
1948	55.89	37.40	58.32	48.38	55.07	86.28	n.a.
1949	52.55	39.34	56.28	49.73	55.73	78.83	n.a.
1950	50.83	41.09	57.76	48.94	61.66	75.74	45.04
1951	51.00	41.86	59.09	48.95	61.66	70.36	46.96
1952	47.37	43.83	61.77	50.28	60.06	65.45	46.08
1953	49.00	44.05	63.98	50.12	60.53	63.04	44.72
1954	50.11	47.31	62.42	49.81	61.00	58.73	44.54
1955	52.36	49.65	61.46	48.21	62.62	57.35	44.99
1956	52.53	50.07	60.76	47.42	62.15	54.63	46.10
1957	53.73	52.44	62.20	47.36	62.96	50.55	47.79
1958	55.02	54.58	62.19	47.68	62.62	48.82	45.43
1959	50.96	55.25	61.86	50.03	62.20	46.00	46.17
1960	52.46	58.14	62.75	50.42	63.50	50.67	45.85
1961	53.06	61.42	63.15	50.99	63.44	52.35	46.10
1962	50.16	62.03	63.00	51.90	63.41	53.89	48.02
1963	48.12	60.86	62.51	52.29	64.80	53.26	48.96
1964	51.98	60.55	62.29	53.73	67.53	54.46	51.50

(continued on following page)

226

TABLE E16 (continued)

Year	Argentina	Brazil	Chile	Colombia	Mexico	Peru	Venezuela
1965	55.16	60.47	62.55	54.29	67.25	54.04	52.35
1966	53.98	60.87	64.24	55.53	67.22	53.99	51.82
1967	53.78	61.27	63.24	56.02	66.34	52.92	52.78
1968	53.42	63.25	62.38	56.96	66.58	53.10	52.15
1969	55.62	64.68	63.19	58.16	65.70	53.06	50.59
1970	55.32	62.11	65.29	59.10	65.16	55.24	49.28
1971	54.97	60.13	66.34	59.24	63.28	56.83	47.97
1972	53.89	57.81	63.82	60.66	63.21	58.32	46.30
1973	54.98	56.88	62.72	61.76	63.05	57.73	44.85
1974	55.81	52.21	63.71	62.07	61.49	56.05	44.16
1975	53.30	47.93	57.15	62.71	58.95	53.49	43.95
1976	50.52	46.26	59.32	62.54	56.36	51.52	44.28
1977	50.47	44.07	64.49	62.68	55.07	49.92	42.78
1978	47.12	41.99	68.51	65.02	55.34	49.04	39.91
1979	48.95	40.87	72.31	64.72	55.10	49.72	37.85
1980	47.48	39.66	74.56	63.56	54.12	49.81	35.94
1981	43.27	37.70	75.53	61.67	53.05	49.34	34.53
1982	40.82	36.33	64.14	59.19	49.68	47.59	33.64
1983	41.93	34.36	62.69	57.55	46.94	41.49	31.61
1984	42.98	35.12	66.42	57.08	47.44	43.46	31.43
1985	42.00	36.79	67.47	56.60	47.26	44.83	31.64

n.a. = not available.
SOURCES: Tables E1–E7 and E14.

TABLE E17 Index of Real Monthly Wages in Selected Years, 1940–1980 (1960 = 100)

Year	Argentina	Brazil	Chile	Colombia	Mexico	Peru	Venezuela
1940	82.9	49.2	n.a.	75.3	80.2	n.a.	n.a.
1950	111.1	51.8	n.a.	68.0	66.8	n.a.	n.a.
1960	100.0	100.0	100.0	100.0	100.0	100.0	100.0
1970	150.1	52.8	140.0	106.3	170.3	139.5	88.4
1980	157.8	46.2	100.0	130.7	170.8	106.0	64.2

n.a. = not available.
SOURCES: See Tables E10–E13.

TABLE E18 Real Gross Rate of Return to Fixed Capital, 1940–1985 (annual percentage)

Year	Argentina	Brazil	Chile	Colombia	Mexico	Peru	Venezuela
1940	22.62	n.a.	24.33	n.a.	n.a.	n.a.	n.a.
1945	28.10	n.a.	n.a.	n.a.	n.a.	n.a.	n.a.
1946	n.a.	n.a.	n.a.	n.a.	n.a.	n.a.	n.a.
1947	32.25	n.a.	26.15	n.a.	40.44	n.a.	n.a.
1948	29.17	17.77	30.55	n.a.	40.37	n.a.	n.a.
1949	24.49	18.90	28.65	n.a.	40.33	n.a.	n.a.
1950	25.55	20.13	30.90	31.30	45.50	48.30	23.40
1951	26.83	20.57	28.30	31.23	46.68	n.a.	25.31
1952	23.79	20.06	25.17	32.43	44.38	n.a.	25.71
1953	24.65	20.06	31.98	43.82	43.82	43.60	23.96
1954	24.65	21.43	n.a.	32.12	43.55	41.44	24.16
1955	27.41	21.97	n.a.	30.27	45.15	40.51	25.05
1956	28.72	21.30	n.a.	30.53	42.66	38.60	26.23
1957	30.18	22.11	n.a.	30.92	45.39	34.88	28.72
1958	30.58	23.80	n.a.	30.85	43.64	33.43	25.33
1959	31.71	24.40	n.a.	32.20	42.85	31.05	23.73
1960	32.52	24.75	35.58	31.90	42.86	34.40	22.93
1961	31.41	25.17	34.61	31.66	43.11	35.02	23.14
1962	30.20	25.67	35.15	31.38	42.48	36.42	24.96
1963	29.34	25.68	36.31	31.27	43.16	35.30	24.72
1964	31.76	25.47	36.38	33.13	45.83	35.99	28.17
1965	32.71	25.03	34.53	33.00	45.02	34.24	28.53

(continued on following page)

TABLE E18 (continued)

Year	Argentina	Brazil	Chile	Colombia	Mexico	Peru	Venezuela
1966	30.38	26.48	34.82	33.63	44.49	35.86	27.92
1967	29.31	25.92	34.40	33.39	43.56	34.54	27.76
1968	29.70	27.07	31.87	34.46	43.89	34.88	30.63
1969	31.53	27.68	32.79	34.26	43.03	32.18	28.94
1970	29.97	36.79	32.71	34.81	42.64	34.25	28.28
1971	29.41	n.a.	n.a.	34.87	41.32	34.40	27.63
1972	30.88	n.a.	n.a.	36.40	41.65	33.82	26.85
1973	29.20	n.a.	n.a.	38.47	38.30	33.62	27.37
1974	30.86	n.a.	35.60	39.51	37.37	34.28	n.a.
1975	30.18	29.53	31.22	36.97	34.43	30.17	26.22
1976	36.44	n.a.	32.94	40.84	31.43	31.11	25.94
1977	36.97	n.a.	34.80	40.76	32.43	30.75	24.68
1978	33.18	n.a.	37.89	41.18	n.a.	31.87	21.73
1979	33.18	n.a.	41.04	n.a.	n.a.	33.38	22.00
1980	29.85	24.64	42.23	34.18	32.99	33.45	20.57
1981	n.a.	n.a.	39.83	n.a.	n.a.	32.48	19.59
1982	n.a.	n.a.	33.34	31.26	n.a.	30.82	18.22
1983	n.a.	n.a.	n.a.	30.01	32.02	26.61	19.20
1984	n.a.	n.a.	n.a.	29.77	32.62	29.32	18.27
1985	n.a.	n.a.	n.a.	30.94	32.32	32.18	18.02

n.a. = not available.
NOTE: The gross rate of return is computed by dividing the capital income on the capital stock of the end of the year.
SOURCES: Tables E1–E7 and E14.

Estimates of the Econometric Growth Model

TABLE F1 OLS Estimates of the Reduced Form for the Rates of Growth of GDP (y) and Capital (k), Argentina, Colombia, and Mexico, 1956–1980

Equation	Population (Z_2)	Energy price (Z_3)	Exchange rate (Z_4)	Real wages (Z_5)	Interest rate (Z_6)	GDP gap (Z_1)	R^2	DW
Argentina								
y	0.26	0.06	−0.05	0.15	1.45	0.56	0.41	2.05
	(0.16)	(0.89)	(0.98)	(2.01)	(2.07)	(2.58)		
k	0.27	0.02	−0.02	0.04	0.29	0.17	0.46	0.83
	(0.59)	(0.97)	(1.64)	(1.81)	(1.50)	(2.75)		
Colombia								
y	−0.12	−0.01	−0.03	−0.13	0.24	0.04	0.34	1.85
	(0.10)	(0.21)	(1.28)	(1.71)	(1.13)	(1.07)		
k	−2.90	0.01	−0.01	0.07	0.05	−0.03	0.68	2.40
	(4.24)	(1.50)	(0.87)	(1.89)	(0.49)	(1.47)		
Mexico								
y	−0.63	−0.01	−0.26	−0.23	0.20	0.02	0.86	1.03
	(0.72)	(0.08)	(1.68)	(1.41)	(0.66)	(7.29)		
k	−0.30	0.01	0.03	−0.07	−0.21	0.02	0.51	1.03
	(0.69)	(0.65)	(0.43)	(0.90)	(1.35)	(1.50)		

NOTE: Absolute value of the t-test statistics in parentheses.
SOURCE: Author.

232

REFERENCES

Abramovitz, Moses. 1956. "Resources and Output Trends in the United States since 1870." *American Economic Review* 46, no. 2 (May): 5–23.

———. 1986. "Catching Up, Forging Ahead, and Falling Behind." *Journal of Economic History*, 46 (June): 385–406.

———. 1988. "Thinking about Growth." Center for Economic Policy Research Publication no. 115. Stanford, Calif.: Stanford University.

Anderson, M. 1972. "The Planning and Development of Brazilian Agriculture: Some Quantitative Extensions." Ph.D. diss., Cornell University.

Ardito-Barletta, N. 1971. "Costs and Social Benefits of Agricultural Research in Mexico." Ph.D. diss., University of Chicago.

Arranz, Juan M., and L. R. Elías. 1984. "Ciclos de Referencia para la Economía Argentina, 1960–1982." *Estudios Técnicos*, no. 60 (July). CEMYB, Banco Central de la Argentina, Buenos Aires.

Arrow, Kenneth J. 1964. "Optimal Capital Policy, the Cost of Capital, and Myopic Decision Rules." *Annals of the Institute of Statistical Mathematics* 16: 16–30.

———. 1969. "Transmission of Technology." *American Economic Review* (May).

Baer, W. 1965. *Industrialization and Economic Development in Brazil*. Homewood, Ill.: Irwin.

Ballesteros, M. A. 1958. "Argentine Agriculture 1908–1954: A Study in Growth and Decline." Ph.D. diss., University of Chicago.

———. 1963. "The Growth of Output and Employment in Basic Sectors of the Chilean Economy 1908–57." *Economic Development and Cultural Change* (January).

Banco Central de Chile. 1975. *Boletín Mensual* 48 (October).

Banco Central de la República Argentina. 1975. *Sistema de Cuentas del Producto e Ingreso de la Argentina*. Vol. 2. Buenos Aires: Banco Central de la Argentina.

———. 1976. *Series Históricas de Cuentas Nacionales de la Argentina*. Vol. 3. Buenos Aires: Banco Central de la Argentina.

Banco Central de la Reserva. 1961. *Renta Nacional del Perú 1952–59*. Lima: Banco Central de la Reserva.

———. 1968. *Renta Nacional del Perú*. Lima: Banco Central de la Reserva.

Banco Central de Venezuela. 1974, 1975. *Informes Económicos*. Caracas: Banco Central de Venezuela.

———. 1986. *Boletín Trimestral*. (October–December).

Banco de la República. 1973. *Síntesis de las Cuentas Nacionales de Colombia, 1950–71*. Bogotá: Banco de la República.

Banco de México. 1969. *Cuentas Nacionales y Acervos de Capital, Consolidados y por Tipo de Actividad Económica, 1950–67*. Mexico City: Banco de México.

———. 1975. *Informe Anual 1974*. Mexico City: Banco de México.

Banco Nacional de México. 1981. *México en Cifras, 1970–1980*. Mexico City: Banco Nacional de México.

Barger, H. 1969. "Growth in Developed Nations." *Review of Economics and Statistics* 51 (May): 143–48.

Baumol, William. 1985. "Productivity Growth, Convergence and Welfare." *American Economic Review* 76 (December): 1072–85.

Becker, Gary. 1988. "Family Economics and Macro Behavior." *American Economic Review* 78 (March): 1–13.

Berglas, Eitan, and Ronald Jones. 1977. "The Export of Technology." Carnegie-Rochester Conference Series on Public Policy, vol. 7, Supplement to the *Journal of Monetary Economics*.

Bergson, A. 1974. "Soviet Post-War Economic Development." *Wicksell Lectures 1974*. Stockholm: Almqvist and Wicksell.

Berry, R. A. 1972. "Some Determinants of Changing Income Distribution in Colombia, 1930–70." Discussion Paper 137. New Haven, Conn.: Yale University, Economic Growth Center.

———. 1973. "Patterns and Trends in the Utilization of the Labor Force in Colombia." Department of Economics, University of Western Ontario. Mimeo.

———. N.d. "Changing Income Distribution under Development: Colombia." Department of Economics, University of Western Ontario. Mimeo.

Blau, David M. 1987. "A Time-Series Analysis of Self-Employment in the U.S." *Journal of Political Economy* 95, no. 3 (June): 445–67.

Boatler, R. W. 1976. "Trade Theory Predictions and the Growth of Mexico's Manufactured Exports." *Economic Development and Cultural Change* 23, no. 3.

Brady, E. 1967. "Production Functions for the Industrial Sector of Peru." Monograph 5. Ames, Iowa: Department of Economics, Iowa State University.

Bruton, Henry J. 1967. "Productivity Growth in Latin America." *American Economic Review* (December): 1099–1166.

Buttari, Juan J., ed. 1977. *Empleo en América Latina: Una Visión de Conjunto.* Vols. 1 and 2. Rio de Janeiro: ECIEL, Programa de Estudios Conjuntos sobre Integración Latinoamericana. March.

Carnoy, Martin. 1964. "The Cost and Return to Schooling in Mexico: A Case Study." Ph.D. diss., University of Chicago.

Carré, J., P. Dubois, and E. Malinvaud. 1975. *French Economic Growth.* Stanford, Calif.: Stanford University Press.

Ceballos, María Beatriz. 1985/1986. "Aspectos Demográficos de Algunos Países de América Latina." *Ensayos en Economía* (Universidad Nacional de Tucumán) 8: 37–109.

Centro de Investigaciones Agrarias. 1970. *Estructura Agraria y Desarrollo Agrícola en México.* Mexico City: Centro de Investigaciones Agrarias.

Centro Latinoamericano de Demografia (CELADE). 1969. *Población Económica Activa, Migración, Seguridad Social, Fecundidad, Mortalidad: Fuentes de Datos Demográficos.* Santiago: CELADE.

Chinloy, Peter T. 1980. "Sources of Quality Change in Labor Input." *American Economic Review* 70: 108–19.

Christensen, Lauritus R., Dale W. Jorgenson, and Lawrence J. Lau. 1973. "Transcendental Logarithmic Production Frontiers." *Review of Economics and Statistics* 55: 28–45.

Christensen, Lauritus R., Diane Cummings, and Dale W. Jorgenson. 1980. "Economic Growth, 1947–1973: An International Comparison." In *New Developments in Productivity Measurement*, edited by John W. Kendrick and Beatrice Vaccara. Chicago: University of Chicago Press.

Coeymans, Juan E. 1989. "Allocation of Resources and Sectorial Growth in Chile: An Econometric Approach." Ph.D. diss., Oxford University.

Consejo Nacional de Desarrollo (CONADE). 1965. *La Mano de Obra en el Sector Agropecuario.* Buenos Aires: CONADE.

———. 1968. *La Distribución del Ingreso en la Argentina.* Buenos Aires: CONADE.

Contador, Claudio. 1975. "Tecnologia e Rentabilidade na Agricultura Brasileira." Rio de Janeiro: Instituto de Planejamento Económico e Social.

Contador, Claudio, and Claudio L. Haddad. 1975. "Producto Real, Moeda e Precos: A Experiencia Brasileira no Periodo 1861–1970." *Revista Brasileira de Estatística* 36, no. 143 (July–September): 407–39.

Corbo, M. 1974. "Schooling, Experience, and Wages in Santiago, Chile." Ph.D. diss., University of Chicago.

Correa, Héctor. 1970. "Sources of Economic Growth in Latin America." *Southern Economic Journal*: 17–31.

Cossio, L., and R. Izquierdo. 1962. "Estimación de la Relación Producto-Capital de México 1940–60." *Trimestre Económico* (October–December).

Cuca-Tolosa, L. 1972. "Demography of Brazil: A Regional Study." Ph.D. diss., Princeton University.

Dagnino Pastore, J. M. 1966. *La Industria del Tractor en la Argentina*. Buenos Aires: Instituto Torcuato Di Tella.

Davis, T. 1966. "Capital y Salarios Reales en la Economía Chilena." *Cuadernos de Economía* (Universidad Católica de Chile) (January–April).

———, ed. 1967. *Mexico's Recent Economic Growth: The Mexican View*. Monograph 10. Austin: Institute of Latin American Studies, University of Texas Press.

de Alba, Enrique, and Ignacio Trigueros. 1986. "Estimacíon de un Ciclo de Referencia para la Economía Mexicana." Mexico City: Centro de Análisis e Investigación Económica, Instituto Tecnológico Autónomo de México.

Denison, Edward F. 1962. *Sources of Economic Growth in the United States and the Alternatives before Us*. Supplementary Paper 13. Washington, D.C.: Committee for Economic Development.

———. 1967. *Why Growth Rates Differ*. Washington, D.C.: Brookings Institution.

———. 1985. *Trends in American Economic Growth, 1929–1982*. Washington, D.C.: Brookings Institution.

Departamento Administrativo Nacional de Estadística (DANE). 1972. *Industria Manufacturera Nacional 1969*. Bogotá: DANE.

———. 1982. *Colombia Estadística 1982*. Bogotá: DANE.

———. 1985. *Cuentas Nacionales de Colombia, 1970–1983*. Bogotá: DANE. June.

Díaz Alejandro, C. 1970. *Essays on the Economic History of the Argentine Republic*. New Haven, Conn.: Yale University Press.

Dirección General de Cuentas Nacionales. 1980. *Cuentas Nacionales del Perú 1950–1979*. Lima: Oficina Nacional de Estadística.

Dirección General de Estadística y Censos Nacionales. 1964. *Anuario Estadístico de Venezuela (1957–1963)*. Caracas: Ministerio de Fomento.

Domar, Evsey. 1961. "On the Measurement of Technological Change." *Economic Journal* 71: 709–29.

Domar, E. S., M. Eddi, G. H. Herrick, P. M. Hohenberg, M. D. Intriligator, and I. Miyamoto. 1964. "Economic Growth and Productivity in the United States, Canada, United Kingdom, Germany, and Japan in the Post-War Period." *Review of Economics and Statistics* 46 (February):33–40.

Dornbusch, Rudiger. 1985. "Policy Performance Links between LDC Debtors and Industrial Nations." *Brookings Papers on Economic Activity*.

Estudios Conjuntos sobre Integración Económica Latinoamericana (ECIEL). 1974–1977. *Ensayos ECIEL*. Washington, D.C., and Rio de Janeiro.

Economic Commission for Latin America (ECLA). 1951. *Estudio Económico de América Latina 1949* (in Spanish and English). New York: United Nations.

———. 1967. *Analysis and Projections of Economic Development III: The Economic Development of Colombia*. Geneva: United Nations Department of Economic Affairs Document E/CN 12/365/Addl. 1957.

————. 1968. *El Desarrollo Económico y la Distribución del Ingreso en la Argentina*. New York: United Nations.

————. 1986. "Balance Preliminar de la Economía Latinoamericana, 1986." *Notas sobre la Economía y el Desarrollo*, no. 438/439 (December).

————. 1988. "La Distribución del Ingreso en Colombia: Antecedentes Estadísticos y Características Socioeconómicas de los Receptores." *Cuadernos Estadísticos* (Santiago, Chile), no. 14.

————. 1989. *Statistical Yearbook for Latin America and the Caribbean*. Santiago, Chile: United Nations.

Elías, V. J. 1969. "Estimates of Value Added, Capital, and Labor in Argentine Manufacturing: 1935–1963." Ph.D. diss., University of Chicago.

————. 1972. "The Contribution of Foreign Trade to National Income." In *International Economics and Development: Essays in Honor of Raúl Prebisch*, edited by L. E. Di Marco. New York: Academic Press.

————. 1974. "Sources of Output and Input Growth in LA Countries." Harvard University. Mimeo.

————. 1975a. "Education and Growth Accounting." Cuaderno no. 75–2. Tucumán, Argentina: Instituto de Investigaciones Económicas, Universidad Nacional de Tucumán.

————. 1975b. "Fuentes del Crecimiento Económico Argentino y Perspectivas Futuras." *Ensayos en Economía* 1 (December): 1–46.

————. 1975c. "El Insumo Capital en Latinoamérica." Cuaderno 75–3. Tucumán, Argentina: Instituto de Investigaciones Económicas, Universidad Nacional de Tucumán. November.

————. 1975d. "The Labor Input in Latin America." Paper presented to the Third World Congress of the Econometric Society, Toronto, August.

————. 1978a. "Comercio e Crescimento na America Latina." *Revista Brasileira de Economia* (April–June).

————. 1978b. "Sources of Economic Growth in Latin American Countries." *Review of Economics and Statistics* (August).

————. 1985. *Government Expenditures on Agriculture and Agricultural Growth in Latin America*. Research Report 50. Washington, D.C.: International Food Policy Research Institute. October.

————. 1986. "Productividad en el Sector Industrial Argentino: 1935–1985." Paper presented at the Congress on Productivity, CERES, Montevideo, Uruguay, November 12–14.

Enberg. 1970. "Agricultural Productivity and Economic Development in Mexico." Ph.D. diss., University of Texas, Austin.

Fabricant, Solomon. 1959. *Basic Facts on Productivity Change*. Occasional Paper 63. New York: National Bureau of Economic Research.

Figueroa, A. 1972. "Income Distribution and Development: The Case of Peru." Ph.D. diss., Vanderbilt University.

Findlay, R. W. 1978. "Relative Backwardness, Direct Foreign Investment, and the

Transfer of Technology: A Simple Dynamic Model." *Quarterly Journal of Economics* (February).

Fuchs, Victor R. 1964. *Productivity Trends in the Goods and Service Sectors, 1929–61: A Preliminary Survey.* Occasional Paper 89. New York: National Bureau of Economic Research.

Fundação Getúlio Vargas. 1973. "26 Años de Economia Brasileira." *Conjuntura Económica* 27 (December).

———. 1984. "Contas Nacionais." *Conjuntura Económica* 38, no. 6 (June).

Fundação Instituto Brasileiro de Geografía e Estatística. 1970. *Brasil: Series Estatísticas Retrospectivas—1970.* Rio de Janeiro: Instituto Brasileiro de Estatística.

———. 1974. *Anuário Estatístico do Brasil.* Rio de Janeiro: Fundação Instituto Brasileiro de Geografía e Estatística.

———. 1984. *Conjuntura* 38, no. 6 (June).

Garcés Voisenat, Juan Pedro. 1983. "Inversión y Capitalización en el Sector Agropecuario Chileno, 1950–1980." Tesis de Ingeniero Comercial Mención Economía, Pontificia Universidad Católica de Chile.

García Rocha, A. 1970. "Las Diferencias Salariales en México y Su Medición." *Revista de Demografía y Economía* 4, no. 2.

Gayer, Fernando C. 1986. "La Fuerza Laboral en América Latina para el Período 1935–2000." Cuaderno 86–2. Tucumán, Argentina: Instituto de Investigaciones Económicas, Universidad Nacional de Tucumán.

Glick, M. 1963. "The Impact of Economic Development on the Returns to Labor in Agriculture in Mexico." Ph.D. diss., University of Chicago.

Griliches, Zvi, ed. 1971. *Prices Indexes and Quality Change.* Cambridge, Mass.: Harvard University Press.

Gutiérrez, Gabriel. 1981. "Real Investment in Machinery and Equipment: An Estimate for Brazil, 1955–79." Paper presented at the Second Latin American Regional Meeting of the Econometric Society, Rio de Janeiro, July.

Haddad, C. 1975. "Crescimento do Produto Real Brasileiro: 1900/1947." *Revista Brasileira de Economia* 29 (January–March): 3–26.

Hanson, J. 1972. "Agricultural Productivity and the Distribution of Land: The Venezuelan Case." Center Discussion Paper 148. New Haven, Conn.: Economic Growth Center, Yale University. June.

Harberger, A. C. 1960. *The Demand for Durable Goods.* Chicago: University of Chicago Press.

———. 1969. "La Tasa del Rendimiento al Capital en Colombia." *Revista de Planeación y Desarrollo* 3 (October).

———. 1978. "Perspectives on Capital and Technology in Less-Developed Countries." In *Contemporary Economic Analysis*, edited by M. J. Artis and A. R. Nobay. London.

———. 1983. "The Cost Benefit Approach to Development Economics." *World Development* 2, no. 10.

Harberger, A. C., and M. Selowsky. 1966. "Key Factors in the Economic Growth of Chile." In *The Next Decade of Latin American Economic Development*, edited by Tom E. Davis. Ithaca, N.Y.: Cornell University Press.

Heaton, L. 1969. *The Agricultural Development of Venezuela*. New York: Praeger.

Helliwell, John F., Peter H. Sturm, and Gerard Salow. 1985. "International Comparison of the Sources of Productivity Slowdown, 1973–1982." *European Economic Review* 28 (June–July): 157–91.

Hertford, R. 1969. "Sources of Change in Mexican Agriculture Production." Ph.D. diss., University of Chicago.

Hulten, Charles R. 1978. "Growth Accounting with Intermediate Inputs." *Review of Economic Studies* 45: 511–18.

Instituto de Organización y Racionalización Administrativa (INSORA), Departamento de Relaciones Laborales. 1961. "Afiliación y Finanzas Sindicales en Chile, 1932–59." Santiago: Facultad de Ciencias Económicas de la Universidad de Chile.

Instituto Nacional de Estadísticas y Censos (INDEC). 1947, 1960, 1970, and 1980. *Censos de Población*. Buenos Aires: INDEC.

Instituto Nacional de Planificación (INP). 1966. *La Evolución de la Economía en el Período 1950–64*. Lima: INP.

———. 1980. *Cuentas Nacionales del Perú, 1950–1979*. Lima: INP. July.

Instituto Nacional de Planificación (Ordesur). 1971. *Boletín Estadístico* (Lima) 2 (October).

Inter-American Development Bank. 1968. *Venezuela 1950–67. Variables, Parameters and Methodology of the National Accounts*. Washington, D.C.: Inter-American Development Bank.

International Labor Organization (ILO). 1971. *Towards Full Employment*. Geneva: ILO.

Johnson, D. Gale. 1950. "The Nature of the Supply Functions for Agricultural Products." *American Economic Review* 40, no. 4 (September): 539–64.

Jorgenson, Dale W. 1973. "The Economic Theory of Replacement and Depreciation." In *Econometrics and Economic Theory*, edited by W. Selekaerts. New York: Macmillan.

———. 1975. "An Econometric Approach to Economic Growth." Fisher-Schultz Lecture, Third World Congress of the Econometric Society, Toronto.

Jorgenson, Dale W., and Barbara M. Fraumeni. 1988. "The Accumulation of Human and Nonhuman Capital, 1943–1984." Discussion Paper 1413. Cambridge: Harvard Institute of Economic Research, Harvard University. December.

Jorgenson, Dale W., Frank Gollop, and Barbara Fraumeni. 1987. *Productivity and U.S. Economic Growth*. Cambridge: Harvard University Press.

Jorgenson, Dale W., and Zvi Griliches. 1967. "The Explanation of Productivity Change." *Review of Economic Studies* 34 (July): 249–83.

Jorgenson, Dale W., and M. Kuroda. Forthcoming. "Japan-U.S. Industry-Level Productive Comparisons, 1960–1985." In *Productivity and International Competitiveness*, edited by B. Hickman.

Jorgenson, Dale W., and Mikio Nishimizu. 1977. "U.S. and Japanese Economic Growth, 1952–73: An International Comparison." Discussion Paper 566. Cambridge: Harvard Institute of Economic Research, Harvard University. August.

Jorgenson, Dale W., and Kun-Young Yun. 1986. "The Efficiency of Capital Allocation." *Scandinavian Journal of Economics* 88, no. 1:85–107.

Kendrick, John W. 1961. *Productivity Trends in the United States*. Princeton: Princeton University Press.

———. 1976. *The Formation and Stocks of Total Capital*. New York: Columbia University Press.

Knight, Frank H. 1944. "Diminishing Returns from Investment." *Journal of Political Economy* (March): 25–47.

Kogut, E. L. 1972. "An Economic Analysis of Demographic Phenomena: A Case Study of Brazil." Ph.D. diss., University of Chicago.

Kravis, Irving, Zoltan Kenessey, Alan Heston, and Robert Summers. 1975. *A System of International Comparisons of Gross Product and Purchasing Power*. Baltimore: Johns Hopkins University Press.

Kuznets, Simon. 1971. *Economic Growth of Nations*. Cambridge: Harvard University Press.

Langoni, C. 1970. "A Study in Economic Growth: The Brazilian Case." Ph.D. thesis, University of Chicago.

———. 1973. "Income Distribution and Economic Development in Brazil." *Conjuntura Econômica* 27 (September): 3–40.

Lucas, Robert, Jr. 1988. "On the Mechanics of Economic Development." *Journal of Monetary Economics* 1 (July).

Maddison, Angus. 1979. "Long Run Dynamics of Productivity Growth." *Banca Nazionale del Lavoro Quarterly Review* (March).

———. 1987. "Growth and Slowdown in Advanced Capitalist Economies." *Journal of Economic Literature* 25 (June): 649–98.

Mamalakis, Markos. 1967. *Historical Statistics of Chile 1840–1965*. Milwaukee: University of Wisconsin-Milwaukee.

Mamalakis, Markos, and G. Reynolds. 1965. *Essays in the Chilean Economy*. Homewood, Ill.: Irwin.

Matthews, R. C. O., C. H. Feinstein, and J. C. Odling-Smee. 1982. *British Economic Growth, 1856–1973*. Stanford, Calif.: Stanford University Press.

McCulloch, Rachel. 1977. "Technology, Trade, and the Interests of Labor: A Short Run Analysis of the Development and International Dissemination of New Technology." Discussion Paper 489. Cambridge: Harvard Institute of Economic Research, Harvard University. May.

Meller, Patricio, and Carol Rahilly. 1974. "Características de la Mano de Obra Chilena: Período 1940–1970." Documentos de Trabajo no. 26. Santiago: Instituto de Economía, Universidad Católica de Chile. July.

Mincer, Jacob. 1962. "Labor Force Participation of Married Women." In *Aspects of Labor Economics*, Universities-NBER Committee. Princeton: Princeton University Press.

———. 1968. "Labor Force Participation." In *International Encyclopedia of Social Sciences*. New York: Macmillan.

———. 1974. *Schooling, Earnings and Experience*. New York: Columbia University Press.

———. 1988. "Human Capital and the Labor Market: A Review of Current Research." New York: Columbia University. Mimeo. November.

Ministerio de Fomento. 1974. *Anuario Estadístico 1972*. Caracas: Ministerio de Fomento.

Modigliani, Franco. 1986. "Life Cycle, Individual Thrift, and the Wealth of Nations." *American Economic Review* 76 (June): 297–313.

Moore, Geoffrey. 1989. "The Development and Use of International Economic Indicators." In *Statistical Methods for Cyclical and Seasonal Analysis*, edited by R. P. Mentz et al. Panama City: Inter American Statistical Institute.

Morelos, J. B. 1972. "Niveles de Participación y Componentes de Cambio de la Población Activa, 1950–1970." *Revista de Demografía y Economía* 6, no. 3.

Mundlak, Yair. 1984. "Capital Accumulation, the Choice of Techniques and Agricultural Output." Washington, D.C. Mimeo.

Muñoz, O. 1971. "Crecimiento Industrial de Chile 1914–65." *Instituto de Economía y Planificación*. Santiago: Universidad de Chile.

Nacional Financiera. 1969. *Mexico Basic Series*. Mexico City: Nacional Financiera.

Nelson, R. 1967. "A Study of Industrialization in Colombia, Part I: Analysis." Research Memorandum 5412. Santa Monica, Calif.: Rand Corporation. December.

———. 1968. "A Diffusion Model of International Productivity Differences in Manufacturing Industry." *American Economic Review* 58 (December).

Nishimizu, Mikio. 1979. "On the Methodology and the Importance of the Measurement of Total Factor Productivity Change: The State of Art." Washington, D.C.: Development Economics Department, World Bank. October.

Nordhaus, William, and James Tobin. 1973. "Is Growth Obsolete?" In *The Measurement of Economic and Social Performance*, edited by Milton Moss. Studies in Income and Wealth, vol. 38. New York: National Bureau of Economic Research.

Oficina de Planificación Nacional (ODEPLAN). 1973. *Balances Económicos de Chile 1960–70*. Santiago: Editorial Universitaria.

————. 1981. *Metodología y Serie Cuentas Nacionales, 1974–1980*. Santiago: ODEPLAN. June.

Oficina Nacional de Estadísticas y Censos (ONEC). 1971. *Anuario Estadístico del Perú*. Lima: ONEC.

Organization for Economic Cooperation and Development (OECD). 1967. *Human Resources in Peru: Education and Economic Development*. Paris: OECD.

Orozco, Ramiro. 1977. "Sources of Agricultural Production and Productivity in Colombian Agriculture." Ph.D. diss., Oklahoma State University.

Peterson, W. L. 1967. "Return to Poultry Research in the United States." *Journal of Farm Economics* 49, no. 3 (August).

Petrei, A. 1971. "Rates of Return to Physical Capital in Manufacturing Industries in Argentina." Ph.D. diss., University of Chicago.

Programa Regional del Empleo para América Latina y el Caribe (PREALC). 1982. *Mercado de Trabajo en Cifras, 1950–1980*. Santiago: Oficina Internacional del Trabajo.

Ramos, Joseph. 1970. *Labor and Development in Latin America*. New York: Columbia University Press.

Reca, L. G. 1967. "The Price and Production Duality within Argentine Agriculture, 1923–65." Ph.D. diss., University of Chicago.

Reca, Lucio, and Juan Verstraeten. 1977. "La Formación del Producto Agropecuario Argentino: Antecedentes y Posibilidades." *Desarollo Económico* 17 (October–December): 371–89.

Reynolds, C. 1970. *The Mexican Economy, Twentieth Century, Structure and Growth*. New Haven: Yale University Press.

Reynolds, C., and Francisco Javier Alejo. 1987. "Effects of Intersectoral Labor Shifts on Productivity Growth: Mexico's Experience and Implications for the United States." *Indian Journal of Industrial Relations* 23, no. 2 (October): 157–87.

Rodríguez, Carlos A. 1978. "International Technology Transfer." Discussion Paper 78–7906. New York: Economics Workshop, Department of Economics, Columbia University. September.

Rodríguez, F., Miguel Antonio. 1984. "El Ahorro y la Inversión en Venezuela en el Período 1972–82." Paper presented at the Seminar on Saving and Investment in Latin America. Buenos Aires: CEDES. August.

Roemer, M. 1970. *Fishing for Growth: Export-led Development in Peru 1900–67*. Cambridge: Harvard University Press.

Rosas Bravo, Pedro. 1983. "Indicadores Cíclicos de la Economía Venezolana." Paper presented in the Twentieth Technical Meeting of Central Banks of the American Continent, La Paz, Bolivia, November.

Rosende, Francisco. 1988. "Ciclos, Crisis Financiera y Desempleo: Consideraciones sobre el Caso Chileno." *Revista de Economía* (Banco Central del Uruguay) 3, no. 2 (December).

Ruddle, Kenneth, and Kathleen Barrows. 1974. *Statistical Abstract of Latin*

America 1972. Los Angeles: Latin American Center, University of California. January.

Sarmiento, E. 1972. "Crecimiento Económico y Asignación de Recursos." In *Lecturas sobre Desarrollo Económico Colombiano*. Bogotá: Fundación para la Educación Superior y el Desarrollo.

Schuh, E. 1970. *The Agricultural Development of Brazil*. New York: Praeger.

Schultz, Theodore P. 1968. "Return to Education in Bogotá, Colombia." Research Memorandum 5645. Santa Monica, Calif.: Rand Corporation. September.

Schultz, Theodore W. 1953. *The Economic Organization of Agriculture*. New York: McGraw-Hill.

Schydlowsky, D. 1971. "Comment." In *Government and Economic Development*, edited by G. Ranis. New Haven: Yale University Press.

Selowsky, M. 1967. "Education and Economic Growth: Some International Comparisons." Ph.D. diss., University of Chicago.

Servicio del Empleo y Recursos Humanos. 1965. *Población del Perú*. Lima.

Solís, M. L. 1967. "Hacia un Análisis General a Largo Plazo del Desarrollo Económico de México." *Revista de Demografía y Economía* 1: 40–91.

Solow, Robert. 1957. "Technical Change and the Aggregate Production Function." *Review of Economics and Statistics* 39 (August): 312–20.

Stigler, George J. 1982. *The Economist as Preacher*. Chicago: University of Chicago Press.

Stone, Richard. 1986. "Nobel Memorial Lecture 1984: The Accounts of Society." *Journal of Applied Econometrics* 1, no. 1 (January): 5–28.

Sturm, Peter H. 1977. "The System Component in Differences in per Capita Output between East and West Germany." *Journal of Comparative Economics* 1, no. 1 (March): 5–24.

Syrquin, M. 1970. "Production Functions and Regional Efficiency in the Manufacturing Sector in Mexico 1965." Ph.D. diss., Harvard University.

Taylor, L. 1973. "Model-Based Consistency Checks on Medium-Term Growth Prospects in Peru." Economic Development Report no. 229. Cambridge: Center for International Affairs, Harvard University. February.

Teubal, Morris. 1979. "Primary Exports and Economic Development: The Role of the Engineering Sector." Documento de Trabajo no. 91. Buenos Aires: Instituto Torcuato Di Tella.

Thirsk, W. 1972. "The Economics of Colombian Farm Mechanization." Ph.D. diss., Yale University.

Thorbecke, E., and E. Stoutjesdijk. 1971. *Employment and Output: A Methodology Applied to Peru and Guatemala*. Paris: OECD.

Thoumi, F. 1970. "Industria Manufacturera Fabril." Bogotá: Universidad Nacional de Colombia.

Tinbergen, Jan. 1959. "On the Theory of Trend Movements." In *Jan Tinbergen*

Selected Papers, edited by L. H. Klassen, L. M. Koyck, and H. J. Witteveen. Amsterdam: North Holland.

Todd, T. 1972. "Efficiency and Plant Size in Colombia Manufacturing." Ph.D. diss., Yale University.

United Nations. 1972. *Demographic Year Book*. Geneva: United Nations.

U.S. Department of Agriculture. 1970. *Agricultural Productivity in Colombia*. Washington, D.C.: USDA.

Valdés, Alberto. 1971. "Commercial Policy and Its Effects on the External Agricultural Trade in Chile, 1945–65." Ph.D. diss., London School of Economics and Political Science.

Vandendreis, R. 1967. "Foreign Trade and Economic Development of Peru." Ph.D. diss., Iowa State University.

Vázquez Presedo, V. 1968. "Sobre la Estructura de las Importaciones en los Comienzos del Desarrollo Industrial Argentino." Buenos Aires: Instituto de Investigaciones Económicas, Universidad de Buenos Aires.

Webb, R. 1973. "Government Policy and the Distribution of Income in Peru 1963–73." Discussion Paper 38. Princeton: Research Program in Economic Development, Woodrow Wilson School, Princeton University.

World Bank. 1973. *El Desarrollo Económico de Colombia: Problemas y Perspectivas*. Bogotá: Biblioteca Banco Popular.

————. 1984. *Colombia: External Sector and Agriculture Policies for Adjustment and Growth*. Vol. 2. Washington, D.C.: World Bank.

ABOUT THE AUTHOR

Victor J. Elías received his Ph.D. in economics from the University of Chicago in 1969. Since 1965 he has been a full professor in the Department of Economics of the National University of Tucumán, in Tucumán, Argentina. He has been a visiting fellow at Harvard University and Stanford University; a visiting researcher at the International Food Policy Research Institute in Washington, D.C., and the Instituto Torcuato Di Tella in Buenos Aires; and a visiting professor at several institutions in Brazil. Elías was a Ford Foundation Doctoral Dissertation Fellow (1964–1965), a Social Science Research Council Fellow (1973), a Guggenheim Fellow (1974), and one of the "Ten Outstanding Young Men of Argentina" (1976). He served as president of the Argentine Economic Association for two terms (1970–1972 and 1978–1980) and as president of the Latin American Standing Committee of the Econometric Society (1984). He is married to Ana M. Ganum, and they have two daughters and one son.

INDEX

Abramovitz, Moses, 25, 26, 27,
  107n4, 151, 152, 154
Adam Smith effect, 175
Age, 77–78, 94–95
Agricultural sector
  input contributions of, 116, 127
  as source of growth, 115
  sources of output growth of, 116–18
Alejo, Francisco J., 99t
Argentina
  agricultural, manufacturing, and
    public output growth for, 116–20,
    125, 127–30
  basic data for, 188–90
  business cycles in, 12, 17
  comparison of growth rates of GDP,
    132, 138, 148
  components of labor quality for, 74–
    81, 90–99
  contributions to output growth in,
    43–44
  employment and population ratios
    for, 72–73, 87
  employment, population, and labor
    force participation in, 210–12
  foreign trade contribution to growth,
    39–40, 56–57
  GDP estimates and rates of change,
    60–61, 64–68
  GDP growth rate, TFP, and input
    contributions, 34–37, 50–54, 232

growth of agricultural sector in, 116–
  18, 122, 125–26, 127
growth of manufacturing sector in,
  118–19, 129
growth of public sector in, 119–20,
  130
growth rate of prices, productivity,
  and capital stock, 38–39, 55–57
income distribution of labor and
  capital for, 61–62, 69
inflation rates in, 15–16
occupation classification I and II,
  78–79, 96, 184–85
partial productivity of labor and
  capital, 37–38, 48–49
predicted GDP growth for, 164–65, 168
trends in labor productivity in, 153–
  54, 158
Arranz, Juan M., 17t
Arrow, Kenneth J., 133
Australia, 153–54, 157

Ballesteros, M. A., 215t
Banco Central de Chile, 196t
Banco Central de la República
  Argentina, 14t, 56–57t, 190t, 209t,
  223t
Banco Central de la Reserva (Peru),
  56–57t, 129t, 204t, 209t, 223t
Banco Central de Venezuela, 56–57t,
  129t, 206t

Banco de la República (Colombia),
  56–57t, 199t, 209t, 223t
Banco de México, 56–57t, 114t, 129t,
  201t, 209t, 223t
Banco Nacional de México, 129t, 201t,
  223t
Barger, H., 26
Barrows, Kathleen, 14t, 190t
Baumol, William, 151, 152
Berglas, Eitan, 133
Bergson, Abraham, 26
Berry, R. A., 82n8, 209t, 215t
Blau, David M., 82–83n10
Brady, E., 97t
Brazil
  agricultural, manufacturing, and
    public output growth for, 116–20,
    127–30
  basic data for, 191–93
  comparison of growth rates of GDP,
    132, 139, 148
  components of labor quality for, 74–
    81, 90–99
  contribution to output growth in, 43–44
  employment and population ratios
    for, 72–73, 87
  employment, population, and labor
    force participation in, 210–12
  foreign trade contribution to growth,
    39–40, 56–57
  GDP estimates and rates of change
    for, 60–61, 64–68
  GDP growth rate, TFP, and input
    contributions, 34–37, 50–54, 232
  growth of agricultural sector in, 116–
    18, 122, 125–26, 127
  growth of manufacturing sector in,
    118–19, 129
  growth of public sector in, 119–20,
    130
  growth rate of prices, productivity,
    and capital stock, 38–39, 55–57
  income distribution of capital and
    labor for, 61–62, 69
  inflation rates in, 15–16
  occupation classification I and II,
    78–79, 96, 184–85
  partial productivity of labor and
    capital, 37–38, 48–49
  predicted GDP growth for, 164–65,
    168

trends in labor productivity in, 153–
  54, 158
Bruton, Henry J., 27
Business-cycle analysis, 2
Business cycles, 12, 17

Capital
  accumulation of, 102
  in agricultural sector, 116, 117
  concept of total, 26–27
  contribution to growth of, 4
  contribution to output growth of,
    122, 124, 126
  estimating depreciation of, 102
  growth by country of, 34, 42
  growth of quality of, 114
  weights for changing composition in,
    104
Capital, educational
  estimates of stock of, 181–82
Capital, fixed
  basic data for stock of, 221–23
  composition of, 105–6, 111
  data for real gross rate of return on,
    229–30
  rates of return on, 105, 113–14, 229–
    30
  stock and composition of, 103, 111–
    13
Capital input
  classification of, 104
  components of, 101
  defined, 108
  definition and diagram of, 101
  quality components of, 103–6, 108,
    114
Capital stock
  estimate of aggregate, 102–3, 111
  estimates of depreciation, 102–3
  estimates of value in components of,
    101–2
  rate of growth of, 103, 109–10
Carnoy, Martin, 92t
Ceballos, María B., 212t
Centro Latinoamericano de
  Demografía (Chile), 215t
Chile
  agricultural, manufacturing, and
    public output growth for, 116–20,
    127–30
  basic data for, 194–96

comparison of growth rates of GDP,
132, 140, 148
components of labor quality for, 74–
81, 90–99
contribution to output growth in, 43–44
employment and population ratios
for, 72–73, 87
employment, population, and labor
force participation in, 213–15
foreign trade contribution to growth,
39–40, 56–57
GDP estimates and rates of change
for, 60–61, 64–68
GDP growth rate, TFP, and input
contributions, 34–37, 50–54, 232
growth of agricultural sector in, 116–
18, 122, 125–26, 127
growth of manufacturing sector in,
118–19, 129
growth of public sector in, 119–20,
130
growth rate of prices, productivity,
and capital stock, 38–39, 55–57
income distribution of capital and
labor for, 61–62, 69
inflation rates in, 15–16
occupation classification I and II,
78–79, 96, 184–85
partial productivity of labor and
capital, 37–38, 48–49
predicted GDP growth for, 164–65,
168
trends in labor productivity in, 153–
54, 158
Chinloy, Peter T., 77
Christensen, Lauritus, 26, 37, 60,
62n1, 73, 75, 76, 145t, 151
Coeymans, Juan E., 129t
Colombia
agricultural, manufacturing, and
public output growth for, 116–20,
127–30
basic data for, 197–99
comparison of GDP growth rates in,
132, 141, 148
components of labor quality for, 74–
81, 90–99
contribution to output growth in, 43–
44
employment and population ratios
for, 72–73, 87

employment, population, and labor
force participation in, 213–15
foreign trade contribution to growth,
39–40, 56–57
GDP estimates and rates of change
for, 60–61, 64–68
GDP growth rate, TFP, and input
contributions, 34–37, 50–54, 232
growth of agricultural sector in, 116–
18, 122, 125–26, 127
growth of manufacturing sector in,
118–19, 129
growth of public sector in, 119–20, 130
growth rate of prices, productivity,
and capital stock, 38–39, 55–57
income distribution of capital and
labor for, 61–62, 69
inflation rates in, 15–16
occupation classification I and II,
78–79, 96, 184–85
partial productivity of labor and
capital, 37–38, 48–49
predicted GDP growth for, 164–65,
168
trends in labor productivity in, 153–
54, 158
Consejo Nacional de Desarrollo
(CONADE), 97t
Contador, Claudio, 193t
Convergency phenomenon, 152
Corbo, Mario, 215t
Correa, Héctor, 27
Cossio, L., 201t, 223t
Cuca-Tolosa, L., 99t, 212t
Cummings, Diane, 26, 37, 60, 62n1,
73, 75, 76, 145t, 151

Dagnino Pastore, J. M., 223t
DANE. See Departamento
Administrativo Nacional de
Estadística
Data
in country comparisons, 30, 31n7
for GDP estimates, 59
Davis, T., 56–57t, 201t, 223t
de Alba, Enrique, 17t
Denison, Edward, 25, 27–28, 75, 76,
107n4, 152, 160t
Departamento Administrativo Nacional
de Estadística (DANE, Colombia),
91t, 129t, 223t

Díaz Alejandro, Carlos, 190t
Dirección General de Cuentas
    Nacionales (Peru), 204t
Domar, Evsey, 26

ECIEL (Estudios Conjuntos sobre
    Integración Económica
    Latinoamericana), 62
ECLA. See Economic Commission for
    Latin America
Economic Commission for Latin
    America (ECLA), 14t, 56–57t, 87t,
    89t, 91t, 129t, 190t, 199t, 209t
Economic growth
    analysis of, 2
    comparison of sources and stages of,
        154–55, 160–61
    foreign trade as source of, 39–40
    of output, labor, and capital, 42
    rate of average annual input and
        output, 35–36, 53
    sources of, 34–36, 43–44, 50–52, 53
    See also Business cycles; Growth
        theories
Economic policy recommendations,
    165–67
Economic sectors
    as components of labor quality, 79–
        80, 82–83nn10, 11, 97–99
    labor composition in, 82–83nn10, 11
Economic stability measures, 12
Education, 74–75, 90–93
Educational level
    change in quality component of labor
        by, 93
    labor force composition by, 90–91
    relative wages by, 92
Elías, V., 17t, 31n6, 103, 114t, 127t,
    128t, 129t, 182t, 223t
Employment
    rate of, 210–20
    rate of growth in, 81–82n4
    as ratio of population, 87–88
Equilibrium models, 20
Equilibrium theory of economic
    growth, 19–20

Fabricant, Solomon, 25
Figueroa, A., 209t
Findlay, R. W., 133
Fisher, Irving, 26

Foreign trade
    contribution to national income of,
        107n6
    as growth source, 29–30, 39–40,
        41n7, 56–57
Fraumeni, Barbara M., 27, 63n14,
    107n3, 176
Fuchs, Victor, 82n10
Fundação Getúlio Vargas, 129t, 193t,
    209t, 223t
Fundação Instituto Brasileiro de
    Geografía e Estatística, 56–57t,
    99t, 129t, 193t, 209t, 223t

Garcés Voisenat, Juan Pedro, 121n3,
    223t
García Rocha, A., 218t
Gayer, Fernando C., 164, 212t
Gender
    as component of labor quality, 75–
        77, 93–94
    wages by, 76–77, 93
    women in labor force, 93
Gollop, Frank, 63n14, 107n3, 176
Griliches, Zvi, 26, 28, 60, 169
Gross domestic product (GDP)
    average annual growth rate of, 34,
        50–52
    basic data for capital income in,
        208–9
    changes in public output and total,
        61, 66
    defined, 59
    determinants of growth of, 20
    econometric growth model to
        estimate, 134–36, 146–47, 149–50,
        232
    estimates and rates of change for,
        60–61, 64–65, 66–67, 68
    growth rates of, 4, 11–12, 14, 50–54
    input contributions to, 50–54
    national accounts in estimating, 59
    predicted growth (1990–2000), 164–
        65, 168
    rates of change for, 64–65
Growth cycle, global, 135
Growth model, econometric, 134–35,
    149–50
Growth theories, 20–22
    See also Sources-of-growth method
Gutiérrez, Gabriel, 223t

Haddad, Claudio L., 193t
Harberger, Arnold C., 63n7, 92t, 114t,
    154, 174n1, 196t, 215t, 223t
Helliwell, John F., 107n4
Hertford, R., 31n6
Heston, Alan, 62n4

Income distribution, 61–62, 69
Inflation rates, 12, 15–16
Input growth, 35, 50–52
Instituto de Organización
    Racionalización Administrativa
    (Chile), 215t
Instituto Nacional de Estadísticas y
    Censos (Argentina), 91t, 99t
Instituto Nacional de Planificación
    (Peru), 204t, 223t
Inter-American Development Bank,
    56–57t, 114t, 129t, 206t, 223t
International Labor Organization
    (ILO), 91t, 92t, 212t, 220t
International Monetary Fund (IMF), 150t
Inventory method, 101–2
Investment goods
    basic data for, 207
    share in GDP of, 60–61, 68–69
Italy, 153–54, 157
Izquierdo, R., 201t, 223t

Japan, 153–54, 157
Johnson, D. Gale, 25
Jones, Ronald, 133
Jorgenson, Dale W., 26, 27, 28, 37,
    60, 62n1, 63n14, 73, 75, 76,
    82n10, 107n3, 136n2, 145t, 151,
    169, 176

Kendrick, John, 25, 26, 82n10
Kennessey, Zoltan, 62n4
Knight, Frank H., 26
Kogut, E. L., 212t
Kravis, Irving, 27, 62n4
Kuroda, M., 82n10
Kuznets, Simon, 26

Labor
    contribution to output growth of,
        122, 123, 124, 125
    frequency distribution by country of,
        34, 42
    quality of, 71, 93

reallocation of, 80
    as source of economic growth, 71
    See also Age; Economic sectors;
        Education; Gender; Migration;
        Occupation
Labor force
    in agricultural sector, 116, 117
    concept of, 72
    educational level composition of, 90–
        91
    occupation classifications I and II in,
        78–79, 96, 183–86
    participation rate of, 72–73, 87
    in three economic sectors, 79–80,
        98, 99
    See also Employment;
        Unemployment rate
Labor input
    definition and diagram of, 71, 84
    gross components of, 72
    quality components of, 71, 74–81,
        93
    See also Age; Economic sectors;
        Education; Gender; Migration;
        Occupation
Labor productivity comparisons, 153–
    54, 157–59
Land, 116–17
Langoni, C., 31n6, 56–57t, 77, 91t,
    92t, 99t, 103, 114t, 209t, 223t
Latin America
    sources of economic growth in seven
        countries, 9
    trends in labor productivity in, 153–
        54, 159

McCulloch, Rachel, 133
Maddison, Angus, 37, 73, 107n4, 135,
    152, 155, 159t, 160t
Mamalakis, Markos, 196t
Manufacturing sector, 118–19, 137
Marshall, Alfred, 78
Meller, Patricio, 129t, 215t
Mexico
    agricultural, manufacturing, and
        public output growth for, 116–20,
        127–30
    basic data for, 200–201
    business cycles in, 12, 17
    comparison of GDP growth rates in,
        132, 142, 148

Mexico (*continued*)
  components of labor quality for, 74–81, 90–99
  contribution to output growth in, 43, 45
  employment and population ratios for, 72–73, 87
  employment, population, and labor force participation in, 216–18
  foreign trade contribution to growth, 39–40, 56–57
  GDP estimates and rates of change for, 60–61, 64–69
  GDP growth, TFP, and input contributions, 34–37, 50–54, 232
  growth of agricultural sector in, 116–18, 122, 125–26, 127
  growth of manufacturing sector in, 118–19, 129
  growth of public sector in, 119–20, 130
  growth rate of prices, productivity, and capital stock, 38–39, 55–57
  income distribution of capital and labor for, 61–62, 69
  inflation rates in, 15–16
  occupation classification I and II, 78–79, 96, 184–85
  partial productivity of labor and capital, 37–38, 48–49
  predicted GDP growth for, 164–65, 168
  trends in productivity in, 153–54, 159
Migration
  effect of domestic, 80
  effect on labor force of, 117
  See also Reallocation by region
Mincer, Jacob, 75, 77, 78
Ministerio de Fomento (Venezuela), 56–57t
Moore, Geoffrey, 12, 63n10, 135
Morelos, J. B., 218t
Mundlak, Yair, 121n4
Muñoz, O., 56–57t

Nacional Financiera (Mexico), 56–57t, 129t, 201t, 209t, 223t
National accounts
  in estimating GDP, 59
  in sources-of-growth method, 22, 23, 24, 28–29

National Bureau of Economic Research (NBER), 24–25
Nishimizu, Mikio, 136n2
Nordhaus, William, 27

Occupation, 78–79, 96–97
Occupation classification
  in labor force (I), 78–79, 96
  in labor force (II), 183–86
Oficina de Planificación Nacional (Chile), 56–57t, 196t, 209t, 223t
Oficina Nacional de Estadísticas y Censos (Peru), 204t, 218t
Organization for Economic Cooperation and Development (OECD), 218t
Orozco, Ramiro, 31n6
Output
  contribution of labor, capital, and TFP to growth of, 34, 43
  frequency distribution by country of, 34, 42
  public and private sectors in aggregate, 59
  See also Gross domestic product
Output-capital ratio, 38, 49

Partial productivity
  basic data for labor and capital, 224–27
  of labor and capital, 37–38, 48–49
  See also Output-capital ratio
Peru
  agricultural, manufacturing, and public output growth for, 116–20, 127–30
  basic data for, 202–4
  components of labor quality for, 74–81, 90–99
  contribution to output growth in, 43, 45
  employment and population ratios for, 72–73, 87
  employment, population, and labor force participation in, 216–18
  foreign trade contribution to growth, 39–40, 56–57
  GDP estimates and rates of change for, 60–61, 64–68
  GDP growth, TFP, and input contributions, 34–37, 50–54, 232

growth of agricultural sector in, 116–18, 122, 125–26, 127
growth of manufacturing sector in, 118–19, 129
growth of public sector in, 119–20, 130
growth rate of prices, productivity, and capital stock, 38–39, 55–57
income distribution of capital and labor for, 61–62, 69
inflation rates in, 15–16
occupation classification I and II, 78–79, 96, 184–85
partial productivity of labor and capital, 37–38, 48–49
predicted GDP growth for, 164–65, 168
trends in labor productivity in, 153–54, 159
Peterson, W. L., 28
Petrei, A., 114t
Policy recommendations, 165–67
Population growth, 12, 14
Prices
growth rate of labor and capital input, 38–39, 55
of labor and capital input, 55
Programa Regional del Empleo para América Latina y el Caribe, 89t, 215t
Public sector, 59, 119–20, 124, 130

Rahilly, Carol, 129t, 215t
Reallocation by region, 80, 99
Reca, Lucio, 118
Residual. See Total factor productivity
Reynolds, C., 56–57t, 99t, 114t, 201t, 223t
Reynolds, G., 196t
Rodríguez, Carlos, 133
Rodríguez, F., 223t
Rosas Bravo, Pedro, 17t
Rosende, Francisco, 215t
Ruddle, Kenneth, 14t, 190t

Salow, Gerard, 107n4
Sarmiento, E., 199t
Schultz, Theodore W., 26, 92t
Selowsky, M., 31n6, 91t, 92t, 196t, 215t, 218t, 223t
Servicio del Empleo y Recursos Humanos (Peru), 218t

Smith, Adam, 78
Solís, M. L., 201t
Solow, Robert, 25
Sources-of-growth analyses, 3–4, 59
Sources-of-growth method, 163–64, 169–74
advantages of using, 38
basic formula of, 22–23
development of, 24–27
estimating TFP using, 38–39
to integrate analyses of public sector, 121n5
organization of information in, 23–24
predecessors of, 24–27
refinement of, 27–30
total factor productivity (TFP) in, 24–29, 117–18, 128
Stigler, George J., 121n5
Stone, Richard, 63n14
Stoutjesdijk, E., 218t
Sturm, Peter H., 29, 107n4
Summers, Robert, 62n4

Technology. See Total factor productivity
Technology transmission models, 133
Teubal, Morris, 133
TFP. See Total factor productivity
Thorbecke, E., 218t
Tinbergen, Jan, 24
Tobin, James, 27
Total capital concept, 26–27
Total factor productivity (TFP), 20
in agricultural sector output, 117–18, 128
comparison of growth rates of, 133–34, 148
contribution to growth of, 4, 34–37, 43, 44, 50–54
determinants of behavior of, 27, 29
estimates of growth for, 132–34, 143–45, 148
explanation of, 26
as residual component in economic growth, 24–25, 29, 128
See also Partial productivity
Total factor productivity (TFP) index, 36–37, 46–47
estimates of growth rate of, 38–39, 46–47, 55–56

Total factor productivity (TFP) index (*continued*)
sources-of-growth method to estimate, 38–39, 46–47, 56–57
Trade, foreign, 29–30, 39–40, 41n7, 56–57, 107n6
Trigueros, Ignacio, 17t

Unemployment rate, 73–74, 89
United Nations, 91t, 212t, 220t
United States
trends in labor productivity in, 153–54, 157

Valdés, Alberto, 31n6, 215t, 223t
Vandendreis, R., 56–57t
Vásquez Presedo, V., 223t
Venezuela
agricultural, manufacturing, and public output growth for, 116–20, 127–30
basic data for, 205–6
business cycles in, 12, 17
components of labor quality for, 74–81, 90–99
contribution to output growth in, 43, 45
employment and population ratios for, 72–73, 87
employment, population, and labor force participation in, 219–20
foreign trade contribution to growth, 39–40, 56–57

GDP estimates and rates of change for, 60–61, 64–68
GDP growth, TFP, and input contributions, 34–37, 50–54, 232
growth of agricultural sector in, 116–18, 122, 125–26, 127
growth of manufacturing sector in, 118–19, 129
growth of public sector in, 119–20, 130
growth rate of prices, productivity, and capital stock, 38–39, 55–57
income distribution of capital and labor for, 61–62, 69
inflation rates in, 15–16
occupation classification I and II, 78–79, 96, 183–86
partial productivity of labor and capital, 37–38, 48–49
predicted GDP growth for, 164–65, 168
trends in productivity in, 153–54, 159
Verstraeten, Juan, 118

Wage index, 228
Wages
differentials by gender in, 76–77, 93
differentials by occupation in, 78–79
by economic sector, 79–80, 98
by educational level, 92
Webb, R., 209t
World Bank, 97t, 114t, 129t

ICEG Academic Advisory Board